Our Hymn Tunes

Our Hymn Tunes

Their Choice
and
Performance

Foreword by
Lionel Dakers

Donald Webster

THE SAINT ANDREW PRESS

First published in 1983 by
THE SAINT ANDREW PRESS
121 George Street, Edinburgh EH2 4YN

Copyright © Donald Webster 1983

ISBN 0 7152 0552 8

Printed in Great Britain by
Bell and Bain Ltd., Glasgow

CONTENTS

FOREWORD

by Lionel Dakers, CBE, Mus.D., FRAM, FRSCM, FRCM, FRCO(Ch.M.), ADCM
Director of The Royal School of Church Music

The past thirty years have witnessed what has been aptly termed "the hymn explosion". Much of this has been the result of a growing awareness of the role hymnody plays as an essential—and inescapable—factor in worship.

Although many books have been written about hymnody, a glance at the chapter headings of Donald Webster's book will quickly reveal the extent of his awareness of the many-sided aspects of the subject. The great virtue of this book, as I see it, is that it has the distinction of being not only comprehensive, informative and scholarly, but also easy to read. This latter is so important, especially since organists and choirmasters are not always renowned for being all that informed—or even sometimes interested—in hymnody.

Perhaps this book will also help to whet the appetite of those who view hymns and hymnody as something little more than a necessary evil.

I have every confidence that *Our Hymn Tunes* will prove to be an up to the minute resource book providing under one cover the background to what many of us view as an intensely absorbing subject. It certainly deserves to be.

Addington Place,
Croydon.

PREFACE

In the following pages will be found reference to all those matters which concern the choice and performance of hymns. This is believed to be the first book which is devoted wholly to this matter; even in books of church music practice, the hymns have been treated of in all too cursory a manner.

Numerous books exist which refer to the words of hymns, their history and that of the tunes. These matters should receive the interest and attention of every earnest church musician, but because of their scholarly treatment elsewhere, they are not discussed here, save where they affect the choice and performance of the music.

It is the tune which rightly or wrongly has the primary appeal where hymns are concerned, and this becomes evident when people are invited to choose their favourite hymns.

Few will disagree with Arthur Hutchings' remark that very rarely do hymns fire the imagination by the words alone. Music can add a whole dimension to the words, but to consider a tune merely as a piece of music is also a doubtful criterion.

Fundamental to our musical ministry is the question, "Is God really interested in our musical offerings?" Since Old Testament times we have found that man has expressed himself in song in his religious observances. Our Lord and his disciples sang a hymn before going into the Mount of Olives to pray (Matthew 26: 30).

Archbishop Temple wrote: "Hymns enable us to come and truly open our hearts to Him, to acknowledge our dependence upon Him, and to fix our thoughts upon Him for another period."

C. S. Phillips in *Hymnody Past and Present,* (SPCK, 1937), wrote: "The bulk of the public that we have to cater for judges more by the tune than by the words.... For the ordinary man, music has a wider range of expression than language."

C. Henry Phillips in *The Singing Church*, (Faber, 1945) wrote: "It is true that the man in the street knows and loves certain hymns better than any other music. They are indeed the only music in which he ever takes part." This being so, it behoves us to treasure and use rightly our great heritage.

ACKNOWLEDGMENTS

The following pages contain material taken from my doctoral dissertation on contemporary hymnody, and I would like to take this opportunity of thanking my supervisors, Dr Denis Cowan of Pacific Western University, California, and Dr Melville Cook, organist of the United Metropolitan Church, Toronto. I would also like to thank Dr Cook for his guidance and example throughout my whole life concerning music in general, and hymnody in particular, not least in its practical aspects.

No one can study this fascinating subject without being greatly influenced by, and indebted to the writings of the late Rev. Dr Erik Routley, and I thank him for the use I have been able to make of his work respecting direct quotation and summarized opinions. Nevertheless, the responsibility for the views expressed in the present book rests with myself alone.

Thanks are due also to the Epworth Press for permission to quote from A. S. Gregory's *Praises with Understanding* (1936), the Scripture Union Publishing for an extract from the preface to *Hymns of Faith*, and to the Oxford University Press for extracts from the preface to the *English Hymnal*. Other writers to whom I make particular acknowledgment are Mr Charles Cleall and members of the 20th Century Light Music Group, together with those whose works are listed in the bibliography.

I would also wish to thank my Edinburgh friends for their sundry kindnesses, and whose informed interest in the book's progress was "an ever present help". These include the Rev. John W. Cumming, minister of Palmerston Place Church; the Rev. Thomas Cuthell, minister of St Cuthbert's Church; Sir Ronald Johnson; Mr Ian Macpherson, organist and choirmaster of Cramond Kirk; and Dr Dennis Townhill, organist and master of the choristers of St Mary's Episcopal Cathedral.

My thanks are also due to the staffs of the Leeds Music Library and New College Library, Edinburgh; Mr Simon Lindley, master of the music of Leeds Parish Church; Mr Douglas Law of The Saint Andrew Press, whose kindness along with that of his editorial staff throughout all stages of the book's preparation was a constant source of encouragement.

In the compilation of the book's indexes I have been greatly helped by David W. Perry's *Hymns and Tunes Indexed,* that indispensable work of hymnological reference, which sets such a high standard of accuracy.

Lastly, the deepest indebtedness is due to my wife, Joan, whose constant help and support sustained me through many a difficult day in the writing and preparation of both the manuscript and the dissertation, and to whom this book is dedicated with deepest affection.

1

The case for reform — some considerations

I have written this in the hope that it may be instrumental in raising the standard of hymn singing from its present generally low level to one which is a vital and enriching experience for all participants. Most of the great evangelical movements in the past have been assisted by fine hymns and now the world-wide Church is the possessor of a vast heritage of Christian song, which expresses a wide range of spiritual experience and covers many centuries, but of which unfortunately only a small part is known generally.

Today, in churches of all denominations, hymn singing constitutes the congregation's main opportunity for musical participation in the service. It is, therefore, all the more necessary that the singing of the congregation should be of the highest possible standard, and that the hymns chosen be of corresponding value. Very often the spiritual life of the parish is reflected in its hymn singing. Psychology asserts that we are moved to action more by our emotions than by our intellect, and we all know how true this is.

Most people would agree that the purpose of music in worship is to create an atmosphere that is conducive to reverence, as an offering to God and as a corporate affirmation of religious beliefs. This being so, there are those who would aver that it is irrelevant whether the congregation enjoys its worship or not, that the congregation does not assemble to enjoy itself. Indeed it is no doubt true that where a church consciously uses bad music in preference to good the

1

motive is self-gratification rather than the praise of God. Fortunately, we are not in the position of having to choose between enjoying ourselves with the second-rate, and worshipping without enjoyment using the first-rate. We can say today, as did the psalmist 2,500 years ago: "O praise the Lord for it is a good thing to sing praises unto our God; yea a joyful and pleasant thing it is to be thankful."[1]

It is, therefore, my aim to show what some of this material is. It is neither complicated nor without enjoyment, and I believe that once church people accustom themselves to a worshipping climate which uses only the good, they will feel an instinctive repugnance towards the bad.

Music for ordinary people need not always be great art in the sense that Beethoven's late quartets and Bach's *St Matthew Passion* are great works of art, in either a secular or a sacred context, but we should not however exclude the opportunity for great art from the Church's life.[2] The surest way to bring about this exclusion is to make people think that the perpetuation of the transient is the proper business of the Church, and that it is the Church's habit to make do with the conventionally inadequate where its music is concerned. As I wrote elsewhere: "I do not believe that the church can survive for very long if it lives solely on its accumulated financial and artistic capital" — particularly if some of it is of a debased kind. We render our religion grave disservice when our music is an amalgam of the second-rate and the second-hand. Such a piece as the "Old Rugged Cross" with its exaggerated emotion and its over-ripe fervour makes for intellectual and artistic corruption.

Good music is neither dull music nor difficult music. What could be finer and simpler than the "Old 100th"? Congregations may say with a fair degree of justice that they don't wish church attendance to become akin to belonging to a musical appreciation class, and that if they wish to extend the range of their musical sympathies they can do so in the recital room or the concert hall. Only some churches can be pace-setters in their utilization of the latest in contemporary art.

Theirs will be the heady joy of startling musical discovery, and also the responsibility for jettisoning that which has been weighed in the balance and found wanting. Past experience teaches us that only a small amount of the output of a generation, even when it is produced with eternity in view, is worthy of survival. Nevertheless, we have a duty to be aware of contemporary composition and to find a place in our services for the finer examples.

My own church congregation has always taken a keen interest in the choir's work, and has not failed to express its appreciation verbally. I will admit, therefore, to some anxiety as to the likely reaction of the former, following our first performance of a work by Kenneth Leighton. My fears were groundless and, following this experience, I wonder if we are too timorous in our approach to contemporary art. We should perform it only when we are absolutely convinced as to its merit, since only then have we the equipment to defend our action and the incentive to give of our best in preparation and presentation. To perform it simply in order to show that we're "with it", or that it's expected of us, or so that we can boast of it subsequently, is a betrayal of our vocation as servants of the Church.

A service in which the hearts of those present are gladdened and stimulated by fine music, sung with enthusiasm, is likely to be a more worthy offering to God, and a more vital experience than one where such conditions do not obtain. Indeed, failure to improve the quality of congregational participation in recent years is no doubt partly responsible for the marked decline in church attendance. A failure to reform *within* the idioms the Church has traditionally deemed suitable for its worship has resulted in the "Pop Revolution".

G. K. Chesterton said: "It is as much an error to say that the people liked bad music, as to say that they naturally took to good music. What they liked was music with a lively rhythm, but not necessarily at a fast speed or with a martial tread."[3] Vaughan Williams expressed the view that the average congregation likes fine melody when it can get it, but it is apt to be undiscriminating and will often take to a bad melody when a good one is not forthcoming. "Is it not worthwhile making a vigorous effort today for the sake of establishing a good tradition?"[4]

Although these words were written as long ago as 1906, there is still the feeble singing of tunes which are enervating, sickly sentimental, cliché-ridden or downright dull. Surely these must create a very unfavourable impression on visitors to our churches. Habitual worshippers, long familiar with such conditions, are perhaps no longer disturbed by the earsores in their church, any more than they may be by possible eyesores. That does not absolve those responsible from the need to effect further reforms.

Whether the congregational singing is good or bad in a church seems curiously unrelated to the standard of the choir or of the music it sings. In some churches the choir sings well and the congregation badly or vice versa, but in few churches is the singing of choir and congregation both good, and very often they are both bad.

Canon A. J. Green wrote: "The better and more expensive the choir and the more elaborate the settings of the canticles and the anthem, the more certain one is to get nothing but the commonplace of hymns, both tunes and words." Broadcast Evensongs are seldom distinguished by good hymn singing.

Arising from this, and as a reaction from the Cathedral type of service to which a number of choirs aspired, many clergymen have insisted on a congregational type of service, presumably on the fallacious assumption that if the choir's contribution is weakened, the congregation's part would be strengthened automatically. All church musicians who are staunch churchmen before all else acknowledge the need for corporate worship, but too often attempts to achieve this have resulted in the discontinuance of anthems etc., and the choir, who, after all, has its contribution to make to the service and feels that the congregation's rights have been purchased at its expense, has either resigned, joined other choirs, or lost interest in its work.

I resent very deeply on behalf of thousands of choristers of all ages the impression that anthems exist chiefly as a sop to the choir's vanity, or as a source of sophisticated entertainment of dubious relevance to the rest of the service for the congregation. A carefully prepared anthem of high quality is an act of worship on behalf of *all* the worshippers. In these days where congregational participation in everything is regarded as a matter of right, it must be said that in order to be involved in the journey one does not necessarily have to drive the train.[5]

Of course, in some instances, the congregational type of service has been put forward as a justification on liturgical grounds for checking a choir that is over-ambitious in its choice of music. No one wishes to excuse this, but I wonder if we pay sufficient regard to the fact that mistakes in the performance of anthems may be due to a variety of causes other than incapacity on the choir's part, or insufficient rehearsal, e.g. nervousness when the time for performance occurs, illness or sheer accident. Whilst it would appear wrong that a choir should regard the performance of anthems as its *raison d'être,* one must remember that the average choir member is more gifted musically than the average member of the congregation. Choirs may think that if they and the congregation are to sing identical music, and the latter is not required to rehearse, neither should they. They expect something interesting to sing and do not like to spend time merely practising hymns to the exclusion of all else.

This apparent digression has been made to emphasize the roles of choir and congregation in musical worship, to show that these should not, and need not be antagonistic, and that if genuine reform of the hymn singing is to be undertaken, a combined effort is necessary. It cannot be stressed sufficiently that the choir's chief duty is to lead both the spoken and sung corporate worship, before the performance of elaborate music is considered.[6]

All changes in service procedure are fraught with difficulties, but no self-respecting minister or organist should let them stand for ever as insuperable. The zeal for reform must be tempered with patience and commonsense. "We need someone who will meet the congregation where it is, and lead it a step or two forward on its own road."[7] The organist, by virtue of his specialized knowledge, will have the lion's share of the responsibility, and his tact and convictions must needs be of the highest. In the Church of Scotland, the control of the praise is in the hands of the minister and it has to be admitted, sadly, that at present few have sufficient musical training to discharge this vital task. It is most unlikely, therefore, that they would be dismissive of an organist/choirmaster's suggestions on praise content.

Many organists find it difficult to work up much enthusiasm for hymns, and regard them as the least attractive and least important part of their work. This shows itself in the fact that so many traditional hymns are not merely ill-chosen and ill-sung: they are also ill-played. Such an attitude is understandable. At the side of the great symphonies and concerti, hymn tunes seem very small fry indeed. Being forced to play year in and year out a small repertoire[8] of feeble and dull tunes drawn usually from only one period because the congregation knows no others, is bound to influence an organist into an unfavourable attitude towards all hymns. We now have a situation in which the average person thinks of the contents of the average hymn book as idiomatically undifferentiated, vaguely nineteenth century,[9] despite the wide stylistic range between the plainsong melodies of the early Church and the magnificent contemporary tunes of Herbert Howells which are found in the modern hymn book. Yes, we tend to forget that serious composers are making distinguished contributions to contemporary church music. It is not a case of "Pop" or nothing, where the here and now is concerned, though advocates of pop music in church, writing in the popular press, would have us think so. It is profoundly disturbing to witness the arrogance shown by those who proclaim "Pop" as the only authentic contemporary musical idiom for the Church to use.

Yet good solid unpretentious tunes like "Melcombe" and "St Peter" do have a part to play, if only to offset more highly coloured music, and even in the most reactionary hymn books there is an abundance of fine material waiting to be used for the enrichment of our services. The companions of such reforming collections as *Songs of Praise,* the *Church Hymnary* and *Congregational Praise* could well stimulate fresh interest in the subject. *Praises with Understanding* by A. S. Gregory performs a similar function for the *Methodist Hymn Book,* and Erik Routley in *Music of Christian Hymnody* makes the *English Hymnal* his source of reference.[10]

Much parochial strife in the past, attendant upon change and reform, could have been avoided by informal discussion at parish meetings. One organist friend many years my senior said: "If the folk like you, you can get away with murder." And it is possible for an organist, by virtue of his demeanour, to win support for what he wishes to undertake. This need does not involve him in any sacrifice of significant artistic principle. It is often necessary to concede the smaller issue in order to succeed in the greater one. One *does* need to explain the reasons for changes, otherwise people may think that we are prompted merely by whims, and that an attempt is being made to ride roughshod over a congregation's feelings. I believe it is this, more than the changes themselves, which cause resentment. One must accept, too, that most people have had to cope with much unwelcome change in other aspects of their lives over the last fifteen or so years. The non-musical aspects of worship have not been immune from this, in almost all the leading denominations.[11] We live in a world in which the invasion of commercial interests into religious matters is a commonplace experience, where reverence, dignity and spirituality are increasingly lost sight of in modern worship. Against this, the old hymns, the bad and the good, give us a sense of security, tradition and custom, and this in a time such as ours is something not to be despised. The preservation of the great hymns of the past, and even their introduction where they are not already known must, therefore, be part of a worthwhile reforming programme. It is surprising how many retain their relevance to the contemporary life of many subsequent generations, particularly those with a strong scriptural content. Well has it been said that the timeless classics are permanently contemporary. Of others, it may be said that most hymn singers would have difficulty in defending what they sing line by line, but the total product of a great hymn lies at the heart of their belief. We hear much from our pulpits as to the timelessness of the Gospel, and of Eternal Truth. There is truth in music too.

The greatest artistic achievement is not that which blazes its modernity like a meteor shooting its way through the sky: rather is it something that roots itself in a tradition which it thereby expands and enlarges. It puts self-conscious modernism out of court just as it also repels self-conscious archaism. Christianity is a religion of integrity, and that means standards from which one cannot depart, except at the risk of producing something false to its purpose and unworthy of its aim.

"All that is needed at first is a readiness to admit that appreciation is capable of development and bears some relation to knowledge. The effort brings an immediate and increasing reward of heightened joy in worship. The musical tastes and habits of Methodism in common with — until recently — all the other churches, have suffered grievously from lack of good nourishment. We have acquired a liking, even a preference for substitutes, some of which were dessicated, and a few positively unwholesome. Now that new and rich pastures are open to us, it would be little short of sinful to refuse to explore them. Our taste in hymn tunes is capable of extension and enjoyment."[12]

The preface to *English Hymnal* reminds us that in Christian song churches have forgotten their quarrels and men have lost their limitations because they have reached that higher ground where the soul is content to affirm and adore. When Methodists sing and love the hymns of Cardinal Newman, and "Ein' feste Burg" is to be found in a Roman Catholic hymn book of the present day, one may be proud of the way our combined hymnody has contributed to ecumenism.

Having raised some of the issues affecting a reform of hymn singing and the choice of hymns, there are still practical difficulties to face.

One is the difficulty the amateur organist and choirmaster may experience in influencing his choir and congregation — and indeed his minister — in the need for reform. The support of a prominent local musician or Church Music Society representative in addressing a church meeting would probably meet with at least a sympathetic hearing. We hear so much about the evangelizing power of poor music, how music with a beat "packs them in at St . . .'s down the road", that we lose sight of the fact that the Church's outreach extends not merely to the materially, culturally, and spiritually deprived. It also extends to that section of the community whose loss to the Church since World War II has been serious out of all proportion to its numbers. I am referring to the thinking agnostic who would dearly love to believe. Such are to be found working at the factory bench as well as belonging to the University Senior Common Room. If they were persuaded to attend a service of poor musical content — when it lay within people's power to provide something better, whether this poverty was of the "traditional" or "modern" kind — well may they say: "Is this all they thought I was fit for? The propagators of the Christian gospel cannot be entirely convinced themselves, if they think that in order to render it palatable, it has to be presented with a tawdry musical accompaniment."

Secondly, there is the problem of persuading a choir that has been unaccustomed to rehearsing hymns that they are worth practising. The introduction of variety in their performance may achieve this (see chapter 7). Gramophone records of first-rate hymn singing can be a wonderful stimulus to a choir that has never attempted more than a tolerable accuracy of notes in its hymn singing.

Thirdly, before embarking upon learning new tunes, we should consider the extent to which our congregation's knowledge and use of the great standard repertoire is needlessly restricted. It is hard to believe that roughly a hundred hymns per year is all many congregations are offered to sing.[13] It would be good to go through our hymn book and to make a list of the great hymns and tunes, the tunes that "open their arms" to all who sing them, and to introduce them into our worship in the course of a year.[14] We may well marvel at the extent of such a list. So many good tunes are undervalued, or are in danger of becoming so by over-use. Because we have discovered that "Abbot's Leigh" or "Blaenwern"[15] is a great tune, there is a danger that one or other will be used for every 8787D hymn to the neglect of other fine tunes of that metre such as "Austria", "Hyfrydol" or "Rex Gloriae".[16] It is a short step from over-use to denigration and neglect. Does not our Christmas music emerge perennially fresh because it is used only once in the year? And does not its fine quality prove that to deserve that epithet, music need be neither idiomatically remote nor difficult to sing?

The practical matters of introducing new tunes, discarding the weak ones and making hymn singing more vital, will be discussed in later chapters.

Notes

1. Psalm 147, verse 1.
2. E. Routley, *Twentieth Century Church Music,* (Jenkins, 1964), p. 202.
3. G. K. Chesterton, *Life of Dickens,* (Methuen, 1906).
4. *English Hymnal,* (OUP, 1906), Preface, p. xi.
5. See note 6, p. 87.
6. *Principles and Recommendations of the Royal School of Church Music,* 1950, p. 24.
7. E. Routley, *Church Music and the Christian Faith,* (Collins, 1980).
8. *English Hymnal Service Book,* (OUP, 1962), p. 4. Yet Vaughan Williams said that his editorship of *English Hymnal* had entailed examining some of the best tunes in the world, and some of the worst.
9. A correspondent in *Life and Work* wrote that the average person's musical taste is light years away from the *Church Hymnary: Third Edition*—as if one could dismiss all the idioms of that book so summarily.
10. See Bibliography.

11. Principally changes in liturgical language; which have not, as yet, been conducive to the creation of fine church music in any quantity.
12. A. S. Gregory, *Praises with Understanding*, (Epworth Press, 1936), p. 162, (summarized).
13. The cult of the closed canon of hymns is an abuse and a scandal and leads people into settled habits, the divorce from which grows more painful and provokes more resentment the more settled they are — (Erik Routley).
14. In his article on "Literary influences in the English Hymnal", Arthur Hutchings wrote: "We enjoyed Holy, Holy, Holy, tremendously because we hadn't sung it for a year."
15. 334 (*CH3*), 473 (*CH3*).
16. 37 (*CH3*), 381 (*CH3*), 148 (*AMR*).

2

Good and bad tunes — an analysis

Having stated the case for reform, both in the choice of hymn tunes and the manner of their performance, it is now necessary to discuss in greater detail the controversial matter of good and bad tunes.

The preface to *English Hymnal* argues powerfully against the bad tune:

"Many of the tunes of the present day which have become... popular with congregations are quite unsuitable to their purpose. More often than not they are positively harmful to those who sing and hear them... Certain other tunes are worthy neither of the congregations who sing them, the occasions on which they are sung, nor the composers who wrote them."[1]

Vaughan Williams, the musical editor, goes on to say that good taste in church music is a moral not a musical issue. Gerald Knight, the late Director of the Royal School of Church Music, has declared that "only the best is good enough for God. It demands the ultimate in sacrifice".[2]

Against these statements, the 20th Century Light Music Group maintain: "It is easy to declare that only certain types of music are suitable for Christian worship and that other kinds are not. On what grounds are such rulings made? It is said that only the best is good enough... We are not told that the stable was the best stable or Jordan the best water. If it were true, who could have the nerve to offer himself to God at the altar, let alone offer himself as Choirman? And what excuse could be put forward for many of the anthems, chants and hymn tunes that should have been discarded long ago?"

In reply to this, one must say that neither Jordan nor the stable was offered *by believers*. As for offering one's self as server or choirman, the crucial point is that our efforts *may* be acceptable, but only if they are the best of which we are capable. The sin of offering the inferior is committed when we have within us the capacity to offer more, better, with greater care and effort, yet we are satisfied with less. As for the music that should have been discarded long ago, the church musician is at one with the Light Music Group. I am, however, a little suspicious of the group's motives when most of the hymns which first attracted their attention were *already* well served by fine popular tunes, e.g. "At the Name of Jesus", "Now thank we all our God", "Angel voices", and "Lord, thy word abideth".[3]

If a hymn tune devitalizes the words to which it is sung, it is already unworthy of its purpose. Such a tune is "Trentham",[4] which is frequently set to the hymn "Breathe on me, Breath of God". One might conclude from it and the way it is sung that the breath of God was an anaesthetic, not a "Giver of Life". Congregations who have become so conditioned by the use of this tune might consider "Carlisle"[5] to be too vigorous to express "Fill me with life anew"!

Another instance is Joseph Barnby's tune to Walsham How's "For all the saints who from their labours rest".[6] Not only is the accentuation incorrect for numerous verses, but the music throws little illumination on such a verse as:

From earth's wide bounds, from ocean's farthest coast,
Through gates of pearl streams in the countless host,
Singing to Father, Son, and Holy Ghost:
   Alleluia!

Further answers to the questions raised by the Light Music Group are to be found:

1. "It ought no longer to be true that the most exalted moments of a churchgoer's week are associated with music

that would not be tolerated in any place of secular entertainment"[7] — and that is a relevant comment on bad traditional music as well as against bad "Pop" and kindred idioms.

2. Lionel Dakers: "What is considered second-rate elsewhere is often considered first-rate in church music."[8]

3. William Byrd (sixteenth century): "For even as among artisans it is shameful in a craftsman to make a rude piece of work from some precious metal, so indeed to sacred words in which the praises of God are sung, none but some celestial harmony (so far as our powers avail) will be proper."

4. *Handbook to Church Hymnary: Third Edition:* "Weak music is not just bad art, it is bad theology."[9]

So many church musicians of today are aware that just as it has taken the devoted labours of many decades to build up standards,[10] it has been tragically easy to lower them, and over a much shorter period of time. Just as the worst of the nineteenth-century excesses were in sight of being removed, there was a cynical injection of debased so-called light music, which incorporated every corny cliché in the book, and this overturned overnight all the reforming activities of committed church musicians, ministers, choirs and congregations which had been undertaken since the beginning of the century.

The *English Hymnal* has been undoubtedly the great reforming hymn book of the twentieth century, and its influence has extended to all the denominations. But its editorial committee erred in condemning the Victorian idiom somewhat inconsistently, in that they rejected certain good examples (e.g. "Diademata") and reprieved other very inferior specimens (e.g. "Leominster").[11] In reaction, Victoriana was replaced by folk song and Welsh tunes. The giving of blanket approval to an idiom meant the inclusion of weak examples. Some folk songs had strong secular associations, so that it was impossible for many to sing the "Londonderry Air" without thinking of "Danny Boy".[12] Some Welsh tunes seemed distinctly like other Welsh tunes, and the danger arose yet again of condemning a whole idiom because of some poor examples. The Victorians' love of four part harmony was reacted against by the cult of the big unison tune which was associated in many people's minds with the Public School Chapel.[13] It therefore acquired the sociological epithet "Establishment" — along with much of the post-Stanford choir repertoire. Much serious contemporary hymn tune writing represents a reaction against this. Thus we have seen a series of violent swings of the pendulum in twentieth-century musical taste. What we should have done, and what we should be doing now, is to seek a balance and try to examine critically individual examples drawn from all these styles, and to make sure that in our year's praise a proportion is maintained between one idiom and another. When condemning Victorian tunes it is advisable to remember that the verse of the period was often at an equally low level, and these hymns received the tunes they deserved. It is significant that "Nicaea" sung to Heber's great hymn "Holy, holy, holy", and "Dominus regit me"[14] sung to Baker's psalm paraphrase "The King of Love" are among Dykes' best tunes. Much of the prejudice against Victorian music can be explained by the fact that history shows it is a trait of human nature for man to despise the achievements of the century preceding his own. The Victorians were prejudiced against the eighteenth century, and no doubt the music too closely identified with our own time will be a similar target of ridicule for future generations. Indeed, there has already been a reaction against the pseudo-folk song type of tune. The Folk Song Movement thrust some semblance of originality on to third-rate talents who were influenced by it, and thus one excess was combated with another. Now we are beginning to see the sterility of some modal "folky" hymn tunes composed during the 1920s, and to realize that they are even more dated than those of the Victorian period.[15]

The question of balance between the various idioms is not a narrow academic or aesthetic one. Failure to take this into account is responsible, no doubt, for the "man in the pew" feeling a general sense of unease that his worship has a certain sameness, and that certain tunes of undoubted excellence no longer make the impact they once did.

It is interesting to note that when the *English Hymnal* in 1906 referred to the old favourites, none of which appeared earlier than 1861,[16] they were making a tilt at *Hymns Ancient and Modern,* whose first edition appeared then, forty-five years earlier. Almost an exactly similar period elapsed between the appearance of the *English Hymnal* and the revised *Hymns Ancient and Modern* of 1950. Surprisingly, few of the tunes the *English Hymnal* introduced — perhaps not more than a dozen —had become household words by then,[17] certainly far fewer than *Ancient and Modern's* old favourites, some of which still retained a sturdy and deserved popularity. Yet the *English Hymnal's* editors showed courage in rejecting certain other poor tunes which the editors of *Ancient and Modern Revised* deemed it expedient to retain, e.g. "Pentecost", and "For All the Saints".[18] Vaughan Williams believed his reforming crusade need be directed only against apathy and inertia. He believed people could be educated, and that by this process of education they would be grateful eventually for the good new material they had been given. Resistance would come only from the pig-headed and the prejudiced. Today the task of the reformer is much harder. Such basic questions are asked among Christians as: "Do we need hymns?" "Should there be a church?" "Should we go to church?" "Is dignity in worship a desirable element?"[19] Philistinism is supported by vast commercial interests and by some of an educated ministry who look to "Pop" as the panacea for the ills of a failed personal witness.

Questioner: Why do we have that new tune to... instead of the old one? No one likes the new tune, whereas everyone liked the old one.

Organist: The new tune is a very fine one, while the old one is a very poor affair.

Questioner: Who says it's poor? Your opinion? Who are you to judge? I may not know much about music, but I know what I like. I resent highbrows trying to determine the tastes of the worshipper.

The expert judgment of the musician is part of his professional equipment, and if it is ignored, one may wonder why the Church employs highly qualified organists and choirmasters. (One may comment that in an age when all value judgments tend to be suspect, every time a tune is chosen for public worship a value judgment is made. Surely it is desirable that those who make such judgments do so after having given some thought to artistic criteria which their training and skill enable them to do, rather than that the tastes of the lowest common denominator or those of an influential member of the congregation are appeased.)

The above type of question has raged frequently during this century, and usually the questioner has won the day. Perhaps one of the earliest occasions was "Duke Street" v. "Pentecost"[20] for "Fight the good fight" and whilst few would question the superiority of "Duke Street" today, the good has not always triumphed over the bad.

The difficulty is that the "man in the pew" always believes he is the final arbiter on musical affairs even though he is prepared to abide by the opinion of experts in other matters. As for "knowing what he likes", he really means that he likes what he knows, and he does not generally seem disposed to enlarging his knowledge. It is difficult to reconcile such an attitude with the demand for fresh musical material in our services. There is surely the necessity for an all-out crusade against this unwarranted assumption that a man is entitled to sing what he knows and to resent what he doesn't. (See also p. 11.)

"Musical taste has been so greatly educated in the last generation, that for the Church to cling to the old tunes is to flout the best standards of our time."[21] So wrote W. K. Lowther Clarke in *A Hundred Years of Hymns Ancient and Modern* in the early sixties. One wonders if he were writing today if he would take so favourable a view of musical tastes. As has been noted, during the past generation forces have been at work which make the task of the reformer, where hymn tunes are concerned, probably more difficult than it has been at any other period this century.

There is always a halo of sanctity surrounding the hymns we have known since childhood that blinds our critical faculties, and we do not as a rule take kindly to something which is substituted. Yet there are good and bad musical associations, and we tend to forget that a tune may arouse pleasant remembrances in the mind of one person and unpleasant recollections in the mind of another. Those who have no long acquaintance with a hymn are better able to evaluate strictly on merit.

The preface to *Hymns of Faith*, 1964, (published by Scripture Union) contains the following extraordinary passage:

"The compilers have tried to avoid a situation in which young people associate good music with day-school, and second- and third-rate music with Christian worship. To some extent, this situation already exists, and it is felt that everything possible should be done to raise the standards of music generally in public worship.... However, spiritual values have to be taken into account [as though musical values were antagonistic to these] and a number of tunes which cannot be rated very highly when judged by musical standards have been retained because of their long association with words of proved spiritual worth."[22]

This passage overlooks the fact that the young have no such associations, and if they are taught "a number of tunes which cannot be rated very highly", the worship of another generation is debased needlessly.

It may be asked "If these tunes are so poor, how did they become popular in the first place?" The explanation is surely this; that they first gained currency when better material was not readily available, and that mental and spiritual inertia has prolonged their lives.

A note on children's hymns

Nowadays there *is* an abundance of first-rate material in such collections as *Hymns for Church and School* and *Songs of Praise*. Yet even where such books are in use, it is surprising how often a poor tune from some other collection is used instead of the one which is set. How sad it is that for a hymn such as "O Jesus, I have promised" the tune the young are given to sing is so often by Geoffrey Beaumont rather than "Wolvercote" or "Thornbury".[23] These lie well within the capabilities of the young and their capacity for enjoyment; and they have, too, an invigorating effect on the words and the singer, that the Beaumont tune cannot begin to attempt. The most that can be said of the latter is that it is catchy in a superficial sort of way.

I wonder if Sunday School teachers are aware of their responsibility in moulding the tastes of the young. Children of primary school age have no prejudice; and it is they who will be the churchgoers of the next generation. Every time a poor tune is taught, this means that an opportunity for learning a good one is lost. Children of this age are remarkably quick in learning new material. Why not then give them the good? One is alarmed to hear that children in many Sunday Schools are making virtually no contact with the great hymns of the Christian tradition. We tend to think of "the young" as an undifferentiated age group from five to fifteen. Yet children of seven plus, when asked their age, say: "But I'm nearly eight." They cannot reach adolescence fast enough and think of some of the hymns they learned when they were five as being unbelievably "soppy". I am sure I am not alone in having gone through a stage, when I was eight, when I was unable to sing "The little Lord Jesus laid down his sweet head".

It is surely better to teach plenty of adult hymns, even if the subject matter may appear to be rather adult, for once these are acquired, they may be a "joy for ever". One of my favourite hymns of childhood was "Crown him with many crowns", which I loved and still love, partly on account of

Elvey's magnificent tune "Diademata".[24] I could not understand for many years the verse:

> Fruit of the mystic Rose,
> As of that rose the stem;
> The root whence mercy ever flows,
> The Babe of Bethlehem.

— and I suspect neither did many of the adults who sang it. But I believe it *could* have been made intelligible to me, had someone taken the trouble. As it was, I believe it did me good to sing it, and the half understood sonorities of:

> Crown Him the Lord of years,
> The Potentate of time,
> Creator of the rolling spheres,
> Ineffably sublime.

made a deep impression. After that I didn't want "Praise him, Praise him, all ye little children" or "Jesus bids us shine", though I recall that they too had been enjoyable — three years earlier. It is more important for our children to grow into the materials of worship, than that they should outgrow them.

The words of "Lord of the dance"[25] are challenging and sophisticated, but have we discharged our duty to the young merely by teaching them a catchy (though meritorious) tune? What do these words mean to the average child if left unexplained? Nowadays I often wonder if adults enjoy children's hymns more than the children, and to hear elderly folk singing about "At school, at home and play" is, for me, an embarrassing experience.

The Rev. N. P. Goldhawk has observed that perhaps the greatest threat to worship comes from the trivial rather than from the theologically inadequate, and trivial verse has an uncanny knack of attracting trivial music.

It has been said that people cling to the old familiar tunes because of laziness — the old macadamized road of custom. This induces spiritual somnolence. The sensuous pleasure of a "good sing" is not synonymous with worship. It may actually exercise a hypnotic influence, under which the senses are satisfied whilst the spiritual faculty is hushed to sleep.

Walford Davies wrote: "Hymnody is not merely a friendly aid or a disposing influence to prepare us for worship but a vehicle for the very spirit of worship itself, the actual carrier of wonderment and adoration."

These words have come to my mind as I sing and accompany Herbert Howells' great tune "Michael" which is set to "All my hope on God is founded". This is a remarkable instance of a wonderful twentieth-century tune ousting a good one, "Groeswen", which has been known and loved, deservedly, by Scots Presbyterians for several generations. The Howells tune has made its way into the hearts of all who sing it on sheer merit, and has added a further dimension to the meaning of the words.[26] There are literally dozens of tunes waiting in the wings to render a similar service.

A powerful argument against an improvement in the choice of tunes lies in the fact that in some churches we often hear poor music sung with real heartiness. The assumption that bad music generates heartier singing is a fallacious one, for one does not experience any diminution in heartiness in such churches when good tunes are used. A large amount of volume does not in any case necessarily reflect profound religious experience.[27]

What makes a good tune?— Is it one that I like? One that goes well? One that is well-known? One that is musically excellent? Or one people ought to like?

None of these questions may be answered by an unqualified "yes". Is it an artistic creation with which only an expert is familiar? Would this be true of "Down Ampney",[28] written for "Come down, O Love Divine"? Are people conscious of quality when singing? Yes, I think they are. The difficulties of the fourth line of "Westminster Abbey" (Christ is made the sure foundation) are worth mastering because we *are* conscious of the tune's excellence, even whilst it is being sung.[29] A good tune is one that wears well, and it comes to mean more to one as the years progress. That is why I for one cannot subscribe to the "planned obsolescence" theory of church music. If we

B

are to make the effort to learn something, let it be something worthwhile and likely to remain of longterm value. "Time may indeed make ancient good uncouth"[30] but for us to bother with the ephemeral, knowing it to be so, is a waste of time and talents.

What price sincerity in evaluating a musical composition? This is something I choose to leave out of account, since only our Maker knows what is genuinely sincere. We don't always know it ourselves. However, if I had to choose *between* one who is sincere in his art and one who is sincere in his faith, I would prefer the former. There have been too many monstrosities conceived by people who claimed to be motivated by the latter, whereas the dedicated artist may lead others to something he has been unable to find for himself. Parry's "Blest pair of Sirens" is one of the great British choral works, and few can sing or hear his setting of "O may we soon again renew that song, and keep in tune with heaven till God e'er long to His celestial consort us unite. To live with Him and sing in endless morn of light", without being moved to the very depths of his being. Yet Parry believed not one word of it!

Archbishop Temple wrote: "A good tune should not be too difficult, but it demands a worthy effort of mind and spirit as well as voice. It shouldn't be a beguiling and catchy musical experience which would lead the singers to wallow in their own feelings." A good tune impresses by its memorability, and the fact that not all its secrets are revealed immediately. Many opponents of reform are apt to say: "What does it matter? I enjoy singing certain tunes, and it never occurs to me to ask if they are good or bad. I can't see what harm is being done. This question of bad or good hymn tunes may cause musicians to tear their hair, but it leaves me cold ... and even the musicians cannot always agree."

There are also those who prefer a verse on a Christmas card to a Shakespearian lyric, and cannot understand the enthusiasms of the literary scholar for the latter, but that is no excuse for condoning low literary standards, or accepting in our services what is mentally and spiritually undemanding, and tasteless. The claim of people that they are "all right as they are" is one of the reasons put forward for not attending church. One can appreciate what has been missing from one's life only *after* experiencing something wonderful. There exists among musicians remarkable unanimity as to what is considered to be first-rate; the disagreements arise as to the extent to which they are prepared to compromise their standards to meet popular demand. The ultimate aim of all Art is the attainment of Truth, Beauty and Goodness, and the achievement of this depends on the existence of objective values. It is not simply "a matter of opinion". Perhaps for the first time we are witnessing the deliberate exploitation of bad taste in worship, and this by people who, by their education, should know better.

One must warn against the mistaken idea that the eminence of a composer, or the fact that a tune is widely represented in contemporary hymn books gives any clue as to its value. Arthur Sullivan was unquestionably the greatest English composer of his day, "A born melodist" one might say after listening to one of the Savoy operas; yet it is the *poverty* of his melodic lines which is so conspicuous a feature of his hymn tunes. "St Gertrude"[31] written for "Onward! Christian soldiers" is the only indispensable one from his entire output. Notwithstanding his fine choir pieces, the hymn tunes of S. S. Wesley are likewise of very variable quality.

In an attempt to revive some tunes that should have been allowed to die, a patching-up process has been undertaken. This has taken the form of arranging "Pentecost" in quadruple time and re-harmonizing "St Oswald".[32] Whilst the result is an improvement, one is left with the thought that, with so much good material available, there is not much point in making what can only be the best of a bad job. (The removal of a diminished seventh chord at the beginning of the fourth line of Henry Smart's "Misericordia" may be regarded as an exception. In any case, only one chord is involved in this "improvement".)[33] A. H. Brown's "Saffron Walden"[34] may be considered a better choice for "Just as I am, without one plea".

Few greater acts of musical sacrilege have been committed than in the adaptation of themes from the great masters as hymn tunes.[35] It is a matter on which one cannot be dogmatic, since some adaptations need little alteration. The least successful themes are the instrumental subjects from the Viennese classics, since these were conceived as material for thematic development, and need to be butchered somewhat savagely in order that they may fit into the hymn tune mould. The more successful ones are those from vocal sources. Much discussion has centered round the classical source of "Walton" ("Fulda"),[36] which is described in some hymn books as "from Beethoven". The nearest classical connection that has been found is between the first line and the introduction to "O Isis and Osiris" in Mozart's *Magic Flute*. The remainder of the tune, which is an excellent one, appears to derive from no classical source.[37]

Sir Walford Davies has described three types of good music:

1. that which is discernible only by a trained musician;
2. that which can be appreciated by the crowd — but only on thorough acquaintance;
3. that which has instant appeal to the untrained no less than to the trained musician.[38]

I believe that only categories 2 and 3 are relevant to hymn tunes. Many of Stanford's tunes fail because they "lack the common touch" — in the Kiplingesque sense. However, the Church is entitled to expect a reasonable willingness to learn on the part of its adherents. "It is readily to be observed that the tunes have greater influence than the words in this process [of becoming known] and no tune, however excellent according to the prevailing canons of musical taste, survives without the elusive but quite distinctive quality of singability."[39] Sir Sydney Nicholson in *Quires and Places where they Sing* has stated: "If music is bad, there are some definite musical faults which may be discovered by close analysis, and a similar method of investigation will make clear beauties that may pass unnoticed by the casual hearer."[40]

The Archbishop of Canterbury's Report on Church Music, 1951, mentions (a) the need for the emotional content to be appropriate to its plan and occasion; (b) strong harmonies, especially a vigorous bass; (c) the melody should not be made up of notes that have no close relationship to one another; (d) the melody to be strong enough to stand without harmonic support; (e) the rhythm to fit the words but to be neither trivial, obtrusive nor dull; (f) the pattern to be simple but definite; (g) the climax to be well planned; (h) the range should not exceed an octave (but there are so many fine tunes of greater compass!). The rising major 6th, a Walford Davies mannerism, has been mentioned by Dr Routley as a danger sign.

Professor W. K. Stanton, himself a writer of many fine twentieth-century hymn tunes, said: "An awkward interval should never occur in an ideal tune."

Analysis

Although no rule of thumb method can be given for testing a tune's merits conclusively, certain aspects of a composer's technique tend to produce strength, and others to produce weakness in a composition.

A melody should have good shape, i.e. the line which the notes trace should have a smooth curve and not a jagged line. Movement by step and by leap should be combined judiciously. The tune's various sections should balance one another and there should be a definite climax (see "St Magnus").[41] Sequence, if not overdone, is a valuable means of achieving this (see "Carlisle").[42] A tune should have some definite point of interest (see the suspensions in "Hereford"),[43] and some memorable, in the sense of being easy to remember, feature (see "Abbot's Leigh").[44] The flow of the tune tends to be restricted if the cadences are insufficiently varied (see

"Dix") but note also Nicholson's harmonic revisions.[45] These latter are not entirely convincing, and offer further illustration of the point made earlier about patching-up poor tunes. Despite all this, it would be unrealistic to expect "As with gladness men of old" to be sung to another tune. A tune in which the notes of the tonic chord are featured prominently is almost invariably strong, e.g. "St Anne", "Hanover", and "Regent Square".[46] Continuity of movement is well preserved in lines where there is no separating cadence, as in "Fulda",[47] lines three and four. See also "St Botolph"[48] for another beautiful instance, also in lines three and four. Unfortunately, this device has been used too freely by some twentieth-century composers, and occasionally the result has tended to be contrived.

Signs of weakness include obviousness (see "Salzburg" lines two, four and eight).[49] But the tune has a "certain something" in stateliness, particularly when J. S. Bach's harmonies are used. Other poor features include note spinning and repetition, especially to fill out a line (see "St Hugh");[50] repeated notes and phrases, e.g. "Arizona";[51] especially at a cadence (see "Stockton");[52] hovering around one or two notes (see "Eardisley");[53] a quick return to a secondary degree of the scale, especially the leading note (see "Sandys");[54] and awkward intervals in a misguided search for originality (see "Praise").[55] This is perhaps the commonest weakness in modern tunes. They sound as if the composer had originally conceived a phrase which he thought subsequently to be too conventional, and then replaced it by a strained idea which is out of keeping with the rest. Hymn tune melodies should always carry about them an air of spontaneous creation.

These apparently academic points *are* borne out in performance, and are compounded each time a tune is repeated during the course of a hymn.

Rhythm is the life-blood of all music. It is the difference between what propels a tune forward, and what breaks it up and checks its progress. Older writers have stressed the need for rhythm in church music to be sober and dignified, but since the "hymn explosion of the seventies" this is hardly a tenable position to take any longer, at any rate as concerning *all* church music. Nevertheless, rhythmic vitality is something which needs to be cultivated in slow tempi, as in quicker speeds. The absence of rhythm in so much of the music we sing in church (both inherently, and in the manner of performance), has come to be taken for granted by the people, but musicians are and should be deeply concerned about it. The attempt to restore rhythm to the old Psalter tunes has taken two forms: (a) the adoption of a stereotyped sequence of minims and semibreves (or crotchets and minims according to the type of notation used) and (b) the use of original versions of these tunes, which often have a subtle rhythm. There is much to commend in these moves, but often the attempts to make a tune rhythmical have resulted in the most hopeless verbal distortion. Books on church music, when discussing this development, have been at pains to select lines where the accentuation is happy, e.g.:

Time like an ever rolling stream
Bears all its sons away.

But in the majority of cases, as indeed is unavoidable in Iambic C.M., the accentuation of the words follows this pattern.

The race that long in darkness pined
Have seen a glorious light.

See *English Hymnal*, No. 43, where these words are set to "Dundee".

It is almost impossible for a congregation to sing these lines without reproducing the accents as marked. Indeed one of the greatest difficulties in the interpretation of all sixteenth-century vocal music is the allotment of the correct accents to the words. If a highly-trained choir experiences difficulty in this matter, how much more will an untrained congregation? There is a growing school of thought which feels that it is in order for the correct verbal accentuation to be overlooked for the sake of overall design. Thinking of a C. M. Psalter tune as being in

3 time has often been advocated, e.g.:

Perhaps at this juncture I may mention that I have long wished for a new musical sign — particularly where vocal music is concerned — the "non-accent" which would be placed over notes and words wherever there is a tendency to accent an unimportant syllable, either because it fell on an accented part of the bar or because it was set to a relatively high note: "Yet in thy dark streets shin*eth*" (when sung to either "Forest Green" or "Christmas Carol");[56] "New every morning is *the* love".[57]

In *Hymns Ancient and Modern Revised,* the presence of the "hook" sign to denote the continuation of the sense between one line and another of a hymn was criticized in some quarters, because it removed the need of a congregation to think. Yet there is little doubt that hymns are sung in churches with more intelligent phrasing than they were a generation ago. I believe the "non-accent", though a more sophisticated device, could have equally beneficial results.

I would agree that a rigid adherence to verbal quantities, and the consequent avoidance of melismas in extended musical composition, is unnecessarily cramping to a composer's inspiration, and prevents him from reaching the sublime heights of the great periods in church music where verbal quantities were occasionally overlooked.[58]

But a hymn tune is quite another thing. Its very simplicity makes it imperative for its accents to coincide with those of the words. In our zeal for historical accuracy in rhythm we must remember that *many* famous tunes date from a time when regular barring was quite unknown. Present-day congregations are so used to mensural music that rhythms in free time often strike them as being incoherent and arbitrary. I feel that Bach had an acute appreciation of this problem. Many historians comment on the loss of rhythmic interest of the Chorales in Bach's hands,[59] and indeed one can appreciate the fact for one's self by comparing the Bach and pre-Bach versions of Chorales in Woodward's *Songs of Syon*.[60] Is it not likely that Bach ironed out the rhythms of these melodies in order that they would fit the words better? In the same way we can examine the rhythmic unorthodoxy of the standard Psalm tunes as reprinted in Terry's edition of the 1635 *Scottish Psalter*. The editors of *English Hymnal* may be very proud of having restored "Commandments" to its original metre,[61] but their spirit of enterprise does not extend to all these Psalter tunes. Moreover the gathering note semibreve has not always the sanction of tradition. Sometimes one suspects that it is editorial tampering, e.g. "St Anne".[62]

One cannot devise any dogmatic solution of the problem beyond saying that the gathering note should not be used where gross misaccentuation is likely to result.

Similarly, one must ask if there is not at times a conflict between zeal for historical accuracy and artistic result. Tunes such as "Franconia", "Narenza", and "St Michael",[63] in the form we have them today, are the result of much butchery and adaptation of their originals. Instead of condemning such nineteenth-century practices, should we not simply evaluate the tunes as we have come to know them, and ignore their antecedents? If we do this, we shall be obliged to rate them at least as serviceable and unpretentious S.M. tunes. A tune moving entirely in crotchets is less monotonous than one moving in alternate minim and crotchet rhythm[64] — or some other cliché. A jigging rhythm is perhaps worse than no rhythm at all, and certain folk melodies have a rhythm which is too trite to make them suitable vehicles for adult worship. Then there are those tunes whose repeated lines exude a certain extrovert vulgarity. I wonder what Vaughan Williams thinks in his Elysian shade about the inclusion of "Lyngham"[65] for "O for a thousand tongues, to sing", where it is the first tune and "Richmond" the alternative? Is it too puritanical to condemn all such tunes? Perhaps. Certainly we should draw the line at tunes whose repetitions make nonsense of the words:

Bring down Sal-
Bring down Sal-
Bring down Salvation from the skies.

One of the reasons why dignity is no longer the respected commodity it once was is because it can lapse so easily into pomposity (see "Lux Eoi"),[66] and this in its way is every bit as bad as the tawdry jingle of the Gospel Chorus.

What is really needed from rhythm in hymn tunes is that it shall possess some interest on its own account, and yet be able to accommodate satisfactorily the rhythm of the words. Many modern composers when writing in the standard metres do so with the distinctive stresses and no-stresses of a particular lyric in mind, e.g. "Dunedin",[67] (which reminds us that tunes in the standard metres are not always interchangeable).

Of course the accentual pattern of a hymn is not always constant throughout its verses. It has been suggested that alterations such as the following be made:[68]

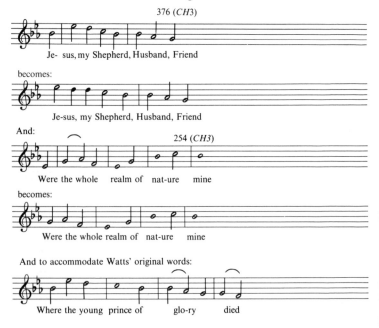

376 (*CH3*)

Je- sus, my Shepherd, Husband, Friend

becomes:

Je-sus, my Shepherd, Husband, Friend

And: 254 (*CH3*)

Were the whole   realm of   nat-ure   mine

becomes:

Were the whole realm of   nat-ure   mine

And to accommodate Watts' original words:

Where the young prince of   glo-ry   died

For my part I feel this is a counsel of perfection, and would point out that the omission or addition of notes to a tune can upset its balance. We can scarcely criticize those who amend the metres of Bach Chorales so that they may fit English words and then commit our own tunes to even worse treatment. Even those tunes which are legitimately irregular are seldom sung correctly. How often, for instance, is "Sine Nomine" sung correctly, even though the alterations from verse to verse appear to be of the most obvious kind? Perhaps one solution would be for metrically irregular verses to be treated by the choir only, in a musically satisfying version, e.g. a faux-bourdon. Even then it should be reserved for those occasions when words and music are greatly at variance with one another.

A tune should not rely on its harmony to get by. "Rivaulx", "St Andrew of Crete" and "St Aelred"[69] are instances where the melody acts as a kind of inverted pedal whilst the underparts take over the tune. Since hymn tune writing is essentially a melodic art, these Victorian part songs can hardly be described as successful. However, a fine melody can be enhanced by strong harmony, e.g. the use of diatonic seventh chords in "Sine Nomine". (The technical term is introduced deliberately, so that the musically untrained churchman may know that his emotional response to the harmony is complemented by the more intellectual response of the professional musician.) Just as the layman may not be able to analyse the effect, but still appreciates the musical sound, so he is able to distinguish between harmonic strength and ear-tickling clichés of the kind found in "Rimington".[70] A vigorous bass part usually denotes harmonic strength, e.g. "Truro",[71] whilst a stationary bass is a sign of weakness, as it is in "St Oswald".[72] The stagnant bass which includes a second inversion chord approached and quitted on its own bass (as at the beginning of "St Clement")[73] is also very weak. Unfortunately the harmony and the melody of many Victorian tunes[74] are so intimately connected that when an attempt is made to improve the harmony there is an uneasy feeling about the inappropriateness of these revisions.

Melodies and under parts that slither in chromatic semitones are bad, because their arresting quality (when they *are* arresting, that is) is vitiated by repetition through the verses (see "St Andrew").[75] There are any number of superior alternatives for "Jesus calls us". Even worse is F. C. Maker's tune "Rest" which lives up to its name all too much. Recently a friend told me that it was, in his opinion, a better tune for "Dear Lord and Father of mankind" than Parry's "Repton"! The reader may wish to compare *Methodist Hymn Book Additional Tunes,* No. 23 — "Rest" is also to be found in *seven* other contemporary hymn books — and Repton in *CH3*, No. 76. The need for "reform" could hardly be expressed more eloquently.

Chord sequences that "harp" on dominant, dominant seventh, and diminished seventh harmonies are usually to be regarded as warning signs (see line five in what is otherwise a fine tune, "Evelyns").[76] Sullivan's "St Gertrude"[77] offers us numerous examples too. It is curious how this tune flaunts virtually every canon of academic criticism, and yet is irreplaceable for "Onward! Christian soldiers". What *is* the secret of its success, that has enabled it to withstand a challenge from an alternative in virtually every book in which it has appeared? "St Dunstan"[78] is the only rival I have seen that merits consideration.

Notes

1. *English Hymnal,* (OUP, 1906), Preface, p. ix.
2. *English Church Music,* (RSCM, 1968), p. 3.
3. 300 (*CH3*), 368 (*CH3*), 455 (*CH3*), 130 (*CH3*).
4. (*AT, MHB*), and five other contemporary hymn books.
5. 39 (*CH3*).
6. 527 (*AMR*), and five contemporary hymn books.
7. *English Hymnal,* (OUP, 1906), Preface, p. ix.
8. L. Dakers, *Handbook of Parish Music,* (A. R. Mowbray, 1976), p. 62.
9. Ian Pitt Watson in J. M. Barkley, *Handbook to Church Hymnary: Third Edition,* (OUP, 1979), p. 69.
10. ... in the work of the Royal School of Church Music and other agencies.
11. But note A. Hutchings, *Church Music in the Nineteenth Century,* (Jenkins, 1967), p. 143. "Since the Lutheran Chorale there has been no finer

treasury of popular hymnody than the Victorians garnered into the first edition of Hymns Ancient and Modern 1861."

12. Not every secular tune's associated words are known to every worshipper. However, I am opposed to the use of secular folk songs in church where there is a danger of this arising. For instance the words "Waly, waly" are anything but Christian, and they remain insistently in the mind even when the tune is sung to other words.

> "O love is handsome and love is kind
> And love's jewel while it is new
> But when it's old, it groweth cold
> And fades away like morning dew."

This is set to a Baptismal hymn in *CH3*, No. 554.

In any case we are not impoverished where fine L. M. tunes are concerned. The use of the Dam Busters' March, Trumpet Voluntary, and Land of Hope and Glory as hymn tunes (see *Songs of Worship,* Scripture Union, 1980) are open to similar objection.

13. E. Routley, *Church Music and Theology,* (SCM Press, 1959), p. 75. See also p. 86 of the present work.

14. 352 (*CH3*), 388 (*CH3*).

15. C. V. Taylor's contention was that *EH* was "more than doubtfully enriched" by over 100 tunes in 1933; (*ECM*, 1976), p. 60.

16. *English Hymnal,* (OUP, 1906), Preface, p. ix.

17. It is interesting to observe that many older tunes usually regarded as *EH* discoveries were included in *AMS*, e.g. "Quem Pastores" 622, "Surrey" 554, and "Ach Gott und Herr" 415. Their widespread adoption occurred only when they came to be associated respectively with "Jesus, good above all other", "The Lord my pasture shall prepare" and "Strengthen for service". In each case the *EH* harmonizations were superior.

18. 304 (*AMR*), 527 (*AMR*).

19. E. Routley, "On Congregational Singing—the next chapter", Vol. 7, *HSB*, p. 115.

20. 304 (*AMR*).

21. W. K. Lowther Clarke, *A Hundred Years of Hymns Ancient and Modern,* (Clowes, 1960), p. 52.

22. *Hymns of Faith,* (Scripture Union, 1964), p. iii.

23. 508 (*CH2*), 434 (*CH3*).

24. 224 (*AMR*).

25. 39 (*EP*).

26. 405 (*CH3*). It has caught on by a kind of musical osmosis. But we should not rely on this process when introducing new tunes (see chapter 6 on hymn practices).

27. The deliberate and defiant use of bad music, inferring for that very reason it will be praise of greater worthiness, is still encountered in many Nonconformist chapels. Such inverted taste no doubt accounts for the use of "Lloyd" (29, *AT, MHB*) for "Fill Thou my life". There are no worries here about reaching the top F in line three, when considering the pitch of tunes! (See chapter 10.)

28. 115 (*CH3*).

29. 10 (*CH3*). A. Hutchings, *Church Music in the Nineteenth Century*, (Jenkins, 1967), p. 149.
30. 563 (*EH*).
31. 480 (*CH3*). See further comment on p. 32.
32. *A Student's Hymnal*, (OUP, 1923), Nos. 39, 179.
33. C. V. Taylor, *Way to Heaven's Door*, (Epworth Press, 1955), p. 31.
34. 79 (*CH3*).
35. See p. 33. The whole matter is discussed at some length by E. Routley in *Companion to Congregational Praise*, (Independent Press, 1953), pp. 66 et seq.
36. 258 (*CH3*).
37. See the unbelievable monstrosity "Elgar" in the élitist *Cambridge Hymnal*, No. 89, taken from the composer's "Dream of Gerontius". It is similarly a source of amazement that the holders of copyright could agree to this being done.
38. Walford Davies and Harvey Grace, *Music and Worship*, (Eyre and Spottiswoode, 1935), p. 187.
39. C. D. Parkes, Vol. 8, *HSB*, p. 71.
40. Nicholson quoted in A. S. Gregory, *Praises with Understanding*, (Epworth Press, 1936), p. 187.
41. 286 (*CH3*).
42. 39 (*CH3*).
43. 338 (*CH3*).
44. 334 (*CH3*).
45. 200 (*CH3*), 79 (*AMR*).
46. 611 (*CH3*), 35 (*CH3*), 289 (*CH3*).
47. 258 (*CH3*).
48. 674 (*CH3*).
49. 131 (*AMR*).
50. 606 (*EH*).
51. 343 (*CP*).
52. 82 (*MHB*).
53. 601 (*EH*).
54. 153 (*CH3*).
55. 535 (*EH*).
56. 172 (*CH3*), 48 (*CH2*).
57. 47 (*CH3*).
58. See Cranmer's letter to Henry VIII quoted in A. Dunstan, *These are the Hymns*, (SPCK, 1973), p. 2.
59. e.g. E. Routley, *Church Music and Theology*, (SCM Press, 1959), p. 74.
60. G. R. Woodward, *Songs of Syon*, (Schott & Co., 1919).
61. The ironing out of "Commandments" as in 551 (*CH3*) seems very difficult to justify when there are so many fine tunes of this metre waiting to be used. Compare the version given in 554 (*AMR*) and 277 (*EH*). There is a precedent for an L.M. version in Ravenscroft's Psalter of 1621, but *CH3*'s version owes nothing to it. In the latter there is no stylistic distinctiveness of any period, and there are even some consecutive fifths!

E. Routley, Vol. 4, *HSB*, p. 21. "Look at the old psalters and you will find wide variations in the rhythmical patterns of the old tunes; you will find as often as not it is the second note, not the first that is lengthened in a C.M. psalm tune, e.g. Dunfermline 378 (*BBC*)... It is, we think [safe] to assume that these early printings of psalm tunes were considerably influenced by printers' conventions, and did not necessarily represent precisely what was sung everywhere."

Because congregations have become so used to the worshipping customs of their particular denomination, any attempt at uniformity creates perhaps more difficulty than is justified. Even on great national occasions, a large congregation finds the singing of the "Old 100th" with reasonable unanimity something of a problem, when the original rhythm is attempted.

62. 450 (*EH*).
63. 74 (*CH3*), 456 (*CH3*), 46 (*CH3*).
64. One line was enough for Purcell in "Westminster Abbey" (10, *CH3*). In his original (the anthem "O Lord Thou art my God") the last pair of notes in line one is in an order opposite to the version found in the hymn books (Ernest Hawkins' arrangement of 1842).
65. 170 (*EHSB*).
66. 137 (*AMS*).
67. 127 (*MHT*).
68. Henry Coleman, *The Amateur Choir Trainer*, (OUP, 1932), pp. 93–104, where similar instances are quoted.
69. 5 (*CH2*), 91 (*AMS*), 83 (*CH2*), (but see notes 11 and 74).
70. 15 (*AT, MHB*), especially the fourth line.
71. 446 (*CH3*).
72. 61 (App. *EH*). See also p. 23.
73. 646 (*CH3*).
74. In *Music of the English Parish Church*, (CUP, 1979), pp. 303–9, Nicholas Temperley argues that the great appeal of the Victorian tune lay in the fact that it made congregations feel that when they were singing them they were in fact taking part in a sophisticated musical performance, supported as they were by a choir singing in harmony and organ accompaniment.

The pros and cons of the nineteenth-century hymn tune are discussed by Donald Webster in "Those Victorian Tunes", *Musical Opinion*, June 1981.

See also the harmonizations of Dykes' "Strength and Stay" in *AMR* and *AHB*.

See p. 23.
75. 211 (*CH3*).
76. 225 (*AMR*).
77. 480 (*CH3*).
78. 379 (*HF*).

3

What can't be analysed — and the human element

If we seriously examine the tunes we are proposing to use we eventually come up against one of undoubted excellence that defies one or other of the academic criteria laid down in the previous chapter. Goss's tune to "Praise, my soul, the King of heaven" begins with four repeated notes.[1] Yet if we play the first line, we sense that tension is being built up during those notes till it finds release in the fifth. Similarly, when played in D major, the notes A and B occur frequently in "Down Ampney".[2] The melody notes of the first two cadences are identical. Are these features to be regarded as points of weakness when making an academic judgment? Yet "Down Ampney" is regarded as "perhaps the most beautiful hymn tune composed since the Old 100th",[3] and this is a view shared by many people.

Does that then mean that academic criteria are nonsense? No, for they have a validity in the vast majority of cases, and they are useful in that they cause us to stop short when we are in doubt, and to see if there are compensating virtues in a hymn tune, qualities which may or may not subject themselves to minute analysis. There is no doubt that if one lives constantly in a worshipping atmosphere of fine hymn tunes, one instinctively spots the shoddy and rejects it, just as the minter of coins can reject the duds quickly, because he sees so many good ones.

We may be aided in the development of our taste by heeding the views of others who are engaged in the pursuit of excellence. There may be some who find their first encounters with the symphonies of Sibelius a chilling experience, and yet who persevere on the recommendation of those whose judgment they respect, and are eventually glad that they did so. So, I believe, it is with fine hymn tunes, which may not yield all their secrets at one performance, and are possibly finer for this very reason.

Hymn singing may be like politics, the art of the possible, in which compromises in choice have to be made. But the goal of excellence is worth seeking because the rewards are so great. It requires courage to say "No" to a tune that is well represented in contemporary hymnody; but if it fails to make the grade, we should reject it, because there are so many fine examples waiting to be used, and there simply isn't room enough for them all.

Then there are tunes we like, that in our hearts we know to be poor. There are tunes towards which eminent musicians are prejudiced — in both directions. Sometimes this "devil's advocacy" is amusing, and finds its parallel in secular life, when people surprise us by showing enthusiasm for something which is hardly consistent with other aspects of their taste and personality.

I would love to hear and sing Sullivan's "Lux Eoi"[4] again in all its appalling vulgarity, but because I know it to be a poor tune I would not inflict it on others. That may give some comfort to the reader who thinks that good taste in hymn tunes is "What I like".

Nobody, then, can devise a recipe for making a good tune. Many tunes are found which embody most of the virtues we have been discussing and virtually none of the faults, yet they will never be popular because they are manufactured rather than inspired. A whole line may be treated sequentially, not as a result of artistic conviction but because the composer doesn't know what to do next. Some, no doubt, come within Dr Routley's theological strictures of "Blamelessness is not enough", "Tunes which don't go the second mile" and "Tunes where the new wine is poured into the old wineskins".[5] The reader is referred enthusiastically to these books, but because the reaction to these criteria is necessarily subjective, I believe people need some Levitical dogmatism to go along with it.

In order to be successful, a tune must contain conventional and novel elements in the correct proportions, which means that the former should predominate.

Notes

1. 360 (*CH3*).
2. 115 (*CH3*).
3. E. Routley, *Companion to Congregational Praise,* (Independent Press, 1953), p. 118.
4. 137 (*AMR*).
5. E. Routley, *Church Music and Theology,* (SCM Press, 1959).
   E. Routley, *Church Music and the Christian Faith,* (Collins, 1980).

4

Organ (and other kinds of) accompaniment

To hear a series of organ accompaniments to a service is to look at a case history of psychological maladjustments

The Rev. Romilly Micklem

Every time you play the organ you give yourself away

Dr Erik Routley[1]

In many churches a congregation does not stand until the first chord of the hymn is played (i.e. after the playing over). This is to be deprecated, as it tends to cause a ragged start to the hymn. The congregation should be requested to stand with the choir, immediately the hymn is announced. In most churches, the numbers are displayed prominently, and there is no reason why congregations should not be encouraged to find their places at the conclusion of the previous hymn, and not wait until the current hymn is being played over.[2]

The manner of playing over should reflect the character and tempo of the hymn (so many organists use the same combination of stops when playing over all hymns). A penitential hymn should be played softly, but not at a slower pace than that at which the hymn will be sung. The organist should be ready to play over, immediately after the hymn is announced. This alertness will be reflected in the people's response. A hymn of praise can be introduced by playing over the first few notes on a solo reed. An unfamiliar hymn may be played over in full, but it is unwise to rely solely on this when

39

introducing a completely unfamiliar tune. Generally speaking, however, the first two lines will form a suitable introduction.[3] Even if at this point the tune seems to have no point of repose, it is better to play it as written than to add a cadence or some other modification, as this will confuse the congregation.

Of course there are exceptions. It would be clearly absurd to play over the first two lines of Elvey's "St George"[4] since, in melodic terms, they are identical and this would result in m m s m d r m being performed in fact four times in succession. In such a case the last two lines would form a suitable introduction. A similar procedure could be adopted where it would be difficult to pitch the first note after hearing the final note of line two of a tune, or where the second line ends on a discord. I have never been able to discover anything untoward about ending an introduction with a feminine cadence (e.g. "Nativity", "Hereford", or "Wiltshire"),[5] but there are those who frown upon it.[6] Some tunes, e.g. Webbe's "Veni Sancte Spiritus" and Vaughan Williams' "Down Ampney",[7] are so structured that a one line or three line introduction is advisable.

The absolute co-ordination of hands and feet in playing the initial chord, and releasing the final one of a verse after sustaining it strictly for the required number of beats is essential. It is also necessary to warn against the abitrary conversion of dominant chords into dominant sevenths.

A short pause should precede the first chord of the first verse and the organist must wait for the people's entry before moving on to the next chord. (In many churches this "waiting period" is unnecessarily long, and could be high on the list of matters to be dealt with at a congregational hymn practice.) Opinions vary as to what constitutes a suitable tempo; size of congregation, character of tune, acoustics of the church, must all be taken into account, but it is safe to say that a musically untrained person should be able to sing a line of a hymn comfortably in one breath. The suggestion that "Niceae" with its twelve syllable lines should be sung $\stackrel{\scriptstyle J}{=} 40$,[8] strikes me as absurd. Equally depressing is to hear, "When I survey [breath] the wondrous cross", which is unavoidable if too slow a tempo is taken.

The presence of a strong cadence progression in the middle of a line is, in itself, a temptation to take a breath, whether one needs it or not, and this is to be resisted. In hymns with long lines, e.g. "Maccabeus",[9] a mid-way mark of punctuation occurs frequently. It is, therefore, all the more important to sustain fully those lines whose sense is continuous, otherwise the majestic sense of progression is lost. The organist must contrive to make the time of the tune clear by implying the accented beat. This can be done by making the note before the accent slightly staccato. It is, of course, not necessary to do this in every bar. Some first beats obviously require more stress than others, but sufficient indication must be forthcoming to ensure a rhythmic performance, especially if the last beat of one bar has the same melody note as the first beat of the next, and generally one should not tie repeated notes.

The organist must regard himself as the leader of the hymn singing. His function is not comparable with that of the accompanist of a highly trained body of singers; in other words, the initiative must rest with him not with the singers. *He* must decide when to move on to the next note or line, and not leave the decision with the congregation. He must coax and help the congregation all he can, without bullying it.

The use of a staccato right hand against a legato left hand is helpful. Confidence is maintained if there is no loss of rhythm when stops are changed, and when the breaks between verses are of uniform length.

A fairly strict tempo is essential, and there should be no change in tempo between the first and last verses of a hymn. So often we feel that the organist is dying of exhaustion from playing a long hymn. On the other hand, there is no virtue in keeping half a beat ahead. Once the tempo is decided, it should be maintained throughout the hymn.

The choice of an appropriate tempo is a matter that requires careful thought, and it is well if the organist *thinks* very carefully before beginning to play over his introduction. The entire character of a tune can be destroyed by an unsuitable tempo. Choosing and keeping a suitable tempo is one of the hardest tasks which the orchestral conductor has to face, as it is for the hymn accompanist. Triple time tunes can be robbed of their dignity and made to sound like waltzes, and triumphal hymns degenerate into a "rant". Such tunes as "Blaenwern" and "Diademata" are cases in point.[10]

The occasion is important too. "Nun Danket"[11] can be a thing of great stateliness on an important national occasion, but the hymn is equally suitable for an occasion of personal thanksgiving as, for instance, at a wedding, where a slightly quicker tempo is more appropriate. On such occasions less ornate harmony (i.e. chords bereft of passing notes) may be justified.

The habit of playing as though the organist's fingers were glued to the keys is undoubtedly responsible for much slovenly singing.

If a congregation can be trained to sing a verse or part of a verse without accompaniment the result can be very thrilling, particularly when the organ resumes. For this to be effective it is desirable for it to sit in a fairly closely-knit group. Of course, old habits of where people sit die hard, and if a compact seating arrangement is not possible, an unaccompanied effect may be simulated by the organist supporting the singing by means of pedals only, or tenor and bass parts (manuals only or manuals and pedals). When the pedals are used, they should be employed consistently at the correct octave, and not invariably using stops of only 16 foot pitch.

Many writers on church music would have us believe that hymns are played too quickly rather than too slowly. Yet my own observations in many places of worship cause me to feel that in general the opposite is true.[12] It is stated that we would not prevent a soloist from making a rallentando, so why deny a congregation the same privilege?[13] The answer surely is that the singer's rallentando is a conscious act, and that subsequently a return to the original tempo will be made, whereas the congregation's rallentando springs from inertia and is persistent if unchecked. Similarly, it is said that when we listen to irregular barrings in Debussy the remark is made, "How delightfully elastic", and yet we deny our congregation the right to make similar adaptations by the introduction of pauses (of indeterminate length). Surely one must remember that irregular barring is merely one facet of Debussy's impressionist technique, and is appropriate to the idiom. What would one think of a performance of the "Hallelujah Chorus" in which every fourth bar was in 5/4 time in the interests of "delightful elasticity"? Some musicians will dismiss these remarks as savouring of "steam-roller" methods, but the fact remains that the rhythmic sense of many people is undeveloped, and if congregations are "given their head", hymn singing will become a very fatiguing business. Anyone who makes an effort to avoid breathing, except at a point which makes sense, will feel exhausted. Tunes moving entirely in crotchets require a pause of course (at the end of the second line), e.g. "Melcombe",[14] and so do tunes where the final note of a line is of only one beat duration. It is advisable in these cases for the organist to raise his hands at the end of a line so that the succeeding line can be taken up with perfect unanimity. On the other hand, a hymn tune which has a long note at the end of each line, e.g. "Eventide",[15] must be held its full length, otherwise the rhythmic flow is disturbed.

It will be helpful to think of tunes whose movement is almost entirely in crotchets, and psalm tunes, as having two slowish minim beats in the bar rather than four crotchets.[16] In selecting a suitable tempo for tunes in triple time, it must be remembered that each eight-syllable line will occupy twelve beats, whilst a quadruple time tune to the same words occupies only eight beats. In order not to overtax our singers, we should adopt a fairly brisk tempo for triple time tunes. How often have we suffered the monotony of hearing a tune like "Hyfrydol"[17] sung with breaths taken every two bars — though sometimes this is the result of thoughtlessness rather than the adoption of too slow a tempo. There is a real danger of this where a line divides naturally into sub-phrases, especially where the second sub-phrase rises to a climax, e.g. "Rockingham",[18] third line.

The second and fourth lines of C. M. tunes in triple time have only three bar phrases, and singers have therefore to be coaxed into beginning the third line promptly.

The Chorale is a type of tune whose tempo presents problems. Many people feel that most of Bach's harmonizations are too elaborate for congregational use, and prefer versions with few passing notes. Yet they claim that the slow tempi adopted for Bach must be adopted for the simpler versions, with consequent breathing difficulties. Surely, the reason for the slow tempo in Bach's versions is so that his elaborate passing notes and changes of harmony on the second half of beats have time to register. If a simpler harmonization is used, I feel that one is entitled to adopt a tempo which is convenient for untrained singers.

Punctuation marks in a hymn are of two kinds; those which are essential for grammatical requirements, and those which are observed in deliberate reading. It is the second class only which concerns the organist, and must be observed by him, as the congregation takes its lead from the organ.[19] It is important that the note *before* the comma be shortened by an amount corresponding to the break, as the rhythm of the tune should not suffer undue disturbance. It is a good plan for the organist to mouth the words whilst playing, as this helps to ensure a consistent tempo; for it is reasonable to suppose that the physical effort of playing and singing reduces the organist's breath control to the level of the average member of the congregation. One particularly bad habit to which choirs as well as congregations are prone is to shorten excessively the final note of a phrase, and give it a heavy staccato thump before taking a breath. The cure for this is to encourage our singers to give a fraction more value to the vowel sound, to take the breath more quickly and sing the note lightly. This may seem to be a counsel of perfection, but if choirs are trained to do this, especially when singing hymns as anthems, some congregations may acquire the habit. A 45-minute rehearsal before a broadcast "concentrates the mind wonderfully", and it is surprising how a significant amount of choral refinement may be acquired during a short, purposeful congregational hymn practice, and how much can be "suggested" by an alert accompanist. Rhythm and phrasing are infinitely more important than fussy registration.

Registration

Organists tend to be unduly influenced by piston selection in their choice of stops. The use of uncoupled manuals, diapasons only, single stops, stops drawn from only one tonal family, some relief from incessant four foot sound, playing senza pedal, or with only eight foot pedal stops, using eight foot and two foot omitting the four foot rank, and playing the melody an octave higher are just a few of the resources available to the imaginative player. The variety of sound on even the smallest organs is greater than we tend to think.[20] It is the sound above and below one's own singing that is really heard and which for this reason can sound oppressive. High pitched mixtures and reeds tend to pall if used too frequently in too long stretches. In general much organ accompaniment is too loud. It does not support the congregation; it stifles the singing and the congregation surrenders in a hopeless struggle by not singing at all.

Whatever virtues the Baroque organ may have for delineating contrapuntal lines in recital pieces, it has serious limitations as an accompanying instrument. Variety of texture, and a continuo approach with frequent inversion of upper parts, are more fruitful ways of securing variety of sound than in changes of registration.

In normal circumstances a *four part texture should be adhered to*, but a gradual thickening at climaxes is a useful way of building up volume quickly without the necessity for awkward stop changes. Similarly, a paring down of the texture can be useful in securing a diminuendo. Playing a line or two in two or three part harmony provides textural variety. Care needs to be taken that thirds from chords are not omitted.

In most verses it will not be necessary to change stops more often than at a verse end. Frequent changes in volume tend to perplex a congregation, particularly a sudden "piano". Increases can be introduced successfully during a verse, provided that they are not too violent, but the start of a new verse is the best place for a return to the former level. It is customary nowadays to point the finger of scorn at the type of expression marks found in the editions of *Hymns Ancient and Modern,* but I feel that the pendulum has swung so far in the opposite direction that many organists feel that it is a point of honour to show an almost callous disregard for the expression of the words. Changes of volume can be undertaken without any diminution of support by soloing the melody. A word of warning must be uttered against the ultra-legato playing on Full Swell closed, with octave and sub-octave couplers. Such playing is unhelpful to the congregation and effectively swamps whatever lead may otherwise be forthcoming from the choir.

In his desire to avoid monotony, the organist may wish to play something other than the harmonized version of the hymn sung by the choir. Four possibilities may be considered:

1. Soloing the tenor;
2. Playing the melody in the tenor register as a solo;
3. Inversion of parts, preserving the original harmonies;
4. Free harmonization, with or without the melody in the top part.

1. The tenor is the most convenient part to solo. Occasionally, a few notes may be borrowed from the alto to add to the melodic interest, but care must be taken to ensure that the four parts are at all times present in either solo or accompaniment. The solo stop should be approximately equal in strength to the accompaniment yet tonally contrasted with it. It must be remembered that this device is only a decoration to the congregation's part, not a rival.

The soloing may be done either at normal pitch or an octave higher.[21]

2. This method is a kind of organ faux-bourdon. To do this straight from an ordinary version of the tune requires an advanced organ technique. At first the organist may find that his left hand is wandering off on to the tenor part, or that his right hand is playing the melody also. He may find it more convenient to play the melody with the right hand an octave lower, and to adapt the alto and tenor parts on the accompanying manual with the left hand. However, the former technique is the more valuable, especially in extemporizing and in gaining independence of hands, and should be practised seriously.

3. This is the easiest method to adopt. One must remember that *the bass part must be unaltered,* and the chord structure of the original must not be altered, save for the introduction of an odd passing note. Some writers stress the need for avoiding consecutive fifths and octaves which are apt to arise, particularly when consecutive first inversions are found in certain spacings but, except between outside parts, they sound quite harmless against a choir singing in harmony.

4. This is the most dangerous type of accompaniment and in its name we are often subjected to the most frightful outrages. Unless the organist has a real flair (a rare gift) for this type of work, he is advised not to rely on his own premeditated efforts. Even some of the published efforts are very fussy, and require a disciplined body of singers to withstand them.[22] Each free harmonization should be rehearsed with the choir, if it is thought that it may be taken unawares. It is advisable to avoid harmonizations which contain an over-liberal use of chromatic chords which obscure the tonality, and therefore distort the character of the tune.[23] A free harmonization which overtaxes the organist's ability must inevitably slow down the tempo of the hymn. At the same time, chords must have the

opportunity to register. There is of course much difference between the deliberate adoption of a *slow* tempo and a rhythmically uncertain tempo, which a free harmonization forces on an incompetent organist, and this difference is apparent in performance. In the abundance of accidentals found in many versions, wrong notes are apt to be played, and what should be a magnificent climax becomes mere discordant noise, accompanied by a few brave souls fighting a losing battle, trying to sing the tune at a funereal tempo.

Clarity in playing, and avoidance of low pitched reeds, are even more important than usual, and where a counter melody overlaps the lines, there must be no uncertainty on the part of the congregation as to where the various lines begin. It will be appreciated how important it is to keep strict tempo at the ends of lines as a general rule, for a congregation at a church where the lengths of notes at ends of lines are left to chance can hardly be expected to keep strict time in unison verses when no help is forthcoming from the organ.

Although the choirs may have certain verses marked "Unison" in their books or service sheets, it is often desirable to play the first few notes of a unison verse in octaves. This has a two fold effect: (a) it reminds them that the verse is to be sung in unison and (b) it gives a bold, confident start.

Lastly, one must err on the side of moderation. Good relations between organist and congregation can easily be disturbed on account of too advanced harmonizations, and the majority of choirmen dislike a great deal of unison singing.

In the preface to *Songs of Praise,* Dr Vaughan Williams stated that strict time at the ends of lines is artistically bad and congregationally impossible. Anyone is at liberty to test the "impossibility", which I would question. In any case, how is an overlapping descant line treated, unless the melody is sung in strict time? (There are numerous examples of this in *Songs of Praise*.)[24] I cannot see how confident hymn singing can be developed if the rhythmic pulse is disturbed every three or four bars.

Accompaniment by other instruments

The *Motu Proprio* of 1903 issued by Pope Pius X stated that instruments other than the organ were not to be used without the bishop's special permission, and the organ was to play a modest role in accompanying, and not to be allowed to cover up the singing. The *Oxford Companion to Music,* in the person of its first editor, Percy Scholes, wrote: "It laid down general principles recognised everywhere by cultured intelligent and devout musicians as being sound." Although much water has flowed under the bridge since 1903, or 1938 when Scholes' words first appeared in print, this is a view which would command the support of many churchgoers of all denominations today.

But clearly there are occasions when other instruments may have to be used, and are being used, sometimes in an attempt to be "with it", and these may be considered briefly.

Because the piano is a percussive instrument, it can score over the organ in its ability to impart rhythmic vitality into singing with comparative ease. Its disadvantage is that sustaining power is virtually impossible without recourse to the pedals, and that the tone may become harsh and metallic whilst a lead is being given, especially in a reverberant building, where the sound can also seem disembodied. The need to re-edit the hymn book textures is even more necessary than is the case with the organ. Playing the melody in octaves and rearranging the other parts so that they can be played by the left hand, or playing the bass in octaves and the three upper parts in the right hand are skills on which it is frequently necessary to draw.

As an addition to the organ, strings are invaluable. They can enrich the texture enormously. One has only to listen to, say, the middle movement of Bach's Cantata No. 140, "Sleepers Wake, a Voice is Calling", where the written parts consist merely of violins I and II and violas playing in unison, and a cello/bass continuo line, to notice how strings and organ together can sound very rich indeed.

So many children begin to learn stringed instruments nowadays, and the number of those who give up is disappointingly high. For children to be asked to play in hymn performances would give them an incentive to persevere, in that the result would sound pleasing and effective out of all proportion to the effort involved.

Simple parts which use only the open strings can be devised easily; for example, here is one for "St Ethelwald":

The use of descants and a reinforcement of the melody at the higher octave are effective devices for more advanced players.

Trumpets to give melody and/or descant support is also a thrilling device provided that it is not overdone. The need to choose practicable keys for the B flat trumpet has to be borne in mind. An occasional verse in a festive hymn accompanied by a brass ensemble is also extremely effective.

Next to the organ, the guitar is the commonest form of accompanying instrument. Virtually no contemporary hymn collection is without its guitar symbols. Let me say at once that I find nothing inherently improper in the guitar. It is an excellent instrument for supporting "folk" singing, either religious or secular in the informal Youth Group. Its use in church is another matter. Amplification distorts the guitar's sound and exposes its lack of tonal variety. More seriously, many of the arrangements which seek to cater for the limited skill of the beginner, simplify, and in the process seriously cheapen, the harmonic content — either that written by the original composer or implied in a modern melody. It is a convention of Western music that harmonic rhythm (the rate of chord change) increases as the cadence (the point of musical punctuation that ends a phrase) is reached. Many arrangements seek to minimize the frequency of such a chord change.

As the cadence points are approached, sensitive souls may wince at the harmonic "fudging" that is taking place to produce a slower rate of chord change to accommodate guitarists' technical limitations. One grows tired, too, with the poverty-stricken monotony of the type of figuration indulged in by so many players. Of course, skilled guitar playing is not open to this objection, but the tonal limitations of the instrument still apply, though to a lesser extent.

Notes

1. E. Routley, *Church Music and the Christian Faith,* (Collins, 1980), pp. 99–100.
2. The custom of having duplicated pew sheets is an excellent one, and the prominent display of hymn numbers should eliminate the need for announcements, which can have a disruptive effect on a service, and impede its momentum.
3. Generally I prefer to play over two lines, because it is a convention in Western music for the announcing phrase to require a response. To play over only one phrase leaves matters "in the air" and fails to establish the tune in the minds of the congregation.
4. 627 (*CH3*).
5. 48 (*CH3*), 338 (*CH3*), 387 (*CH3*).
6. See E. Routley, *Organist's Guide to Congregational Praise,* (Independent Press, 1957).
7. 156 (*AMR*), 115 (*CH3*).
8. 162 (*EH*).

    John Curwen, in *Studies in Worship Music,* (Curwen, 1880) states that psalm tunes were sung $d = 30$ until 1848.
9. 279 (*CH3*).
10. 473 (*CH3*), 298 (*CH3*).
11. 368 (*CH3*).
12. Most churches are required to sing hymns more quickly than is their custom when taking part in radio and television hymn broadcasts.
13. This matter is discussed at some length in Harvey Grace, *The Complete Organist,* (Richards, 1947).
14. 47 (*CH3*).
15. 695 (*CH3*).
16. See p. 28. This helps to reduce the number of accented notes and thus improve the flow.
17. 381 (*CH3*).
18. 237 (*CH3*).

19. Consider the absurdity of observing every mark of punctuation in this verse from 376 (*CH3*):

Jesus, my Shepherd, Husband, Friend,
My Prophet, Priest, and King,
My Lord, my Life, my Way, my End,
Accept the praise I bring.

20. H. Coleman, *The Amateur Organist,* (OUP, 1955), quotes twenty alternative schemes without physically changing stops.
21. In either case the treble and alto will be at normal pitch.
22. Bairstow's arrangements (OUP) are too intricate for normal church use.
23. Organists must decide for themselves on the type of harmonic language in relation to the style of the tune and its period. No one ruling meets all circumstances or type of tune.

Both in his theoretical writings, *Varied Harmonisation to Hymn Tunes,* (OUP, 1934), and in his practical examples, *Varied accompaniments to 34 well known hymn tunes,* (OUP, 1937), and *44 Hymn Tunes Freely Harmonised,* (Novello, 1969), Eric Thiman was an admirable mentor.

To play the organ part of a descant arranged on free harmonies without the descant being sung is often useful.

Hymn Tune Accompaniment for Unison Singing, (RSCM, 1971), is recommended.
24. e.g. 437.

5

New words

Much of the contemporary "hymn explosion" has resulted from a desire to expand hymnody's range of subject matter. The hymns of previous generations have assumed a predominantly agricultural society, whereas ours is predominantly industrial. It is commonly believed that hymns need to express the Gospel in terms of Human Rights, the Third World, Race Relations, Social Justice, etc., in a more explicit manner than say, G. K. Chesterton's "O God of earth and altar".[1] Whilst we may agree with Bernard Manning that the business of a hymn is to strengthen the faith of today and not to present a historical record of the faith of the day before yesterday,[2] there are dangers:

1. that we lose sight of the timeless elements of our faith;
2. that we give musical utterance to matters, e.g. urban housing problems, that can be expressed more appropriately in other ways. The Protest Song is often dispiriting, unredemptive, and negative;
3. that we may sing hymns that are thinly-disguised political propaganda fashioned by non- or even anti-Christians in which God is brought in as an afterthought, if at all.

As Dr Routley has said: "So much is happening now in hymnody that is depressing or strident or mediocre or downright irreligious." Whilst most of us live in towns and cities, surely we are not incapable of witnessing the marvels of God's creation when we visit the country. "God made the

53

country but man made the town" may be a trite expression, but we should be encouraged to step aside from our technological marvels and seek fresh delight in the miracles of nature. Isaac Watts has expressed this in matchless language in hymn after hymn, and it is good to find "Nature with open volume stands"[3] in no fewer than seven of the hymn books and supplements of recent years. The allusions to nature are confined to verse one, in what is essentially a Passiontide hymn.

The best modern hymns are challenging, and we diminish the role of music if we think it is merely a vehicle for the words, rather than an enhancing complement to them. It is desirable to look beyond the confines of one's hymn book and its supplement, and to defer judgment until a new hymn has had one or two "airings". Many of the words are of the carol type, and are written in so distinctive a metre that the choice of tune hardly arises, but such a hymn as "God of concrete God of steel" has attracted a different musical setting in several of the six books in which it has appeared (see the index). Whilst I have doubts as to whether these words, with their strident references to the contemporary urban scene, leave one much edified, the fact that they *are* so widely represented necessitates a decision generally acceptable as to the most satisfactory tune.

It has been said that new words demand new tunes, and the analogy of new wine in old wineskins has already been quoted.[4] Since many of the "standard marriages" between words and music bridge the centuries,[5] to treat contemporary religious verse as a special case seems to be unjustified. In any case, a new hymn is more likely to gain acceptance when sung to an older familiar tune. The idea that the older idiom of the music somehow diminishes the impact of modern words is one that hardly bears close examination.[6] Some new verse has been written which "carries" most effectively a good alternative tune to a standard hymn. For instance, Thalben Ball's "Arthog"[7] fails to rival Monk's for "Angel voices, ever singing". Yet the newer tune hardly deserves extinction. It may now enjoy an independent existence in company with David Mowbray's words, "Come to us creative spirit".[8] Some present-day writers have used the standard metres with a high degree of flexibility, and only the freer rhythms of the modern tune can cope with them effectively. In general, one should warn against the automatic assumption that words can always be sung to tunes of identical metre. Some writers, notably the Rev. Caryl Micklem,[9] have written their tunes with specific words in mind, and we should endeavour to respect these associations.

Nevertheless, we should avoid giving too uncritical a welcome to post-war hymns and tunes, lest in the end all this material, the good and the bad, be subsequently lumped together as "contemporary" or "modern" or "twentieth century", using those terms pejoratively as some people, equally irrationally, talk of "traditional" and "Victorian" hymnody as having equivalent meaning. Just as "bad money drives out the good", so bad contemporary hymns and music may preclude the use of the good, of which there is a substantial amount.

We have to be careful, too, about double standards. There is little point in jettisoning well-loved hymns because of their theological inadequacy, if their replacements are, as Robin Leaver puts it somewhat euphemistically, "not as theologically orthodox as those of earlier generations". He points out that to express modern concerns of urban life "basic theological truths have been distorted".[10] In past times people have gone to the stake for this; it is called heresy.

There are double standards too about altering and modernizing the original words of hymns. Percy Dearmer declared that he had, whenever possible, printed the words of hymns as their authors had left them as a matter of editorial principle in the *English Hymnal*. He pointed out that often the freshness of the original had been replaced by conventional phrases in other books. In fact, this principle was departed from more often in the *English Hymnal* than that book's admirers find convenient to admit, and in *Songs of Praise* (which Dearmer also edited) we find alterations made which have the effect of weakening doctrine. No later twentieth-century editor has seen fit to adhere to the "original version" principle. The editors of *Ancient and Modern Revised* claim in their preface that in many instances the authors themselves admitted the superiority of the altered version for singing purposes.

With the foregoing in mind, let us compare the Whitsuntide hymn "Come, thou Holy Spirit, come" in *Ancient and Modern Revised* with "Come, thou Holy Paraclete" as it appears in the *English Hymnal.* I have accompanied, as a Wedding hymn, both versions, for which purpose they are appropriate. There is no doubt in my mind which is the more *practical* version — even if it does yield in "freshness" to the other.[11]

> Heal our wounds; our strength renew;
> On our dryness pour Thy dew;
> Wash the stains of guilt away;
> Bend the stubborn heart and will;
> Melt the frozen, warm the chill;
> Guide the steps that go astray.
>   E. Caswall and compilers (*AMR*)

> What is soilèd, make Thou pure;
> What is wounded, work its cure;
> What is parchèd, fructify;
> What is rigid, gently bend;
> What is frozen, warmly tend;
> Straighten what goes erringly.
>   J. M. Neale (*EH*)

Such emendations as have taken place have been usually linguistically consistent with the original. It would appear, then, that this was hardly an issue in our time, but it has been yet another stick to beat the editors of the hapless *Anglican Hymn Book* for their (apparently) doctrinal alterations.[12]

Attempts to modernize older hymns, such as one encounters in *New Catholic Hymnal* are a much more radical matter. If the contemporary hymn writer wishes to use the second person plural when addressing the Deity, that is his affair, but to force other, older hymns into this convention is hardly justified. It is not merely in the last ten or fifteen years that the language of

the *Book of Common Prayer* and the Authorized version of the
Bible have been archaic; they have been in that condition for
three hundred years. What would one think of a similar
"modernizing" process carried out on Palgrave's *Golden
Treasury*? Radically altering the texts of standard hymns is not
only offensive to those for whom they are the treasure of a
lifetime, but it effectively inhibits effective ecumenical worship,
unless one or more of the participants is to make a wholesale
surrender of his tradition. Because the Roman Catholics are
still in the process of discovering the value and the delight of
hymn singing in a vernacular liturgy, they have no such
tradition, and presumably feel free to vandalize anything that
comes to hand.

Modernizing involves so much more than replacing one
pronoun with another. Following scriptural precedent, the
vocative case has been used freely by the older hymn writers,
and when this is modernized, instead of an attitude of praise
or penitence being evoked, we have all too often the image of
the bullying schoolmaster or the demanding child. Our services
will be severely impoverished if we try to reduce our words
and our music to a unified idiom.

Notes

1. 562 (*EH*).
2. John Wilson, *English Church Music*, (RSCM, 1972), p. 39.
3. 164 (*MHT*).
4. See p. 37.
5. "Turn back, O man", 84 (*CH3*), is a happy instance of twentieth-century
   words wedded indissolubly to a sixteenth-century tune.
6. "In most cases I write hymns with a tune in mind", F. Pratt Green,
   quoted by C. V. Taylor in *Church Music Quarterly*, (RSCM, Jan. 1981), p.
   5.
7. 455 (*CH3*).
8. 24 (*PP*).
9. But I think most people would consider that his literary gifts are superior
   to his musicianship.
10. Robin Leaver, *A Hymn Book Survey 1962–80*, No. 71, (Grove Worship
    Series, 1980), p. 20.

11. Compare also: God the One in Three adoring
                  In glad hymns externally   474 (*AMR*)
             with: God the One and God the Trinal
                  Singing everlastingly   170 (*EH*)
              and: Thus unite we to adore Him   161 (*AMR*)
             with: Thus conspire we to adore Him   372 (*EH*).

Clinging tenaciously to archaic and obscure expressions as found in the originals of some hymns, rather than sanctioning a modest revision within the same idiom, is undoubtedly responsible, at least in part, for the much more violent idiomatic revisions of standard hymns that have taken place recently.

12. See Robin Leaver, *A Hymn Book Survey 1962–80,* No. 71, (Grove Worship Series, 1980), p. 8. "It was criticised for radically altering the texts of some of the hymns."

But note also John S. Andrews in the *Evangelical Quarterly,* No. 3, Vol. 52, (Paternoster House, 1980). "The texts of the hymns are accurate, but not pedantically so."

6

Congregational hymn practices

Despite their widespread advocacy, congregational hymn practices do not appear to have been held widely. Perhaps that is because it has been assumed that if hymn practices are announced they will not be supported; surely a rather rash assumption. They must be made attractive for those who attend them. In order to be successful, a sound technique must be adopted to suit the particular conditions, and they must be held at regular intervals so that people become used to their being part of the regular parochial Kalendar.

Much discussion has arisen as to what is the best time to arrange them. Whatever decision is reached, it is bound to be inconvenient for someone. Personally, I believe that before the sermon at a Sunday service once a month is the most suitable time.[1] It avoids the interruptions caused by late comers, as happens when practices are held before service, and it enables some period of time to elapse between practice and performance. People learn subconsciously, and all choirmasters know that a work taken up at one rehearsal is often better known the following week than the way it was left the previous week. If the practice is held before the service, not sufficient time has elapsed for the instruction to register before the congregation is called upon to sing. A hymn practice after a service is inevitably an anticlimax.

The first task of the choirmaster is to encourage the congregation to *sing*. In most churches the standard of singing well-known hymns is far from satisfactory and there is little

hope of new tunes "catching on" if the *good* old favourites are
sung with diffidence. By his encouraging manner the
choirmaster should stimulate confidence. He should make it
obvious to all that hymn singing matters to *him*. By his playing
he can radiate his own enthusiasm by vigorous and imaginative
accompaniment. He should know the hymns he proposes to
practise thoroughly, so that there are no awkward pauses whilst
he refers to his hymn book, and should be clear in his mind as
to what he hopes to achieve. The most satisfactory place to
direct the practice is from a piano in the nave of the church, so
arranged that there is sympathetic contact between choirmaster
and congregation. The percussive tones of a piano are often
more helpful, particularly in rhythm, than the heavier tone of
the organ. Moreover, continuity is likely to be maintained
more satisfactorily than where the choirmaster has to give
detailed instructions to his deputy at the organ each time a
halt is made. The presence of the choir is important, too, as it
can be used for leading and demonstration. At the start of
each practice, the congregation should be asked to move
forward, so that it is in a manageable block. Good singing can
seldom be provided by a scattered congregation.

After the congregation has lost some of its inhibitions, a
start can be made on correcting some of the most common
faults of hymn singing, e.g. sluggish beginnings to verses,
scooping, singing on consonants, clipping semibreves in triple
time tunes, breathing every half line even where the tempo
permits a whole line in one breath, and wrong notes such as
disfigure tunes like "Austria", "St Anne", "Mendelssohn",
"Nun Danket" and "Adeste Fideles". A significant
improvement can often be achieved merely by congregations
being asked to open their mouths and hold up their heads!

During these early stages of hymn practising, the tunes
selected should be those which are particular favourites. The
choirmaster's manner should be reverent yet friendly. He must
be quick to sense the congregation's reactions to the work in
hand and turn to something else, even if the performance is
not to the required standard, if there appears to be lack of

interest. No point should be laboured; a little and often is the precept given to piano pupils, yet many choirmasters fail to carry out their own advice when rehearsing choral music. Minute particularizing is an essential element in the later stages of choral rehearsing, but it is clearly out of place when dealing with untrained singers at a congregational practice. Some attention to phrasing and accentuation (and non-accentuation) can be paid, however.

The choirmaster can avoid a laboured rehearsal by taking careful note of the difficulties encountered by his choir in learning a particular tune. It is safe to say that what will tax it is likely to be an even greater problem to a congregation. Whilst it is said that to anticipate difficulty is to create it, I have found that much routine drudgery can be avoided by singers having their attention drawn to likely stumbling-blocks. Equally, if a choir finds a certain tune very difficult to learn, it may be unwise to introduce it at a hymn practice at all. Such a tune may be quite good as music, worthy of a place in the service but uncongregational, and should be kept in the choir's repertoire of hymn anthems.

Unless a tune new to the parish is very simple or generally well-known, it is not wise to rehearse it with the congregation until it has been performed as an anthem. Even then, every effort must be made to ensure that the congregation will make a reasonable attempt the first time it is called upon to sing. First impressions, where a tune is concerned, are often crucial. One must remember that the congregation's presence is voluntary, and it will make no attempt to learn something that it does not like. It is often possible for the choirmaster to find out what the congregation's reaction to a tune is between its performance as an anthem and the congregational practice.

The best kind of tune to learn is one to an unfamiliar General Hymn, for then it can be repeated at intervals until its place is sufficiently assured for it to be incorporated into the standard repertoire. Not until hymn practices are underway is it advisable to introduce a new tune to displace a bad old favourite. The hymn should not be performed at all during this period.

Not more than two new tunes and preferably only one, i.e. those that the congregation will have to *learn,* should be introduced at a practice, one for performance at a morning service and one for an evening service sometime during the ensuing month.

Vocalizing, reading of words, and other techniques adopted with a choir when learning new music, are clearly out of place at a hymn practice, but asking the congregation to sing the tune "to itself", whilst the piano "soloes" the melody before a performance at full volume, is a sound procedure. It is also desirable to present the tune as a whole in the first instance before treating it a line or two at a time.

Whilst the choirmaster should not be preoccupied with the idea that a hymn practice offers opportunity for self-advertisement, he should remember that the congregation will assess his skill as a choirmaster by the manner in which he conducts the practice, and by the results he achieves.

A verse or two of a well-loved hymn should begin and end all practices. The time taken up by this is well spent, for it ensures enjoyment and can often be used for performing a descant or faux-bourdon.

The task of learning a new tune is greatly helped if copies of the music are available. Many members of congregations like to "sing seconds" or a bit of tenor or bass, thinking that there's something rather inferior about singing in unison. It is said that *Hymns Ancient and Modern* taught English congregations the delights of participating in a harmonized performance,[2] whereas the *English Hymnal* introduced them to the more austere practice of unison singing. The desire to harmonize, found mostly in older members of the congregation, is clearly a survival from *Ancient and Modern's* early days. To avoid an unseemly scramble for tune books before a service — and undue expense — our would-be altos, tenors and basses might be persuaded to buy their own books, and may thus be induced to sing the correct notes. The "fuzz" that they provide for a unison congregation and a choir in harmony is harmless enough, and causes little damage to the overall effect, however disturbing it might be to their immediate neighbours.

Melody only editions are much cheaper, and as words only hymn books wear out, they could be replaced with melody editions as normal congregational policy.[3] Few people nowadays are unfamiliar with at least the appearance of musical notation. They can be encouraged to note the rise and fall of familiar tunes and how this corresponds to the actual sound, and then apply this to the learning of new material.

If a church is in the frequent habit of not singing the tunes set, members of congregations will resent having to look at words in one part of the book and tunes in another, even more than choir members do. Possession of tune books may therefore be an added incentive to churches to be more enterprising in their choice of tunes, but occasions will certainly arise when a tune other than the one set will be needed.

Notes

1. Two particular problems must be faced when hymn practices take place during a service. The first concerns the total length of the service, at a time when pressures of all kinds are towards shorter rather than longer services.

   Without any sacrifice of seemliness, time can be saved by not announcing hymns (see p. 51) and by listing these, and parochial intimations on a pew sheet. In many churches, the latter are now so numerous that when they are announced verbally, many members of congregations "switch off" — thus defeating the object of the exercise. In any case, the mentioning of Treasure Hunts, Barbecues, and Discos at a solemn point in the service strikes a jarring note. Time thus saved could be devoted to a hymn practice. Perhaps on such occasions the choir's anthem performance could be foregone too.

   Some clergy may even be willing to sacrifice a sermon occasionally for such a worthy cause, but if this is not possible, a short address built round the personalities of the author and composer, and an explanation of the text would be an excellent means of integrating the hymn practice into the service, and of providing a teaching sermon.

   Our second difficulty arises from the structure of the services themselves. Where these are of the Free Church type, a "spot" immediately after the Offering is suitable for a hymn practice. The organist's offertory voluntary could take the form of an improvisation on the new tune, and this could be mentioned on a pew sheet. By this means, the congregation's ears can be attuned, before the formal learning process even begins. The last few minutes before a service could also be devoted to an improvisation on a new tune.

Family services, and the Anglican offices of Matins and Evensong similarly present no problem, since a practice conducted after the Grace would in no way disturb the service as set forth in the *Book of Common Prayer*.

However, in many Anglican churches, parish Communion is the only Sunday service at which a sizeable congregation is present. On these occasions a hymn practice near the beginning of the service would be possible, and the new hymn could then be sung by the choir as a Communion motet later in the service during the Administration, if its subject matter is appropriate.

The manner of the performance of music at this point in the service is something that requires much-needed reform. I have never found the singing of hymns (often with long lines, such as "And now, O Father" and "O thou, who at thy Eucharist didst pray") at half-speed, with all the attendant problems of breath control, an edifying experience. The difficulties are compounded when these are sung kneeling.

A comfortable tempo should be chosen, and the choir should stand to lead the singing, as well as to perform its own music.

2. See note 74, p. 35.
3. Words only editions of hymn books are a peculiarly British phenomenon. However, the North American practice of printing the words of a stanza or two between the staves of music is not one to be emulated, since it frequently obscures the meaning.

7

Vocal variety in hymn singing

There is little doubt that varied treatment of verses in hymn singing contributes much to the interest and vitality of the performance. If the organist will stop to consider, possibilities for variation are numerous. For the choir, such devices as descant, solo quartet, solo, faux-bourdon, unison, harmony, unaccompanied singing, women only, men only, readily come to mind. Occasional verses by choir or congregation alone help to make both bodies aware of their individual responsibility in hymn singing. The choir's performance, whether full or sectional, can often serve as an object lesson to the congregation. Whilst broad treatment is required in congregational singing a refined performance of a verse by a trained body of singers in a choir will often reveal fresh beauties in an over-familiar hymn, and each member of the congregation will respond, whether consciously or not, by making his or her contribution a little more worthy.

Numerous services are held when no choir is available and the singing tends to be rather feeble. The experience of singing by itself at Sunday services should help the congregation to sing with more confidence at occasional services. It strikes me as being the height of stupidity to set unfamiliar tunes to hymns which receive only an annual performance, e.g. hymns for Saints' Days. It would be better on these occasions to use a well-known tune to the words set. In many churches feasts are left uncommemorated so far as hymns are concerned because the set tunes are not known, and have little opportunity of ever becoming known. If the using of known tunes is not feasible, the choir could perform the special hymn as an anthem.

Suggestions have been made that the congregation be subdivided into North Aisle, South Aisle, etc., and with a large congregation such a hymn as "All glory, laud, and honour" would sound very fine, but until a strong hymn tradition has been built up in a church any attempt to subdivide the congregation (apart from men and women) is to court disaster.[1]

When the choir is singing by itself, perhaps a more elaborate version of the tune could be sung. For instance, far more standard tunes than are popularly supposed have harmonizations by Bach which are too elaborate for congregational use,[2] but whose superlative beauty deserve performance. (The question of cost is a burden which faces most choirmasters. However, Bach's Chorales are not copyright, and may be duplicated without incurring legal troubles.)

The congregation must be told what verses it is to sing alone, etc., and it is advisable not to have too much complication in any one hymn — at any rate from the congregation's point of view. For instance, supposing in a six verse hymn we adopt the following scheme:

Verse 1	All, choir in harmony
Verse 2	Quartet
Verse 3	Unison
Verse 4	Harmony
Verse 5	Congregation only
Verse 6	Unison and descant.

It is then sufficient to announce only that verse two will be sung by the choir and verse five by the congregation.

Faux-bourdons have never been widely used, and in these days they present added difficulties. The melody is usually assigned to the tenor part — a department which is distinctly light-weight in many choirs. Moreover, the melody often lies in the least sonorous part of the tenor voice, below G. Baritones and basses are fairly plentiful, and it may be possible for some of these to be transferred to the melody in a faux-bourdon. I am aware that many basses, even those who are good sight-readers, have difficulty in holding an inner part, but this difficulty is scarcely likely to arise in the case of a well-known hymn melody. The tunes rarely rise above D, so no difficulty of range is likely to arise for baritones. Yet the fact remains that faux-bourdons were intended to be sung by tenors, and it strikes me as inconsistent that low-pitched tunes should be advocated, alongside the use of faux-bourdons. A low-pitched tenor part requires the surrounding harmony to lie equally low for the individual voices.

The other voices in the choir must be urged to sing sufficiently softly to enable the melody to be heard — otherwise the faux-bourdon loses its point, and it may be advisable for the people's part to be "soloed" by the organist to help the congregation. Most composers find that the writing of a faux-bourdon based on the original harmonies is too restricting, and use a different harmonization. It must be admitted that many of these versions are unsatisfactory, and on melodic grounds leave something to be desired. (Historically, the device is the employment of contrapuntal melody strands rather than blocks of chords accompanying a tenor *canto fermo*.) The *Tenor Tune Book* (Faith Press) and *Songs of Praise* contain a fair number of faux-bourdons, but neither collection can be recommended unreservedly. Faux-bourdons can often by used by the organist for accompanying a unison verse. They have the advantage over other types of "free harmonies" in that the melody can always be kept in the foreground, and seeing that they are intended to be sung, are not "outlandish" in terms of the resultant harmony. However, the tonality is often vague and they may sound falsely archaic.

Descants are much more practicable, yet even these are not used frequently in most churches. It is of course desirable to use descants chiefly for tunes that are used most often so that a fair return is given for the work of learning them. They need careful rehearsal. It should not be necessary for trebles to have to *rely* on the organ for their part (and it should *never* be soloed by the organist). His duty is to give the congregation all possible assistance. In so many churches, one feels that the organist and his trebles are engaged in a conspiracy to annihilate all opposition. No descant should be performed unless (a) the trebles can sing their part confidently and without organ assistance, and (b) they can sing whilst organist, adult choir and congregation are performing the tune. The congregation is more capable of detecting flaws in the choir's work than many choirmasters imagine, and they would prefer choirs not to attempt extras rather than do them badly. They are quick to notice when choirboys are trying to sing an inadequately rehearsed descant.

Those descants which rely on new harmonies are usually more melodious than those based on the composer's harmonies, but it will be appreciated that harmonies which are too far removed from the original make it more difficult for the congregation to sing. (For instance, Vaughan Williams' descant to "Eventide"[3] must be quite a trial for all concerned.) The remarks about free organ harmonies apply here with added force, as a counter melody above the tune makes it even more difficult for the congregation to hold its part.

It is undesirable to have more than one descant per service. The more accustomed a congregation becomes to singing against a descant, the more easily will it hold its part.

The difficulties of learning a descant are twofold. Firstly, there is the problem of learning a strange melody, and, secondly, the problem of high notes. A high note always appears higher in something new, and the task of learning the notes is made doubly difficult. Most descants can be transposed for learning purposes as much as a third down, and when the notes are known, the high notes will appear much less terrifying when the original key is taken up. It is unfortunately necessary to draw attention to the common mistake of allowing choristers to sing the melody note rather than the note below it when the descant crosses momentarily under the *canto fermo*. Such passages are difficult for choristers who are inexperienced in singing an under part, and moreover, they tend to be nervous when the service time comes. In order to avoid drudgery in rehearsal and yet ensure a confident performance, it is advisable to spread the learning of the descant over several weeks. Three sessions of ten minutes are far more valuable than half an hour of continuous rehearsal.

A descant should not be stylistically dissimilar from the tune. Geoffrey Shaw's descants to "Rockingham" and "Wiltshire"[4] are excellent examples of descants which are complementary to their tunes. The various types of descant may be classified as follows:

1. Descant based on original harmonies, note against note;
2. Descant based on simple free harmonies, note against note;
3. Descant based on original harmonies, contrapuntal;
4. Descant based on advanced free harmonies, note against note;
5. Descant based on simple free harmonies, contrapuntal;
6. Descant based on advanced free harmonies, contrapuntal.

The use of two tunes in a hymn performance can be effective in throwing new light on a hymn's meaning. The use of "Buckland" for verses five and six of "Forty days and forty nights" makes a splendid complement to the more sombre "Heinlein" for the first four verses.[5] Similarly the choral performance of "Searching for Lambs" would make an effective contrast to "Crimond" (suitably transposed) in the 23rd Psalm paraphrase. The possibility of the former being sung as a solo verse without accompaniment should not be overlooked.[6]

The singing of "Meine Hoffnung"[7] by the choir for verses two and four of "All my hope on God is founded" would make a marvellous contrast to "Michael" sung for verses one, three and five. See also 73 (*EP*) for a fine descant to the latter It is very difficult but well worth the effort of learning.

Regrettably it is necessary to warn against the tasteless expedient of transposing a tune a semitone higher as a means of whipping up spurious excitement during the course of a hymn. In view of the claims made for the *Cambridge Hymnal,* on the grounds of artistic excellence, it is scarcely credible that they could mutilate "St Ethelwald" in this fashion (see No. 94).

Notes

1. See E. H. Thiman, "Recent Thought and Tendency in Congregational Singing", in W. T. Whitley, *Congregational Hymn Singing in England,* (Dent, 1933), p. 211.

   The simple use of antiphonal singing between women and men and choir and congregation is particularly valuable in the modest four line tune in imparting freshness to a tired tune.

   As Thiman observes, op. cit. p. 222: "There is that about antiphonal singing that seems to spur the congregation on to the best efforts possible; no doubt the natural feeling for emulation and competition is partly responsible; but there is in addition the fact that... the congregation have a chance to rest their voices with the result that when the turn of each section comes round, the allotted verse is attacked [sic] with freshness and enthusiasm."

2. e.g. "Old 100th", "Breslau", Genevan "Psalm 42".

3. 437 (*SP*).

4. 133 (*SP*), 677 (*SP*).

   Shaw's two volumes *The Descant Hymn Tune Book,* (Novello, n.d.), may be generally recommended. These may be used also as "free" organ harmonies.

5. 341 (*BBC*).

6. 387 (*CH3*).

7. 405 (*CH3*).

8

Hymn recitals

As a change from the monthly hymn practice, a hymn recital can be arranged. In drawing up the programme, a just balance between old and new, familiar and unfamiliar, must be made. It is important too to avoid picking too many tunes of the "impressive" kind. Such tunes appear to require certain exclusiveness for their true effect, and two or three in close proximity, e.g. "Nun Danket", "Hanover", and "Laudate Dominum"[1] take the lustre away from one another. Equally important is the need for metrical variety. The writer once played at a service at which four of the five hymns were 66664444, and a very wearisome business it was. Apart from the vocal variety available, as referred to in an earlier chapter, carols, organ Chorale preludes, Chorales, solos of the Schmelli Gesangbuch type and anthems like Bairstow's "The King of Love"[2] could be introduced.

The community hymn singing broadcasts attract peak audiences, and the holding of interdenominational hymn recitals could be very impressive as both a religious and a musical experience. As the index shows, each denomination has much to give and much to learn, and if the good tunes which at present enjoy a purely denominational existence could be turned to the service of all, much good would result.

Two very serious difficulties are at once encountered — the fact that the majority of tunes are harmonized differently in the various books; occasionally melodic discrepancies are to be found too, and often the words differ considerably. In many instances the harmonic differences appear to be purely arbitrary, and one cannot always say that one version is markedly superior to the others. Whilst consideration of the merit of words is outside the scope of this book, it must nevertheless be stated that some verbal differences are of a trifling nature.[3]

The decision to omit verses is, strictly speaking, an amendment. Yet we must admit that white heat inspiration does not always flow consistently through even the greatest hymn. Opinions must vary too as to the sheer practicality of going beyond a certain number of verses in the performance of a particular hymn, unless its narrative would be meaningless if verses were omitted. Many other factors have to be borne in mind beside the doctrinaire preservation of the writer's original in choosing between one version and another.

Taste and propriety presumably influenced the decision to remove

Enough for Him whom angels
Worship night and day,
A breastful of milk
And a mangerful of hay

from "In the bleak mid-winter".[4]

The removal of

And that a higher gift than grace
Should flesh and blood refine,
God's presence, and His very self
And essence all-divine

from "Praise to the Holiest in the height"[5] from the *Church Hymnary: Third Edition* was made on doctrinal grounds because there *is* no higher gift than grace, not even presumably the gift of the Incarnation. There seems to be little doubt that Newman was referring to Transubstantiation, but the fact remains that in less ecumenical times than our own, Protestants[6] have sung this verse without strain on their consciences and have interpreted the words as referring to Our Lord's earthly ministry.

Both omissions in my view are to be regretted.

Notes

1. 368 (*CH3*), 35 (*CH3*), 372 (*CH3*).
2. Based on the Irish tune "St Columba" (OUP).
3. "Him serve with fear" 166 (*AMR*) or "Him serve with mirth" 1 (*CH3*). "Shall sing to Thy praise" 167 (*AMR*) or "Shall lisp to Thy praise" 8 (*MHB*) or "Shall echo Thy praise" 85 (*Camb. H.*).

    See also note 11, p. 56.
4. 178 (*CH3*).
5. 238 (*CH3*).
6. Including the users of *CH2*.

9

Plainsong tunes

The use of plainsong has aroused more ill-feeling among choirs and congregations than probably any other kind of church music. Two reasons may be advanced for this. Firstly, plainsong was introduced in the nineteenth century when its true nature was imperfectly understood, and performances under these conditions then became dreary and inartistic. Even today, the type of "plainsong" found in the *Cathedral Prayer Book* is thought by many to be the "real thing". Secondly, plainsong has been advocated by many prominent church musicians rather stupidly as a panacea for all the ills of church music.

The case for and against plainsong has been admirably made by the late Sir Sydney Nicholson,[1] and his remarks may be summarized as follows: "Whilst it would be foolish to ignore the great sacred music written since the plainsong era, a space should be found for the distinctive song of the church." It is still regrettably true that there is Evangelical prejudice against plainsong because of its "Catholic" origin.

Even the most bigoted person cannot fail to be moved by the ethereal quality of plainsong as performed by the Monks of Solesmes, and one is left with the feeling that this music, more perhaps than any other kind, relies on its interpretation for its effect. A small body of singers carefully trained can best impart the necessary flexibility of style, and it may well be that congregations will appreciate plainsong more as listeners than as performers.

The introductory notes to the music of the *Church Hymnary: Third Edition,* pp. xv — xvi, give excellent directions as to the manner of performance, except that I prefer the division between one group and another to be made consistently at the mid-point of each verse, because this brings out the parallel structure of the poetry.

The widespread revival of Office hymns performed to the ancient church melodies could be undertaken by many churches with choir and congregation, or male and female voices alternating, for it is hard to see how the singing of Office hymns could, in itself, change the theological "colour" of a parish.

When choral settings of the "Magnificat" and "Nunc Dimittis" are being sung at Evensong, an Office hymn at the end of the first lesson is particularly desirable.

The intelligent and artistic performance of plainsong was for a long time inhibited by inappropriate and cumbersome accompaniments as printed in the various hymn books. Happily, that situation has changed and those found in the 1933 edition of *English Hymnal* and in *Hymns Ancient and Modern Revised* are excellent. In performance it is suggested that pedals are not used and that light flute stops are to be preferred to heavy diapasons for the manuals. A rhythmically flexible style of playing is essential. It is neither necessary nor desirable that the melody should remain consistently at the top of an organ accompaniment.

Notes

1. S. Nicholson, *Church Music,* (Faith Press, 1920). See also Harvey Grace, *The Complete Organist,* (Richards, 1947), for a well-reasoned chapter on the defence of plainsong and its use.

10
The pitch of tunes

In favour of low pitch

As the congregation's opportunities for participation in the service are so limited, tunes must be so arranged that they are in a sufficiently low key for untrained singers. Many tunes as printed in the standard collections are in too high a key.

Against low pitch

Most hymns are meant to be sung by a four part choir in harmony. If the melody is lowered, so are the accompanying parts. The higher reaches of the voice are the most sonorous. Hymns sung at low pitch tend to sound colourless. Eric Thiman states that "Not to perform the 'Easter Hymn' in D ruins it",[1] and my own experience confirms this. Most congregations have enough Easter joy in their hearts to reach a top F sharp just as even greater heights are scaled on the last night of the Proms. Lower keys can rob hymn melodies of brightness.

The two principal arguments having been stated briefly, it is now necessary to consider other matters. In determining what key shall be adopted, the tessitura, rather than the actual range of a tune should be examined, and the way a high note is approached in the melody. For instance, to what extent are we justified in grovelling in the depths of C major (or even B flat) when we are singing "Ewing"[2] simply so that we may negotiate the sixth line successfully? Similarly, because of its approach, no one finds the high F in "St Gertrude" unduly difficult — though it is printed in the *Church Hymnary: Third Edition* in E flat.[3]

The editors of the *English Hymnal* and *Songs of Praise* were among the first to express concern about the pitch of hymn tunes, but no consistency was shown. Whilst the customary keys for "Easter Hymn" (D major) and "Nicaea" (E major) were to be found only in the appendix, and versions a tone lower in the body of the book, two of Vaughan Williams' own tunes, "Sine Nomine" in the *English Hymnal* and "Marathon" in *Songs of Praise*[4] contain high Es. It is difficult to see why they shouldn't have been transposed to F major, and indeed, in the *Mirfield Mission Hymn Book*, "Sine Nomine" is printed in that key.

In the Free Churches, with their fine traditions of congregational singing, high notes do not appear to be the problem they are to Anglicans. See the reference to "Lloyd" (29, *AT, MHB*), note 27, p. 33.

Many hymns have to be played in public by pianists and organists of limited attainments, and often at short notice. Are we justified, then, in adding to their difficulty by printing tunes such as "Crediton" in a key of five sharps,[5] merely so that it will be sung a semitone lower, when C major would be so much easier?

I have often believed that certain twentieth-century tunes of great beauty have made far less headway than they should have done because they have appeared in difficult keys. These include "Alberta", "Cornhill", "Oswald's Tree", and "Rochester".[6]

Another problem that has arisen recently is the curious fact that the contralto voice appears to be more and more the "natural" voice for women, particularly young women. Many choirmasters and choral society directors are finding that their soprano lines are the weakest. Even where this is not the case in sheer numbers, it is in terms of vocal output. The cause of this is probably a combination of the discontinuance of serious choral singing in many schools, so that children at an impressionable age are no longer brought face to face with its delights; of the need to "interpret" pop songs with a kind of nasal "grunt" rather than with a properly produced singing voice; of the impression that a deep singing/speaking voice has greater sex appeal, and paradoxically that a deep singing voice reflects an increasingly unisex society.

Whatever sociological arguments may be put forward, one is left with the feeling that much of this low-pitched singing (like other contemporary attitudes to musical worship) arises out of laziness.

Frequently, when a prospective *Music* student is asked at an audition to sing at sight a melody of medium range, a request is made for a lower preliminary chord to be given. This, too, is a recent development. If young men and women who were the leaders of such musical life as their schools possessed are so disadvantaged in the use of their voices, what can one say of the others? Alongside their advanced practical and academic studies many music undergraduates are having to *learn* how to use their voices in a musical fashion. In most cases the basic vocal equipment is of good quality, which has never been allowed to develop.

So, then, this is a complex question on which it is difficult to come down wholly on one side or the other. According to the situation in which a musician finds himself, so will his solution be found. In general I favour thinking *initially* in terms of the higher simpler key, and, if sheer necessity beckons, being prepared to "come down".

Notes

1. E. H. Thiman, *The Beginning Organist,* (Ascherberg, 1954), pp. 8–9.
2. 537 (*CH3*).
3. 480 (*CH3*).
4. 641 (*EH*), 302 (*SP*).
5. 35 (*SP*).
6. 554 (*SP*), 41 (*SP*), 247 (*AMR*), 594 (*SP*).

11
Bach's Chorales

Throughout the book are to found scattered references to Bach's Chorales, and the following is meant to be read as supplementary to these.

The Chorales, nearly four hundred in number, form one of the greatest treasuries of Christian song, and it is regretted that they are not more widely used. Not all, of course, are suitable for congregational use, but the more elaborate ones could be used as anthems, particularly since several of them have more than one harmonization, and each verse could be treated differently where suitable and desirable.

Unfortunately, many of these melodies are set to metres which are strange to Britons, and attempts to fit them to other metres by radically altering the tune, e.g. "Innsbruck",[1] are to be deprecated. Occasionally however, the substitution of two crotchets for a minim and vice versa has no bad effect. For instance, "Mach's mit mir"[2] ("Eisenach") originally 878788 (lines three and four being a repetition of lines one and two) makes a serviceable L. M. tune, without any alteration of melody or harmony being necessary. Indeed, a comparison of the various versions of "Werde Munter" show that Bach did this sort of thing himself. "Ein' feste Burg" has to be altered rhythmically for English performance in the eighth line where we find:

instead of

Another serious problem arises from the fact that Bach's various harmonizations underline the meanings of the words,[3] and these words often express a kind of theological thought which is not favoured nowadays, and it is maintained that if the Chorales are sung to other words, the harmonizations lose their point. Yet if these Chorales are sung to translations of the original, the same objection is likely to arise, since the words chosen for special treatment by Bach may not occur in the same place in both the original and the translation. My own view is that other words may be found which are in keeping with the harmonies, even though they may be completely unrelated to the original text.

Notes

1. 276 (*AMS*).
2. 138 (*EH*) and 459 (*EH*).
3. It would appear from the writings of Schweitzer and other Bach scholars, that the composer's method of setting the Chorales is to treat the words in a detailed, individual manner, rather than by setting the spirit of the text as a whole.

12

Hymns as anthems

It is suggested that the following types should be considered for performance by the choir as an anthem:

1. Tunes with words not found in the congregation's hymn book. It is often desirable for the choir to have copies of an additional hymn book, for the sake of additional tunes, and tunes of unusual metre, which have specially written words. *Songs of Praise,* used as a choir book, together with either the standard or revised edition of *Hymns Ancient and Modern* will combine to include nearly all the great standard tunes and many fine modern compositions. Hymn books are expensive items, and many choirmasters may feel reluctant to spend money on an extra set of books. However, it should be remembered that cheaper treble part editions are sufficient for sopranos.

2. Tunes set to hymns already provided with a good popular tune.[1] It is seldom advisable to have two different tunes for the same hymn for congregational performance, so the newer tune should be used solely for choir performances, e.g. "St Ethelwald" and "From strength to strength" as settings of "Soldiers of Christ! arise".[2]

3. Tunes whose rhythmic complexity make the tune difficult to learn by rote. Many Psalter tunes in their original form fall into this category. Apart from their difficulty, the correct accentuation of words is a serious problem, but these fine old melodies could be sung by a choir.

4. The intimate character and lilting rhythm of some folk song melodies sound rather ludicrous when sung by massed untrained voices.

5. Tunes whose harmonic strength lies in the interplay of contrapuntal lines, rather than in interesting chord progressions, e.g. florid eighteenth-century harmonizations of Chorales.

6. Tunes of the broad unison type. These tunes often lend themselves well to varied treatment.

7. Tunes which are given varied treatments by the composer, e.g. Charles Wood's tune "Cambridge".[3]

8. Plainsong tunes (see special section).

9. Settings of metrically irregular words.

10. Settings of words whose subject matter and idiom render them unsuited to massed singing.

Many church authorities are against the use of hymns as anthems. They maintain that the anthem is something peculiarly English and, this being so, Bach Chorales, carols and hymns are not suitable. There are two answers to this point of view:

1. There is no objection presumably to foreign tunes being used congregationally. What is unobjectionable at one part of the service should be acceptable at another.

2. Many anthems are based on standard church melodies, with varied treatment of each verse. What difference is there in principle between singing a composed "hymn anthem" and the organist arranging one of his own? What sanctity has the octavo sheet?[4]

Many church choirs have suffered a steep decline in the numbers of personnel available over the past thirty years, together with a deterioration in actual singing ability in not a few cases. It has become almost a point of honour to maintain the old repertoire, as "to cut one's coat according to one's cloth" is to admit that the cloth is not what it was. The performance of standard anthems in such churches can be a real trial. Often the singers are incapable of producing the necessary weight of tone; parts are ill-balanced or non-existent and the long-suffering congregation anticipates a breakdown any moment. It is hard to see what value such a performance can have. An Anglican Bishop once said: "Because they knew I was coming to their village church to preach, the choir sang Wesley's 'Blessed be the God and Father' at the evening service. I wish they hadn't." In the choice of anthems too, choirs are often restricted, because in countless churches are to be found the faded pages and faded merits of Victorian anthems of the worst kind, and because they are there, they tend to be used. In fact, because such music exists in some profusion, it is often difficult for choirmasters to obtain money from church treasurers for something better.

This must not be interpreted as opposition to performances of all anthems, such as some writers on church music advocate. A carefully prepared, intelligible anthem makes a noteworthy contribution to any service, and the principle of a choir performing by itself should always be conceded. The use of relatively simple hymns as anthems saves rehearsal time, which can then be devoted to more elaborate anthems, which will then receive occasional performance at other times.

Even choirs of quite moderate attainments can achieve a high standard of performance of hymn anthems when contrapuntal anthems of the orthodox type are beyond them. More can be done in the way of vocal refinements than in bigger works,[5] where tolerable accuracy is as much as is ever attempted. Moreover, as hymn anthems call for broadly similar kinds of technique, the learning of one hymn indirectly assists the learning of others. This type of work can be undertaken by the most modest choirs. The singing of children in schools of unison material, with possibly an occasional descant, can be a thrilling experience, and a church choir of this type would find the performance of a unison hymn by itself a stimulating experience. To sum up, a choir which is never allowed to assume its separate identity in vocal performance soon ceases to be a choir. Two safeguards are necessary: (a) the music chosen should be of high quality and (b) it should lie well within the abilities of the singers.

So far we have discussed this matter from the point of view of the choir, but there is the congregation's point of view to be considered also. An anthem which is unintelligible to a congregation cannot in any sense be an offering on its behalf. So many anthems are "through composed", highly contrapuntal and lacking any sense of unity of form which the "man in the pew" can appreciate. The hymn anthem, with its recurring theme, subjected to varied treatment, and written for the most part in "familiar style" (note against note) fulfils the basic requirement of musical form — "Unity with variety". In some cases, the congregation will be able to follow the words in its hymn books. It can thus be associated with the choir's performance in a real way.[6]

The hymns chosen for performance as anthems will be of two kinds: (a) those which are to remain in the choir's repertoire permanently, and (b) those which are performed by the choir preparatory to their introduction at a hymn practice for subsequent congregational use.

A choir need not feel that the performance of simpler music for the bulk of its anthems necessarily represents a lowering of its standing. There is little doubt that the advent of broadcasting, and the Festival Movement has raised critical standards enormously, and performances which relied on the inability of the congregation to notice anything wrong cannot escape censure today. This fact is often overlooked by those who look with nostalgia on the standards of the "good old days". The congregation, whilst being critical of mistakes, is as a rule not prepared to take into account the difficulty which a certain anthem imposes. It prefers the simple anthem well performed rather than a brave try at the elaborate anthem, and naturally it will judge the choir's standards on the attractiveness of the music performed and the quality of its performance. Whilst a choir's performances in a service should not be looked upon as a mini-sacred concert for the congregation, the latter is a captive audience, and it should not be required to witness performances whose poor quality disturbs its religious devotions instead of assisting them.

The sources discussed in the chapter on "Vocal variety in hymn singing" are, of course, applicable to the performance of hymns as anthems and a selection of these may be undertaken. The possibility of congregational participation in the final verse shouldn't be overlooked.

Forty or fifty years ago it was commonly said that there were only about two hundred first-rate hymns. Today the situation has changed. There is now far more first-rate potentially popular hymnody than any congregation can use. Much of this "surplus" can be used chorally. Perhaps in these ecumenical days, when there is much talk of liturgical and musical experiment, we should look beyond our denomination's own distinctive contribution to Christendom's praise, and explore the idioms of other Churches, whose values have stood the test of time. This would surely be a more valuable exercise than performing ephemeral "Pop".

Much of our hymn singing is mechanical and unthinking. I suspect that many singers are often so delighted by the tune, that the meaning of the words passes them by. How many of us have *really* stopped to consider the full significance of

> As o'er each continent and island
> The dawn leads on another day,
> The voice of prayer is *never* silent,
> Nor dies the strain of praise away.

Perhaps it is only when we read the words that *others* are singing that their sense makes its total impact.

One Christmas I attended a carol concert given by two highly prestigious bodies in Edinburgh. In the hymn "It came upon the midnight clear" the words "O hush the noise, ye men of strife, And hear the angels sing", were accompanied by a fierce roll on the tympani and a full brass chorus. Few people present seemed unduly disturbed by such insensitivity, and perhaps it differs little in kind, if at all, from that which takes place in many churches. The use of the hymn anthem may

D

enable us to use our imagination and our intellect a little more in our singing, both chorally and congregationally.

Whilst all the major hymn books and supplements contain items suitable for performance as hymn anthems, the following may be recommended especially: *BBC Hymn Book* (OUP), *Cambridge Hymnal* (CUP), *Songs of Praise* (OUP), *Songs of Syon* (Schott) and *New Catholic Hymnal* (Faber).

A note on unison tunes

The unison tune has come into vogue mainly during the present century as a result of the influence of *English Hymnal*, and amongst composers there has been rather more enthusiasm for it than there has been in choirs, particularly those on the lower rungs of the doctrinal ladder. It would appear that some modern composers have more skill in devising interesting chord sequences for an organ accompaniment than in writing interesting vocal lines for harmonized singing. This fact is observable in such tunes as "Thornbury"[7] where there are both unison and harmony versions. Many unison tunes are very fine and provide variety in a service. It would be a pity if they were "killed" by prejudiced choirmen who deliberately blinded themselves to a tune's merits.

Recent criticism of the broad unison tune has tended to run on sociological lines — redolent of the Establishment and the Public School Chapel, suggesting a superficial camaraderie rather than anything deeper.[8] As one who repudiates Marxist artistic dogma when applied to certain works of Soviet composers, I find such dismissive dogmatism equally unacceptable when applied to British church music. Religion and moral standards are not the prerogative of a particular social class. One suspects that the omission of "Wolvercote" and "Ladywell"[9] from the *Church Hymnary: Third Edition* after they were pioneered in the *Church Hymnary: Second Edition,* was dictated by such considerations, but I have never found any class barriers set up against "Sine Nomine",[10] perhaps the greatest tune of this type.

Notes

1. One consequence of the "hymn explosion" of recent years has been the writing of new words to carry a redundant second tune originally written for a standard hymn. See note 6, p. 57. So much for the contemporaneity of words and music. Even though a tune may be written in the eighties, its idiom may still be that of the thirties. Herbert Howells' "Michael", (405, *CH3*), has made its tremendous impact only during the last decade even though it was written in 1932. It is not "dated" in the way that pop hymn tunes, in attempting to capture the popular idioms of that time, most certainly are.
2. Compare 303 (*AMR*) and 441 (*CH3*). See also p. 94.
3. 507 (*BBC*).
4. It could be argued, I think, that such an arrangement of a pre-existing tune might have more merit than the hymn anthem in which a *new* tune is treated strophically. This is, of course, a different matter from the anthem in which a composer uses a hymn text for a freely composed anthem of some complexity.
5. Such choral niceties as blend, expressive enunciation, purity of intonation, balance, beauty of tone and, above all, phrase shaping, can all be dealt with more thoroughly than in music of greater difficulty.

   Such rediscovered or underdeveloped techniques can then be applied to all aspects of a choir's work by skill transference. It may even set the congregation a good example.

   Even where there is not a full complement of parts, choral variety from verse to verse is still possible. Men's voices, women's voices, solo voice (with or without a vocalized background), descants, and free harmonization from the organ, are all possibilities.

   Apart from their intrinsic excellence, John Wilson's arrangements of *Sixteen Hymns for Today for use as simple anthems,* (RSCM), are valuable as a demonstration of how organists may go and do likewise with other material.
6. See p. 5.

   In *The Amateur Organist,* (OUP, 1955), Henry Coleman wrote: "It may not be out of place to suggest that undue emphasis is often in these days placed upon the needs and desires of congregations." Dr Coleman stated this in the context of arguing that the more genuinely musical members of congregations may prefer to worship silently in a choral performance than in an inadequate congregational rendering.
7. 434 (*CH3*).
8. E. Routley, *Church Music and Theology,* (SCM Press, 1959), p. 75.
9. 508 (*CH2*), 139 (*CH2*).
10. 534 (*CH3*).

    Does not the folk tune "Portsmouth" partake of similar musical characteristics?

13

Prose settings

The Free Church hymn books contain a generous supply of psalms, passages of scripture and canticles pointed for chanting. In many cases, words are drawn from the Authorized Version of the Bible and not from the prayer book translation, and one feels that these versions are not the best for chanting. The fact that the system of pointing is not always in accordance with Anglican speech rhythm principles need not cause alarm. Speech rhythm is the product of the application of intelligence on the part of the singers and not on the system of pointing adopted. Though this view may appear to be unliturgical, the pointing of scriptural passages other than the psalms would be distinctly useful in Anglican churches. It would appear that although the chant section has been a constant feature of Free Church hymn books for over fifty years, its use is still the exception rather than the rule. Although chanting is difficult, the literary beauty of the prose passages is incomparably superior to the metrical psalms, which are often little better than doggerel,[1] and could be employed to advantage — not as a substitute for a hymn but as an addition — particularly since opportunities for congregational participation in Free Church services are so limited.

Sadly, we have to acknowledge that alongside the choral refinements in psalm singing that have been achieved by speech rhythm in Anglican chanting, there has been a sad decline in congregational vocal confidence during the present century. The so-called "Anglican thump" in the reciting note, followed by the remaining notes sung in strict time in the Old Cathedral Psalter pointing, did have at least a degree of predictability alongside its artistic ugliness, which gave congregations a feeling of security. This was enhanced because most churches used this book, and associated a psalm or canticle with a particular chant. The problem today is compounded by there being a number of differently pointed Psalters in current use in the Church of England — the *Oxford*, the *English*, the *Parish* and the *Worcester*, all of which claim with some justification to be applying speech rhythm principles.

When the revised translations of the psalms are in general use by agreement among the various churches, it is to be hoped that similar agreement can be reached as to the method of pointing. We shall *all* have to learn anew. Perhaps a start could be made by working on the canticles at a congregational practice. Whilst the "Magnificat" and "Nunc Dimittis" are poorly sung, as they are in many churches, there is little hope for an improvement in psalm singing. For some time we may have to be satisfied with a very small repertoire of psalms which will be sung at frequent intervals.

The choirmaster should begin by patterning *in speech* the rhythm he desires and this may then be followed by a choral demonstration verse by verse to the congregation.

A characteristic of Hebrew poetry is its parallel structure, in which the second half of a verse either amplifies or antithesizes the first. There is therefore every justification for using contrasted groups to illustrate this. Furthermore, most problems for congregations arise during the singing of the first half of a psalm verse. If, therefore, the choir were to sing this by itself, and the congregation were to join it for the second half, it would mean the removal of a major hindrance to intelligent and confident psalm singing.

Because of the various drawbacks of plainsong, metrical psalms and the Anglican chant, the Gelineau method has been advocated in many quarters, with as yet disappointing response, considering that this has been in existence for twenty-five years.

Gelineau's method has been to retranslate the psalms into prose following strictly the rhythm of the Hebrew original. The melodies change their notes (or repeat them) to coincide with an accented syllable. Each melody note is equal to four crotchet beats, and the syllables which occur between the accented notes arrange themselves to fit this metrical scheme. The chief drawback to this method arises from the necessity, on occasions, to leave melody notes unsung, or to observe rests in order to satisfy the accentual requirements of verses of varying length.

Fortunately, this is a problem only for a soloist or for a choir, since the congregational part consists of a simple metrical antiphon which acts as a refrain at the end of each verse.

The parallel structure of the verses can be brought out in Gelineau settings too by assigning each half of a verse to a different soloist, e.g. soprano answered by tenor, or soloist and choir, or sopranos and altos answered by tenors and basses. See Nos. 67, 350 and 389 (*CH3*).

Notes

1. Notwithstanding the deeply entrenched historic associations and traditions of Scottish Presbyterianism. It is difficult to justify the retention of these in their present form when other spoken and sung parts of the service are to be modernized.

   Compare: I joy'd when to the house of God
   Go up, they said, to me.   489 (*CH3*)

   with: I was glad when they said unto me
   We will go into the house of the Lord. Psalm 122 (*Book of Common Prayer*)

14

The hymn book and its contents

Following the "hymn and tune" explosion of the last fifteen years, one would like to see some process of ecumenical consolidation in the next major hymn book to appear. Perhaps we could be spared specially commissioned new material, particularly from the editor, whoever he may be. It is possible to predict the winners and the losers from the new material very early in a hymn book's life. The judgments made by Walford Davies and Harvey Grace in *Music and Worship* on the new tunes in *English Hymnal,* precisely one year after its 1933 edition, are still valid. If one were to comment on critics' predictions as to the fate of new tunes, one would say that they have tended to be a little over-generous in their praise of the good, but remarkably prescient in their condemnation of the bad.[1] I must confess a disappointment that "Ladywell" (297, *AMR*) and "Marathon" (303, *SP*) have not been taken up with greater enthusiasm. Whatever academic merits a tune may have to a musician, if it lacks popular appeal after reasonable attempts to make it known, it is a bad hymn tune. We require from our tunes simplicity, fervour and imagination, not facile conventionality, sentimentality or sophistication. Only then can they claim from us a worthy effort of mind, spirit and voice.

One would like to see the choice of musical editor made only from those who have grown up with and *love* hymnody in all its aspects, as distinct from those professional musicians for whom editing and tune writing is merely a professional chore. Some former editors of hymn books have been musicians of the highest distinction but have lacked consistency in their judgments. It is surely no accident that among contemporary hymnals *Congregational Praise* (editors Eric Routley and Eric Thiman), *BBC Hymn Book* (Thalben Ball and Cyril Taylor) and *Hymns Ancient and Modern Revised* (Gerald Knight and John Dykes Bower) should have been so conspicuously successful. A long experience of singing in the pew and accompanying hymns at the organ gives one a sixth sense as to what will permanently enrich and what will not. An editor needs to know intimately the material he intends to discard, as well as what he intends to use, excepting of course the new material. Even today with our dodecaphony and our aleatoric serious music, it is as true as it ever was that the successful hymn tune is a subtle blend of the familiar and the novel, with the former predominating markedly.

It is said that musical excellence means nothing to a congregation. That it may be unconcerned with the minutiae of analysis of the kind we have been considering in earlier pages may be true. But it *is* concerned with the end product and responds to fine melody if it can have it. If this were not so, we would not find so many great tunes among the popular favourites.

Dr Routley said that the following were the guiding principles in selecting tunes for *Congregational Praise*:

1. They are to be appropriate for the occasion on which they are to be sung, and to be capable of being performed by an untrained congregation.

2. Worthy psalmody is not independent of effort and concentration.

3. Therefore no tune should be rejected merely on the grounds of unfamiliarity in usage or idiom.

4. A distinction is to be made between the unfamiliar and the eccentric, the universally sound and the temporarily fashionable.

5. "Compromise items" should be placed in an appendix.

The Rev. E. P. Sharpe, of the *Baptist Hymn Book* editorial

committee, stated that one way of producing a new edition of a hymn book was to start with the existing book, prune it of anachronisms and failures, borrow from the hymn books and supplements of other denominations, and relegate the worn out favourites to an appendix. "We can no longer predict what future needs will be." Since some of those needs will themselves be only temporary, perhaps the major publishing houses could go into the "leaflet business" with their ephemera; but it is disturbing to find ephemera such as Geoffrey Beaumont's tune for "Now thank we all our God" within the hard covers of the *Baptist Hymn Book*.

One disquieting feature of contemporary tune writing is the uneasy feeling that in order to gain publication there is a party line to follow. Dr H. M. Best, Dean of the Music Conservatoire, Wheaton College, Illinois, wrote: "No tune seems to be complete without its token syncopation. These are predictable, usually shoddy and do nothing to revitalise or transform tune styles. They are just another example of the church's superficial attempt at relevance."

Dr Arthur Wills, organist and Master of the Choristers at Ely Cathedral and a distinguished church composer wrote: "So much contemporary church music is based on clichés of rhythmical attractiveness of a rather twee nature, and a harmonic colour which is now beginning to sound decidedly tarnished."

Too high a proportion of poor material in a hymn book can obscure the good that it contains (see "Distribution of tunes", p. 245). Publication is an expensive matter, and one sympathizes with the need to compromise. Nevertheless it is high time editors "came clean" as the Americans say. Instead of airy generalizations in their prefaces about standards and relegating a token number of horrors to an appendix, let them (a) consistently place the poor tune as the second one, though one recognizes that some second tunes may be genuine good alternatives; (b) state clearly in the preface that it was with the greatest reluctance that the words and/or tunes of hymns numbered ... were printed and it is their earnest hope that these will soon be discontinued in worship; (After all, not every user is a graduate musician or littérateur, yet he may genuinely wish to improve his taste, and that of those whom he serves.) (c) state that pressure of space and copyright difficulties prevented inclusion of the following hymns, tunes and arrangements and list where these may be found; (If we are genuinely interested in ecumenical worship we have to begin by exploring the hymnody outwith the book we normally use. Lest this appear to be ultra-idealistic I would cite a precedent. A long list of anthems was included in the early editions of the *Church Anthem Book* to which it was hoped choirs would devote their attention. Details of publishers were also included.) (d) list those items which the editors regard as being particularly practicable among the unfamiliar items (which does not mean necessarily *all* the editorial contributions).

Apart from selecting hymns for a particular service, it is essential to keep some record of the praise for a whole year so that there is a balance between one type of tune and another. The impressiveness of an idiom (even that of the Bach Chorale) can be greatly diminished if it is over-represented in a year's praise.[2]

So far as the individual service is concerned, there has to be regard paid to the acoustics of the church building, the size and age of the congregation, the occasion and worshipping traditions of the users, and the tempo. In practical terms this may mean limiting one's use of brisk folk song tunes in a large reverberant building, using "St Ethelwald" rather than "From strength to strength" for "Soldiers of Christ! arise" with a small elderly congregation, using "Austria" rather than "Abbot's Leigh" if the congregation is likely to include a large number of only occasional churchgoers. Whilst many hymn tunes are taken too slowly, there are a number of tunes which can degenerate into a "rant" if taken too quickly.

The need for variety of type within a service is not an academic one. As was mentioned in connection with hymn recitals, too many tunes of the type that "carry all before them" in one service can only result in none of them making the customary impact. We need variety in length of line, in number of lines, in metre (avoiding for instance a hymn of 8787 followed by one of 8787D), in key, in period, in mood, in not having more than one unison (or unison type) tune per service.

All hymns should be chosen with regard to their relevance to the rest of the service — the lessons and sermon, and this should be true particularly of those in the middle of the service. The post-sermon hymn and the opening hymn should normally be bright, objective and positive. In Anglican churches, an opening hymn before the responses makes little sense of "O Lord open Thou our lips", and there should be no hymn after the Blessing. The singing of hymns in procession simply to accommodate a choir's journey from the vestry to the choirstalls is not approved of liturgically. Processions should begin in the choirstalls. *Ancient and Modern Revised* makes excellent and abundant provision for these.

The actual arrangement of a book's contents shows much diversity. The Free Churches tend to group hymns according to their subject matter, whilst the contents of the Anglican books are arranged according to the Church Year with the remaining hymns grouped under the heading "General Hymns". The latter are often regarded scornfully in Free Church circles, but a collection of all-purpose hymns does ensure that they are used more frequently than might otherwise be the case. For instance, when I sang from *Ancient and Modern Standard* which listed "There is a green hill far away" as "For the Young", it was seldom heard at adult services during Passiontide. Similarly, the inclusion of "Hail to the Lord's Anointed" as a post-Epiphany hymn in *English Hymnal* tended to preclude its use at other seasons. For this reason, there is much to be said in favour of a simple alphabetical listing, provided that an index shows both thematic and seasonal groupings. Specific recommendations in a hymn book Sunday by Sunday do not ensure real relevance, and may result in a mechanical pattern of worship year by year.

Notes

1. Reviewers of hymn books have tended to evaluate them according to the quantity of brand new material they contain and they overlook the question of what is *new* to the congregations who will use the book. Every editorial contribution or specially commissioned piece excludes something that may be just as modern (in the real sense) that has appeared elsewhere, and may be something of infinitely greater quality and value. It is not only in the field of the pop hymn that tunes are appearing that use the musical language of the 1920s. That does not of itself damn them: it simply means that they have to be judged alongside the music of fifty years ago, and used only if they are superior. The preface of *Praise for Today* proclaims the book's modernity in rather strident terms, yet of the book's first thirty tunes, there are at least fifteen that are post-war only in the sense that they were written at that time.

   My own acquaintance with Presbyterian worship is of only six years' standing, and so I am exploring "the new book" *(CH3)* along with my choir and congregation. There is much in it that is new to me, including words — whatever their metrical conventionality — that are relevant to today and poetically competent. Consequently I blinked when I read in *ECM*, 1974, p. 58 that "*CH3* makes ferocious demands in its music [but] in its words it is unadventurous beyond belief". Canon Cyril Taylor, who wrote that, could be criticized for the lack of idiomatic adventure in his own tunes, but while he continues to maintain such a high level of consistency within that idiom, I for one won't mind.

   See also note 15, p. 33.

2. In Vol. 5, *HSB*, p. 128, Canon Noel Boston wrote: "... seeing that the average number of tunes a congregation can be expected to sing without practice is 30." One can only believe that even so far as the humblest village congregation is concerned, this state of affairs can only have been allowed to develop as a result of hymns being chosen without thought, or not even as a serious pastoral duty over a long period of time. At the beginning of the Christian Year it should be possible for the person responsible for the praise to compile a chart for his study wall, consisting of as many numbers as there are hymns in his hymn book. He could at once blank off all the numbers of hymns he would never use. So far as the rest are concerned, these could be divided into the "Golden Oldies" and written in red ink, and those which it would be desirable to introduce during the year written in blue. Each time a hymn was sung the number could be crossed through, and though some popular hymns would perhaps have several crossings during the course of a year, the chart would at least serve as a reminder of what was available, and help to avoid too narrow a choice and too frequent repetition. The new material, perhaps not more than fifteen or twenty items on the chart, would show the evenness in time with which these were introduced.

   See also note 14, p. 11.

15

Poor music and evangelism

Arising from the success of the mission hymn towards the end of the last century and the beginning of this, claims have been made for the evangelizing power of poor music. The material of the mission hymn has always been regarded as of only temporary use, at any rate by the larger denominations. Charles Cleall has written of Gospel songs which, "minister to immaturity and keep people immature... [It is] ambulance work for people in their dreary conditions of industrial Britain, but is too strong in calories and short of protein to make a good diet for those who hope to grow. To seek milk when we ought to be digesting stronger meat is the mark of the voluptuary; of self-gratification; of a determination, like that of Peter Pan not to grow up."[1]

As a development from this, pop music in a variety of idioms has been introduced into our services because it is the only music that seven-eighths of the population ever listen to. It is the background to the lives of people in urban communities. One can point to cultural deprivation in the 1890s when there was *no* demand for the idioms of "Daisy, Daisy" in our churches, or even for the "Holy City" as an anthem; or to cultural deprivation in the 1930s when people were happy enough to have Cole Porter and Irving Berlin confined to their Palais de Danses. The minority who like Bach and Beethoven has never been bigger than it is today, and educational standards are supposed to have increased, and yet...

But historic parallels, we are told, are hardly relevant, because "Pop" is not so much a kind of music but a social phenomenon from which the young cannot escape. Charles Cleall wrote: "Secular Pop is primarily an exhibition of sexual paganism — hot, trivial and unbridled — it is to this kind of music that people inevitably turn when priestly law is absent and discrimination blind."[2] The natural accessibility of "Pop" gives expression to the feelings of ordinary folk who are without culture, secular or religious, but the "natural" in "Pop" is corruptible, and indeed is often corrupt. It can induce attitudes which are not epic but bestial. It exaggerates and associates all too easily with extravagance and infantilism.[3]

Yet because it represents the ordinary and the transient, which is the background to the lives of so many, some maintain that it has a rightful place in our worship. It introduces greater freedom and less stuffiness into our services, and complements to some extent modern liturgical language. Words take on a new meaning when sung to the new tunes. One can also say that they may be trivialized by the same process, e.g. "At the Name of Jesus" when sung to Beaumont's "Camberwell" (115, *HF*). As for the crude materialism in the lives of so many of us, instead of the church mirroring this, shouldn't it be showing us something better, both in its message and in its music?

We may ask, what has Beaumont's "Maiquez" (61, *HF*) *really* to offer, except defiance of most people's sense of musical fitness? In what way is it superior simply in terms of popular appeal over "Angel Voices" (455, *CH3*); or "Pastor" (669, *HF*) over "Dominus regit me" (388, *CH3*)? How many performances will be necessary before even the most musically unsophisticated person winces at the corny linking chords in "Tersanctus" (101, *HF*) for "Holy, Holy, Holy" by Hartless?

Erik Routley has shown greater tolerance and understanding than most hymnologists of the "Pop" phenomena in its musical, liturgical and sociological aspects, and he has written: "Performed in church it has shocked and terrified the conservatives; but we cannot take comfort for long in congratulating ourselves on the great necessity of shocking and terrifying the conservatives. It has not filled the churches with pop worshippers or done anything to transfer their worship away from the pop idols.

"If there is a lack of balance in Beaumont and Co., this could be because of a failure accurately to assess the relative demands of musical integrity and the need for communication. If there is such a lack of judgment it is not for any who are more careful of integrity to throw stones; but it is quite proper to point out that music has an integrity quite independent of the person who uses it for communication, and that if this is corrupted, if music's language is blurred and blunted by careless use, he who does so is at fault, no matter how admirable his personal intentions are."[4]

It is claimed that there is a strong religious empathy in much contemporary "Pop", and as a "bridge" between the classical and contemporary cultures the Gospel should be proclaimed using pop music, particularly where present day issues are concerned. If something brings young people to church, some sacrifice of artistic standards might be a small price to pay. But many teenagers have looked on this as a kind of bribery; they were suspicious and felt they were being "got at". For many of the young it is the group and not the song that interests them. Since it takes time to print, advertise and distribute new musical material, by the time all this has happened another secular style has emerged — and there's nothing so dead as last month's Chart Topper.[5] How many churches can go on buying music in order to chase fashion? It is dishonest to say that it is ephemeral and disposable. As we have seen in the *Baptist Hymn Book* and other hymnals, some has found its way into hardbacked hymn books. If bought with precious funds, it will stay around for fifty years, especially if during that time the congregation has developed an "association" for it.

The pseudo-religious has always been harmful when taken seriously. Fortunately such ballad songs as "The Lost Chord" and the "Star of Bethlehem" were regarded as providers of pleasant entertainment and nothing more, because it was never claimed that they were *church* music. The same arguments against "Pop" in church can be levelled at them — they would rob worship of dignity and a sense of the numinous — and that the "religious elements" in them provided an opportunity for making easy money.

I do not believe that left to themselves the young would have asked for "Pop" in their services. Most young folk are remarkably conformist and accept the environment in which they find themselves, both sacred and secular. The demand for "Pop" in services has been manufactured by an older age group who ought to know better.

It is difficult to escape the feeling that by using pop music, the church is compromising its values to accommodate those of an increasingly pagan world.[6] Throughout the Old Testament one reads of the faithful remnant who sought to preserve the purity of their worshipping ideals, and not to allow them to be polluted by Baal-practices. When Our Lord drove out the money-changers, he was setting his face firmly against those who sought to corrupt worship with blatant commercialism. Yet we are told that pop culture is intolerantly puritanical, and rebels against a society that produced Auschwitz and Hiroshima. Can one say that our pop-orientated society with its drugs, its abortions and its pursuit of the soft buck has helped to bring in a higher standard in international morality or higher standards of personal and social conduct, when muggings and violence are a regular feature of city life — and not confined to poorer areas?

A full house is not sufficient if the people go just for the sensation, or for something controversial, or to be "with it". These are factors which can easily blind people to what worship — and the church — is about. "Pop" is so derivative that it underestimates the powers of almost all who are asked to sing it. Professor Arthur Hutchings has observed: "You cannot effectively 'pep up' what is dull, and much supposedly 'hot' popular music is duller than the dullest hymn tunes."[7] Geoffrey Beaumont's "Peter ad vincula" set to "Fight the food fight" (384, *HF*) is a case in point. Stripped of its gimmicks — its false accents and its cliché-ridden harmony — it could easily be made into a traditional-style hymn tune, and what a poor thing it would be — commonplace to the nth degree! The composer runs out of "modern" resources by the time he reaches lines three and four anyway.

When one examines the quality of the "Pop" we've been given for use in church, it isn't even good of its kind. It is the kind of music that "would be tolerated in no place of secular entertainment" (to quote again from the preface to the *English Hymnal*). As we have seen, many of the tunes of Beaumont don't even fit the words to which they are set easily. They merely use the syncopations that Bertie Wooster might have danced to.

Of course, one can understand the feelings of those who believe that pop music and kindred idioms can once more fill our empty pews, and even that so-called traditional music has driven people away. There is a vast quantity of the latter for which no musician can find any room at all. Yet the musician is expected to defend *all* traditional music when he attacks "Pop". He is absolutely at one with all those who wish to drive from our churches music which has long outlived its usefulness. But we take an over-simplistic view if we believe that music in a traditional idiom is responsible for our half (and more than half) empty churches.

Even if our church were filled for a service of pop music, for how many weeks would this state of affairs continue? Some would be there merely out of curiosity, which when satisfied would no longer interest them. The emotionally charged Gospel song, with a souped up presentation was part of the evangelizing technique of Dr Billy Graham, and many believe that his mission would have had greater lasting effect if less emotionally cosy musical material had been used. This kind of sophistication in presentation is beyond the resources of most, and leaves the church open to the charge, once again, of being associated with the second-rate because generally its financial resources permit of the use of only inadequate electronic hardware.

If we really want to increase our congregations (though I

believe there are more important ideals for the church to have) we may be forced to the conclusion that those denominations who have been most successful in attracting and keeping a large number of adherents are not those who have made worship easier, but those who have been most demanding of time and effort.

Because of the associations of the guitar with "Pop", a much more challenging and worthy type of contemporary Christian song is in danger of similar condemnation. Such contemporary hymn writers as Fred Kaan, Sidney Carter, Brian Wren, Albert Bayly and F. Pratt Green have written religious lyrics which have tended to avoid the traditional hymn metres and require musical settings of the carol type. The intimacy of subject matter requires group performance rather than congregational singing, and even where full congregational rendering is possible, accompaniment by guitars or an instrumental group is more effective than the organ. At the time of writing, not all this verse has received adequate musical treatment any more than the new liturgies have. Nevertheless, it is in some of this work that the late twentieth century will sing its songs worthily to the Lord in its presentation of petitions peculiar to its own time and condition, and find there a true complement to its heritage of the great hymns from the past.

Notes

1. C. Cleall, *Sixty Songs from Sankey,* (Marshall Morgan & Scott, 1960), Preface.
2. C. Cleall, *The Selection and Training of Mixed Choirs in Churches,* (Independent Press, 1961), p. 17.
3. E. Routley, *Twentieth Century Church Music,* (Jenkins, 1964), p. 206.
4. E. Routley, *Twentieth Century Church Music,* (Jenkins, 1964), p. 167.
5. K. R. Long, *Music of the English Church,* (Hodder & Stoughton, 1971), p. 434.
6. "Nothing was further from the Apostolic mind than that Christians should make any concessions whatever to the normal and everyday standards of the non-Christian world. Still less was it a likely notion to be entertained by the Church of the fourth and fifth centuries." E. Routley, *Twentieth Century Church Music,* (Jenkins, 1964), p. 153.
7. Arthur Hutchings, Vol. 8, *HSB*, p. 215.

16

Some hymn book reviews

The Baptist Church Hymnal

Of the hymn books surveyed comparatively, the *Baptist Church Hymnal* (1933) is by far the most disappointing. But for a handful of the great twentieth-century tunes, one could hardly regard the book as a product of this century. It is true that the good standard tunes are fairly well represented, but the rest seems to be a repository of all that is weakest in Nonconformist Hymnody. One is conscious of the fact that no musician of eminence was responsible for the musical editing, and the foreword, including a clever double-edged remark by Sir Henry Coward: "They [the editors] have secured a just balance and blend of the old and new tunes which commands respect, if not admiration", is no substitute.

There are a number of tunes not found in other books but scarcely any of these deserves to gain widespread usage, and the book as a whole has had no influence whatsoever on contemporary hymnody. It cannot have been long before the Baptists themselves were aware of the inadequacy of their book, in that a new edition appeared in 1962, the *Baptist Hymn Book* in which a third of the contents of the older book was discarded. Whilst it is true that each generation needs its own hymn book, it cannot be said that other religious denominations using such books as *English Hymnal,* 1906, *Hymns Ancient and Modern Revised,* 1950, the *Methodist Hymn Book,* 1933, and *Congregational Praise,* 1951, were quite so desperately in need of a new book.

Dr Routley has reminded us that a hymn book should be judged by the good it does rather than by the evil it condones. Certainly in a book of seven hundred and seventy hymns it is possible to find room for the good and the bad. Unfortunately if the latter is well represented, not only does it tend to obscure the good, but it results in the "bad popular" being used, (see "Distribution of tunes" p. 245). If this were eliminated, congregations would then have no option but to use only the "good popular" and every encouragement to explore the new "potentially good popular".

Thus we find some strange bedfellows. Thalben Ball and F. C. Maker, "England's Lane" and "Rimington" facing one another on opposite pages, "Abbot's Leigh" (making two appearances in the first fifty hymns) as an alternative to "Lux Eoi", and "Nun Danket" as the *second tune* to Geoffrey Beaumont's "Deo Gracias", "Repton" alongside "Rest" for "Dear Lord and Father"... and so one could go on.

There are, however, some brave musical gestures: Stanton's "Crudwell" for "Rescue the perishing" and "Ermuntre dich" for "I've found a Friend", and some fine twentieth-century tunes from Norman Cocker, Henry Ley, William Harris and Harold Darke that have made their mark elsewhere. Of the hymn book's "unique" material there are some fine Welsh tunes, e.g. "Dinas Bethlehem" and "Rachie" and the *Baptist Hymn Book* was the first Protestant hymn book to include A. G. Murray's "Anglorum Apostolus" and Richard Terry's "Billing" from Roman Catholic hymnody. Of the new tunes, some use essentially nineteenth-century idioms, e.g. "Thanksgiving", "Bletchley" and "Dear Love", but Greville Cooke's "Ivinghoe" is really a winner and Lyddon Thomas' "Harvest Song" is nearly as good.

Thus whilst one may regret the reprieve given to some of the "old lags", there is ample material here for Baptist congregations to have an exclusive diet of absolutely first-rate material—if they want it... The *Baptist Hymn Book* must be evaluated against the book it replaced and it represents a considerable leap forward.

The Anglican Hymn Book

Of the large modern hymn books, few have been criticized more severely or more irrationally than the *Anglican Hymn Book*, published in 1965. These criticisms included alterations to the words (as if this were something new) and the fact that the title implied a more comprehensive type of churchmanship than that of the Evangelical wing of the Church of England for which it is clearly designed. It may be said that Evangelicals have as much entitlement to a book of their own as the Anglo-Catholics, who find their needs satisfied by *English Hymnal,* and surely the Evangelicals have an equal claim on the title "Anglican".

Though this is a theological matter, it is not one that lies outside the musician's province, especially when he notices the absence of some of the great communion hymns such as "Deck thyself, my soul, with gladness", "Let all mortal flesh keep silence", and those that carry the French "Sapphic" church melodies (though two of the latter ones are included elsewhere in the book). The use of sanserif type gives a certain brash appearance to the book which may cause some to place a corresponding valuation on the material. This would be most unfair since there are some particularly fine tunes which the *Anglican Hymn Book* has pioneered notably Willcocks' "Conquering Love" (No. 205), Gillespie's "Harrowby" (No. 150), Ashfield's "Broadwalk" (No. 125), Finlay's "Hamilton" (No. 12) and Thalben Ball's "Stand Up" (No. 586). Some of editor Robin ˙Sheldon's tunes are spoilt by a sense of strain, aggressive harmonies and restless modulation, but "Maer Down" (No. 53) and "Daymer" (No. 134) are very fine pieces. Llewellyn's "Tidings" (No. 439) is, in my view, the best modern tune yet to appear for "Tell out, my soul".

"Bodley" (No. 440) and "Westron Wynde" (No. 136) are just two of a number of pieces that would make good choir motets and no contemporary hymn book is so well provided with choral settings of standard tunes (some of them quite superb) as this book. Since it has been my contention throughout this book that vital hymn singing is a partnership between choir and congregation, each performing its distinctive role, the importance of this provision can hardly be understated.

Hymns Ancient and Modern

As one examines the various editions of *Hymns Ancient and Modern,* one is conscious of a distinctive aura common to them all. The first edition of 1861 was, in comparison with its rivals, a High Church book, and one that set higher artistic standards. It was responsible for more than two dozen inseparable "marriages" including "Eventide" and "Abide with me", "Melcombe" and "New every morning" and "St Theodulph" and "All glory, laud, and honour". Of these, only eight were specially composed. *Ancient and Modern* has always appeared to be non-party, yet one notices a general avoidance of tunes in the early editions that had strong Nonconformist associations, e.g. "Richmond" and "Helmsley". In subsequent nineteenth-century editions there were more "modern" than ancient hymns, and many of these were Evangelical in character. Thus when the Church of England moved in a Catholic direction in the last decades of the nineteenth century, *Ancient and Modern* appeared to have gone slightly in the opposite direction, and by the time *English Hymnal* appeared in 1906, it seemed to be positively Low Church alongside the newcomer.

Ancient and Modern had by this time become a national institution, and among the proprietors there was felt to be a need for a new edition, which set out to remove the complacency which had surrounded the book, in the opinion of many influential churchmen. Despite a bad press, nearly two million copies of the 1904 edition were sold, but this was counted a failure by previous standards. When one examines that book today, despite the obvious good intentions and reforming zeal of the editors, one is daunted by its forbidding appearance and the seeming anonymity of its contents;

authors' and composers' names appear only in the index. Yet one must pay tribute to the editors' courage in rejecting twenty-six tunes that the editors of *Ancient and Modern*, revised forty-six years later, deemed it inexpedient to exclude. They also had nothing to do with the Gospel hymns of the type found in *English Hymnal*, Nos. 567–585.

The reversion to Standard *Ancient and Modern* plus the 1916 supplement, which salvaged the best of the 1904 material, appeared to symbolize a characteristic conservatism, especially when compared with the seemingly progressive thrust of the *English Hymnal*. Anglicans have tended to overlook the fine tunes in *Ancient and Modern* that *English Hymnal* either did not want or couldn't have, e.g. "Diademata", "Gerontius", "Harewood", "Laudate Dominum" (Parry), "Hereford" and "Crucifer". The inclusion of fifty of these in *English Hymnal Service Book* and *English Praise* gives a clear indication of the extent to which users of *English Hymnal* were inconvenienced by not having them. In fact, apart from the ten out of every thirteen Anglican churches who used *Ancient and Modern,* in a large number of the remainder, the navy blue bindings could be seen in discreet corners of the choirstalls.

Despite the fact that 324 hymns (out of a total of 779) were left out when the Revised Edition appeared in 1950, the distinctive character remained. It is a remarkable fact that *Ancient and Modern's* numbers were so much easier to remember than those of other books, and in recognition of this, eighty-seven hymns were able to retain their former number. Alongside fifteen Stainer tunes and thirty-one by Dykes, there are some fine plainsong arrangements and no fewer than forty-one Communion hymns. All the new material is singable, but some of it lacks individuality and has made little headway either among users of *Ancient and Modern*, or in other books. Such tunes as "Twyford", "Ad Astra", "Sampford" and "Emmaus" would come into this category. Following the success of "Totteridge", a number of tunes with bars of differing lengths have been included such as "Kybald Twychen", "St Nicholas" and "Veryan". Whilst this is a welcome development in the interests of flexibility, some attempts suggest the triumph of ingenuity over inspiration, and result in a mannered end product. But there are also some magnificent tunes making their début including "Swanmore", "Abbot's Leigh", "Wolvercote", "Ladywell", "Golden Grove" and "Nap Hill". "Shrewsbury" is the first real competitor "St Cuthbert" has ever had.

English Hymnal's trump cards have always been "Monk's Gate", "Sine Nomine" and "Down Ampney", and their copyright hold will never be relaxed so far as *Ancient and Modern* is concerned. The substitutes the latter provided in the form of "Bunyan", "Engelberg" and "North Petherton" are fine tunes, but just lack their rivals' magic. Some of *Ancient and Modern's* harmonizations and arrangements of old melodies first popularized by *English Hymnal,* may seem rather tame to some people, despite their idiomatic propriety, e.g. "Easter Song", "Herr Deinen Zorn", but *Ancient and Modern's* Genevan "Psalm 42" is a fine version.

The printing of "Song 34" and "Ave Virgo" with long bars will help to achieve greater flexibility in performance. Most of the psalm tunes are printed without gathering notes, presumably in order not to disturb "hallowed usage", but those that had never made much headway in Standard *Ancient and Modern* such as "Old 120th" and "Caithness" appear with their preliminary semibreves.

Thus whilst one may regret timidity shown in some parts of the book, there is so much first-rate material that it is difficult to see how a successful rival to *Ancient and Modern* could appear.

The canniness in judgment which ensured *Ancient and Modern's* success during the first century of its existence has also been present in the two supplements.

The Public School Hymn Book

Despite its title, there is nothing adolescent about either the words or the music of this fine collection published in 1949.

The type of religious experience it seeks chiefly to promote is a healthy objective one, and there is no doubt that those whose schools use this book will find that their aesthetic as well as their religious outlook will be broadened. Many of the best tunes have already appeared in *English Hymnal* and *Songs of Praise* and yet one notices that ephemeral "folksy tunes" found in those collections have been excluded from this book. An outstanding feature of the book is the large number of fine modern tunes by Public School musicians, among them C. S. Lang, W. H. Ferguson and Henry Ley. They are chiefly of the broad unison variety and sound very impressive when performed under the conditions for which they were created. Few hymn books have been compiled in which a larger number of first-rate compositions have appeared for the first time than is found here. A large number of descants add to the usefulness of the book, though they demand trebles with a good upward range.

A new book, based on the *Public School Hymn Book,* appeared in 1964 under the title *Hymns for Church and School.* The number of hymns was reduced from 554 to 346 and the "school Chapel" ethos of the older book was pared down somewhat. Most of the tunes of C. S. Lang were eliminated because they represented this ethos in an extreme form. The new book is of almost consistent musical excellence. The Psalter tunes are set forth in the original versions, the authentic version of "Gopsal" is here complete with Handel's postlude, and there are fine contributions from Leonard Blake, John Wilson and Herbert Howells, some of which make their hymn book début.

Songs of Praise

The musical excellence of *Songs of Praise* (1931) is generally acknowledged and the words are equally often derided. It is certainly true to say that it is hard to believe that the editor of this book, who saw fit to alter so many standard hymns and translations by inserting weaker versions of his own, is the same Percy Dearmer who twenty years earlier in his editing of *English Hymnal* was vehement in criticizing editors who altered words. Not only is the churchman at liberty to take exception to the multilating of a well-loved hymn, but many fine tunes must needs be left unperformed because the words to which they are set express a very diluted form of religious thought.

Yet in saying all that, one must not lose sight of the many beautiful lyrics found in no other hymn book, and the fine tunes written by the most eminent of contemporary composers to fit them, as well as the process in reverse.

It may be claimed that *Songs of Praise* is not meant to be a church hymn book, yet equally it is unsuitable as the book for an *ad hoc* miscellaneous gathering as the preface suggests. Surely on such occasions something well known is required rather than the intimate treasures of this book.

Yet it forms a first-rate school book, either in its complete form or in one of the smaller books based on *Songs of Praise*. Much in the book is restricted to a purely juvenile appeal and its influence among young people for a generation was a healthy one, certainly from a musical point of view. Recently it has lost favour as a school hymn book, largely because of more informal worship patterns and, in some instances, the discontinuance of daily school prayers. From all points of view these developments are to be deplored.

There is relatively little duplication in the Standard Edition of *Ancient and Modern* and *Songs of Praise*, and it would appear a good investment to buy *Songs of Praise* for use as a choir book.

Not all the music consists of pearls of great price; the folk song bug has bitten even more deeply into this book than the *English Hymnal,* and certain ancient church melodies could have been allowed to sleep undisturbed.

It would be unfair to end a short review of a book of such outstanding musical merit on an adverse note. There remains one other distinguishing feature of the book, which a comparison of other hymn books reveals, namely the excellent quality of the harmonizations of standard tunes. In the vast majority of cases they are the best available.

The English Hymnal

Although nearly eighty years have elapsed since the first publication, the *English Hymnal* still appears to be a modern book. One cannot call to mind any denominational hymn book which has enjoyed so long an existence, without there being urgent need for revision.

In reviewing the book, two quotations from its preface come to mind: "It is not a party-book..." (p. iii) and "This does not mean that austerity has been unduly sought" (p. x).

So far as the first quotation is concerned, one must reply that unless a particular parish belongs to the Anglo-Catholic wing of the Church of England large areas of the book will be left unused, and yet clearly the *English Hymnal* did valuable work in reviving for High Church use so many of the ancient hymns of the Church in fine translations. However, for many churchgoers, the words will often seem too remote for the present day, particularly since the whole drift of contemporary hymnody is away from archaic expression, regardless of what literary beauty it may possess.

Great courage was shown in the rejection of some Victorian "worthies", particularly in view of the hostile reception given to the "reform" 1904 edition of *Hymns Ancient and Modern* only two years earlier. As we look back over the period, it would appear that the reasons for the success of the one book, as against the failure of the other was due to (a) the *English Hymnal's* willingness to be more compromising. Despite all that the musical editors had to say against Victorian tunes, there were a surprising number that survived even the 1933 revision, and held their places in the body of the book, although being as bad, if not worse, than anything found in Standard *Ancient and Modern,* e.g. "Benevento", and "Leominster". (b) *English Hymnal* was superior in layout, type-setting and general appearance to any other hymn book. (c) There were a few outstanding editorial contributions, notably "Down Ampney" and "Sine Nomine".

Beyond this there were some fine hymns introduced to Anglican worshippers, including "Dear Lord and Father of mankind", "Firmly I believe and truly", "Eternal Ruler of the ceaseless round" and "Thy Kingdom come".

The older music included the French Church tunes in the Sapphic metre; the Tallis tunes; seventeenth-century tunes by Clarke and Lawes; correct versions of "Old 124th" and the Gibbons tunes; superior versions of standard tunes such as "Heinlein", "Old 104th", "Hyfrydol" and "Ratisbon"; folk tunes, including "Kings Lynn", "Forest Green" and "Monk's Gate"; Welsh tunes, including "Ebenezer", "Llanfair", "St Denio", "Rhuddlan", and Bach Chorales. Other fine tunes culled from a variety of sources included "Soll's Sein", "Grafenberg", "Stracathro", "Savannah" and "Cranham". All these in aggregate took away from the book the depressing appearance of what Geoffrey Shaw called minimity, which was responsible for much dullness in late-Victorian hymnody. Because of all this, the book has been far-reaching in its influence, even extending to the most reactionary corners of Nonconformity. Its basic fault lay in its excess of doctrinaire zeal, a trait also discernible in its admirers.

One of the disturbing aspects of comparative hymnology is the tendency of writers to hold fixed views and ignore evidence which points in a contrary direction. Robin Leaver in *A Hymn Book Survey 1962–80*, (Grove Worship Series), p. 6 wrote: "Whereas the original [English Hymnal] was adventurous, daring and uncompromisingly an Anglo-Catholic production, the English Hymnal Service Book [which is based on it] is safe, careful and middle of the road. The English Hymnal had an appendix of tunes that people would want to sing, but which the editors did not approve of — they apparently referred privately to this as the 'Chamber of Horrors'."

A second appendix was added in the 1933 edition to make

room for new material and bore no derogatory designation.

The Rev. Cyril Taylor, writing a review of the *English Hymnal Service Book* in the *Hymn Society Bulletin,* Vol. 5, No. 8, pp. 111–8, stated: "The prison gates of EH's appendix sternly locked by Vaughan Williams and Martin Shaw are thrown open and out come the prisoners... Believe it or not Dykes' St Agnes is the only old lag, with her husband outside, who has not been restored to liberty."

In fact, "St Agnes" was *not* included in the 1906 appendix, but occupied a place in the body of the book. The appendix contained sixteen tunes (including "Nicaea" and the "Easter Hymn" in higher keys than the versions in the book). Of the remainder only four were paroled.

The rehabilitation of Victoriana, including some pieces that had never appeared in *English Hymnal,* took place because the editors of *English Hymnal Service Book* realized that Shaw and Vaughan Williams had made serious errors of judgment, and that because of this, users of the parent book had been inconvenienced in their choice of tunes.

The 1933 edition contained no revision of the words, but recast the plainsong accompaniments into a more flexible form, and introduced about a hundred new tunes, most of which had been previously issued in *Songs of Praise.* Those which had been written in a pseudo-folk song style proved to be far less durable than the tunes they sought to displace. (See note 15, p. 33, and note 1, p. 91.)

The BBC Hymn Book

The conditions for which the *BBC Hymn Book* (1951) were compiled are ideal ones for any musical editor bent on compiling an anthology of only the best, for in broadcast services tunes can be sung without any regard for popular taste and they can be repeated until they are known.

Yet in saying this, one must observe that the editors of this book have not abused their position. An admirable sanity pervades the whole, and the odd and perverse find no place here. Equally admirable has been the ecumenical approach to the selection.

It is averred that a hymn book must ultimately stand or fall on the excellence or otherwise of the original material it offers. At first sight it would appear that the musical editors, who have provided fifty per cent of the new tunes, have included a disproportionate amount of their own work but, as this book's index indicates, almost all of them are of the highest quality and fill an acknowledged need.

An interesting feature of the work is the section of choir settings, which could with advantage replace some of the feeble anthems performed in many churches.

One can scarcely conceive of a book compiled for broadcast services fulfilling its function more adequately than the present one.

The Church Hymnary: Second Edition

The *Church Hymnary: Second Edition* (1927) is a sober dignified collection. It contains a large number of Psalter tunes, and no doubt because of its editor's nationality, many Welsh tunes. A very high standard of harmonization is maintained and there are many fine modern tunes. Inevitably, with so large a hymn book, there is a fair crop of weaker tunes, but the book is so generously provided with alternatives that people who wish to raise musical standards have the material to do so.

The Church Hymnary: Third Edition

In its day, the second edition of the *Church Hymnary* was a reforming, challenging book, so it comes as no surprise that its successor fills a similar role today. It would, however, be sad if the *Church Hymnary: Third Edition* (1973) were written off as a highbrow book, when the needs of the humblest congregation are so well provided for.

The new material in an unfamiliar hymn book is always that which one examines first, and much of this has a distinctively Scottish sound — not merely because of the connections of the composers. There is a certain bleak austerity about "Rutherglen" (No. 13) and "Stonelaw" (No. 86 — this is a tune of very great potential) and also in the tunes of Kenneth Leighton, which veer precariously on the side of the possible, "Colinton" (No. 576) being perhaps the easiest. Much the same can be said of Barrett-Ayres' tunes (Nos. 425 and 470). However, to include tunes merely as status symbols when their congregational usefulness is precisely nil is an expensive luxury, and the tunes of Sebastian Forbes (Nos. 141 and 678), John Currie (Nos. 399, 411 and 453), Frederick Rimmer (No. 576), Martin Dalby (Nos. 149 and 647) (but excepting No. 433, an attractive setting of "God be in my head"), and Arthur Oldham (Nos. 177 and 300) clearly come into this category. Frank Spedding's "Mapperley" for the marvellous "Magnificat" paraphrase "Tell out, my soul" faces competition from numerous other modern composers, and Llewellyn's "Tidings" in the *Anglican Hymn Book* is a much more reasonable proposition.

Modern rhythms will attract the young towards Donald Swann's "Jordan" (No. 105), and Malcolm Williamson's "Christ, whose glory" (No. 114). I cannot see John Joubert's "Moseley" (No. 367) making headway (against "England's Lane") as a new tune for "For the beauty of the earth", but Joubert's other tune "Egton Bridge" (No. 401) is a most imaginative piece. This hymn is also served with two excellent Irish settings by James Moore. Riches indeed.

Among future winners, we may safely predict "Laredo" (No. 427). "Searching for Lambs", as an alternative to "Crimond", "Blessing and honour" (No. 299) and, perhaps less certainly, "In armour bright" (No. 288) and "Tredegar" (No. 583). Lennox Berkeley's two evening hymns are worth examination, since their melodies are attractive and the unorthodoxies confined to the harmonies.

One extends a warm welcome to new (or recently fashionable) tunes from other books, notably "Abbot's Leigh", "Michael", "Sancta Civitas", "Chorus Angelorum" and "Westminster Abbey"... and so one could go on. The list is a lengthy one.

"Alberta", Harris's tune for "Lead, kindly Light" and "King's Lynn" for "O God of earth and altar" — or even as an alternative to the ubiquitous "Aurelia" for "The Church's one foundation", are the most notable omissions.

The previous book was perhaps overloaded with Welsh tunes, and it is inevitable that these should now be pruned, some rather unfortunately. But one didn't expect to find "Christmas Carol" (Walford Davies), "Stracathro" and "Galilee" (surely one of the finest nineteenth-century L. M. tunes) among the discards from the *Church Hymnary: Second Edition*.

The *Church Hymnary: Third Edition* contains an interesting collection of prose settings, plainsong tunes, etc., all of which could enrich our worship if performed chorally in the first instance.

The policy of making certain tunes do double or even triple duty, e.g. "Love Unknown", when there are excellent specimens of an identical metre such as S. S. Wesley's "Harewood", is one I would question. It is good to find the Christmas season so well provided. I didn't find more than a dozen "horror tunes", which must be a record in a hymnal for general use, and was amused to find three settings of "The Lord bless you". I doubt if any of them will be more successful, than was Lowell Mason's rival in the *Church Hymnary: Second Edition* in ousting Mason's tune from some churches.

When amendments are proposed to a work which has represented the combined toil and devoted endeavours of a large number of able people, the maker of them leaves himself open to the charge of arrogance. Nevertheless, after some years of close study and working with the *Church Hymnary: Third Edition*, I make the following suggestions with some diffidence. Whilst there may appear to be a degree of dogmatism in the comments, this is not intended. It is simply that one wishes to make points with reasonable brevity. Tunes outwith the *Church Hymnary: Third Edition* are of course found in sources other than those listed, which are quoted merely for reference. It may be said, however, that those mentioned are the best available versions in the writer's opinion.

At first sight the list appears to be a long one, but the hymns and tunes referred to represent a small portion of the total book, which during its short life has contributed significantly to Presbyterian worship.

No. in CH3	*Comment*
4	A mellifluous but rather undistinguished eighteenth-century tune. Try "Sennan Cove" (528, *AMR*).
5	With its ironed-out rhythm "Grafenberg" is seriously impoverished. Could we have the original restored? See 139 *(Camb. H.)* and 421 *(EH)*.
11	A rather ordinary tune, but there's not much to choose from in this metre. See "Gott ein Vater" (666, *CH2*). See also 415 *(AMR)* for harmonized version.
13	A simpler alternative needed for "Rutherglen". Try "Falcon Street" (635, *SP*).
18	"Swabia", with the sixth chord of line three held for three beats would make a splendid 6666 tune. See No. 113.
22	With three perfect cadences out of four it would have been reasonable to make the end of line three an interrupted cadence.
24	Why the parsimony in not providing different tunes for Nos. 23 and 24? See "Rochester" (422, *CH2*).
34	Despite hallowed associations with these words, "Ombersley" has outlived its usefulness. Few L.M. tunes are metrically suitable. "Galilee" (647, *CH2*) is nearly so.
38	"Northampton" (369, *AMR*) is a winner for these words.
40	Key D and a few more passing notes for "Was lebet".
44	"Farley Castle" (No. 649) a possible alternative.
52	"Ach blieb bei uns" (No. 642) or "Jena" (5, *CH2*).
59	"Tres magi" is feeble in the extreme. Try "Bonn" ("Festus") (170, *CH2*).
70	(second tune), 75 (second tune), 77 (second tune) are all poor but the first tunes are all splendid.

E

81	Halting and poverty-stricken harmonies in "Olivet". "Denbigh" is much better.
83	A poor tune but irreplaceable.
84	Incredibly unstylistic harmonies especially at the end of line two. Compare 114 (*EH*).
86	For those whose courage fails, try "All Souls" ("Yoakley"). App. 57, (*EH*).
89	The second chord on line two of "Cwm Rhonnda" should be A flat first inversion.
101	Compare the infinitely superior version of "Dunfermline" (378, *BBC*).
103	Despite the notation, "Wirksworth" shouldn't be hurried. Consider also "Carlisle".
105	Webbe's "Veni Sancte Spiritus" (186, *CH2*) has much beauty, especially for these words.
109	An incredibly monotonous tune with three plagal cadences out of four.
110	Why omit verse two with its inextinguishable blaze, which I have never found unsingable, as is often averred, especially to "Hereford" (No. 338). There is a very hallowed association for many between S. S. Wesley's tune and Charles Wesley's words.
134	With so many first-rate 8787D tunes how has this one crept in? Try "Marathon" (302, *SP*).
141	John Wilson's magnificent modern tune is the one for these words (64, *PFT*). Sebastian Forbes is a non-starter.
143	"London" (170, *AMR*) brings out all the stateliness of Addison's words.
150	Ouseley's gracious tune "Contemplation" (177, *AMR*) fits these words better than the idiosyncratic rhythm of "Nativity".
164	Of the many settings of these magnificent words that I've encountered Llewellyn's "Tidings" (439, *AHB*), is the best.
173	Isn't it a bit mean to remove the traditional harmonies in the refrain? It's good to have a modulation to A but wouldn't it have been better at the end of line three?
178	Are we too squeamish nowadays to sing about "A breastful of milk and a mangerful of hay"?
179	A few more verses of "See amid" wouldn't come amiss.
184	"Was born on Christmas Day" would enable the carol to be sung intelligently on other days during the Festive Season.
200	Plagal cadences in lines one and three would avoid every line ending with a perfect cadence as at present.
207	"Love Unknown" a delicate tune receives too much exposure in *CH3*.
211	"Merton" (47, *AMR)* would stand a better chance of displacing that dreadful "St Andrew".
218	An 8787D tune such as "Hyfrydol" has a sweep that encompasses these words better than a four line tune. Return to line five for final verse.
247	We can't do anything about "Petra" for "Rock of Ages" but we can have "Arfon" for this hymn.

259	Four appearances of "Stuttgart" are three too many. What about "Halton Holgate" (186, *AMR*)?
269	"St John Damascene" (133, *AMR*) deserves a journey over the Border, since "Ave Virgo" is also found at No. 449.
282	Try "Mead House" (98, *BBC*).
285	"Winchester New" in waltz time.
306	"Bishopthorpe" (No. 530) is preferable to the commonplace "Fingal".
314	"Highwood" (32, *BBC)* to these words is superb.
320	Despite its unsavoury associations, "Cross of Jesus" (54, *AMR*) is fine to these words.
324	"Bucer" is a feeble S.M. tune. Try "Camberwell" (679, *CH2*).
325	"Lochwinnoch" hardly compares with "Sheen" (310, *EH*).
329	It is surely an error to set two Whitsuntide hymns to the same tune, even if it is "Gonfalon Royal".
336	"Shrewsbury" (230, *AMR*) is the only plausible rival to "St Cuthbert".
367	Try "England's Lane" (309, *EH*).
370	Try "Laudes Domini" (167, *CH2*). "Psalm 3" is rather an endurance test for any but a large congregation.
379	Tallis' "First Mode Melody" or "St Francis Xavier" (106, *AMR*) gets closer to the words.
381	Rather a poor harmonization for "Hyfrydol". See 301, *EH̄*.
412	*Ugh*!
414	Compare "Gott sei Dank" (552, *EH*) where a superior version is printed.
416	This harmonized version is a poor thing alongside Holst's version. See 502, *SP*.
420	"Kings Lynn" (562, *EH)* is a marvellous replacement for the doleful "Aurelia".
434	Bring "Wolvercote" (508, *CH2*) back into circulation.
467	What a poor thing when there are so many 8787 tunes. Try "Gott wills machen" (364, *AMR*).
482	*Ugh*!
484	What about Smart's magnificent "Rex Gloriae" (148, *AMR*)?
533	Bring "Ladywell" into the fold once more (139, *CH2*).
535	A poor harmonization of "O quanta qualia". See 281, *AMR* or 465, *EH*.
536	Try "Beulah" (32, *AMR*) (without the A # in line four).
552	Arranged in this fashion "Commandments" is a poor thing.
646	If we're looking seriously for a good quality replacement to "St Clement", "Hereford" could be easily adapted.
656	"Shipston" better.
667	Couldn't Scotland come into line with the rest of the U.K. and sing "Martyrdom" in 3/4?
677	It would take a miracle to displace "St Margaret", but "Repton" with the metre of the second line amended might just do it.
681	"Passion Chorale" as an alternative to "Penlan".
682	Why wasn't "Alberta" (298, *AMR*) used?

The Methodist Hymn Book

The present *Methodist Hymn Book* was published in 1933 to coincide with the Methodist Union. The claim that "Methodism has been always able to sing its creed" is a valid one, and clearly the first aim of the editors was to produce a book which would be acceptable to the three uniting churches, whose musical traditions and associations between hymns and tunes differed. The 1904 *Wesleyan Hymn Book* had not been the success hoped for and a second failure could not be contemplated. It seems likely then that popular acceptance, rather than high musical standards, was the principal aim. How well this aim was realized is common knowledge now. The present book is large — incredibly so by Anglican standards. Yet one notices that the average Methodist knows his hymn book, and knows by name far more tunes than the average Anglican.

The system of having more than two-thirds of all Methodist services conducted by visiting local preachers who are entitled to select hymns as they please, makes it imperative for a large number of hymns to be generally known, and in practice even the most popular hymns are not sung more than twice a year.

There is, of course, a tremendous disparity between the best and the worst tunes. Indeed, superficial acquaintance with the book shows that the bad by its sheer abundance tends to obscure the good. Yet it is possible for a selection of the best tunes from the 984 hymns to be made, which would be sufficient for the needs of any church.

The catholicity of taste shown in the tunes is remarkable. Some of the tunes are of a kind that the first edition of *Ancient and Modern* would not have included, whilst others form the best modern tunes in *Songs of Praise*. It is unfortunate however that the harmonizations of the standard tunes leave much to be desired.

If musical standards are to be improved, some directive and guidance should be forthcoming. Many of the worst tunes are sung because of inverted snobbery, or because they are thought of as "Methodist" tunes, and better tunes of Anglican origin tend to be overlooked because they are thought to be outside the Methodist orbit in style. In actual fact it is the florid triple time eighteenth- and early nineteenth-century tune which should have special significance for Methodists, rather than the Moody and Sankey type. At the time of writing, it is understood that a new book is in course of preparation. Such collections as *Hymns and Songs* and the *Methodist School Hymn Book* have clearly been used as proving ground for newer material. It is safe to predict that a new book will cover as wide a range of musical quality as the old, but it is hoped that better versions of standard tunes are provided than in the current book. That is Methodism's greatest musical need.

Congregational Praise

The handsome appearance of this hymn book in 1951 has no doubt contributed to its success, but there have been few new hymn books which established themselves in popular esteem more quickly. This fact is all the more remarkable when it is remembered that it represents a noteworthy advance on the previous Congregational hymn book. The committee were fortunate in having the services of so distinguished a musician as Dr Eric H. Thiman. *Congregational Praise* contains a fine quota of standard and modern tunes, which latter include some particularly attractive ones making their first appearance in a hymn book, e.g. "Cheerful Songs", "Beeding" and "Stokesay Castle". They are modern in style, and yet free from experiment. Whilst there are those tunes which popular sentiment demands, in many cases the modern alternatives stand a good chance of ultimately superseding them.

It is pleasing to note, too, the broadmindedness shown in the choice of words. In choosing hymns which would be acceptable to Christians of all denominations, the book succeeds where *Songs of Praise* fails. This has been achieved not by weakening the doctrinal content of hymns by alteration, but by choosing hymns with a strong scriptural foundation.

Songs of Syon

This fine though little-known book is a collection, published in 1919, for the most part of ancient church melodies of Western Europe. For the historian it is valuable for tracing the evolution of musical idioms, and yet such fine music deserves to be performed. The editor G. R. Woodward, has written words for the unusual metres these tunes demand — words which maintain the medieval atmosphere of the music, without expressing a narrow theological outlook or being precious. In some cases the editors have provided harmonizations of their own, but so thoroughly have they absorbed period style that no trace of anachronism is to be found. Particularly interesting are the pre-Bach Chorales, which help us to realize how Bach altered melodically, harmonically, rhythmically and metrically to suit his purpose. It must be remarked, for motives other than those of artistic snobbery, that these ancient melodies need ancient or quasi-ancient settings for their true beauty to be perceived. Even where the melody has been scrupulously kept in modern hymn books, the treatment, whilst no doubt being "correct" is often unidiomatic and causes one to estimate the tunes unjustly. It must be added, however, that few of these tunes in their appropriate setting are suitable for congregational performance.

The Cambridge Hymnal

This is a collection of just under 200 hymns, songs and carols which it is believed "express Christian thought and feeling appropriate to the twentieth century". The extent to which the editors have succeeded in this is something the individual can decide only for himself. Perhaps more than any other hymn book, it may be regarded as an anthology which reflects the tastes of the editors, rather than a balanced self-sufficient hymn book. Consequently, there is much traditional material of undoubted excellence that has been omitted, and some hymns and tunes included that are either intrinsically of questionable merit, or have been made so by their arrangements. Nevertheless, the enthusiastic reviews of a generation ago were hardly justified in the light of the book's subsequent use. For instance, at a time when so much religious teaching has been in the direction of simplicity and directness, one wonders how intellectually and aesthetically challenging material has fared in schools, colleges and youth clubs, for whom it was intended.

Nevertheless, as a supplementary collection of choir hymn/anthems the *Cambridge Hymnal,* published in 1967, is first class. How good it is to see "Grafenberg" (No. 139) with authentic rhythms, thus adding a whole new dimension to the tune. Splendid arrangements of spirituals, e.g. No. 132; traditional American pieces, e.g. Nos. 32, 117, 134 and 135; Irish folk song arrangements, e.g. No. 131; Campion pieces, e.g. Nos. 75, 92, 127 and 129; two excellent pieces from John Joubert, No. 44 and No. 118, and two from John Gardner No. 101 and No. 113, enrich its contents. There have been some splendid words provided already for Tallis' "Third Mode Melody", and John Mason's "Thou wast O God" is yet another instance.

Whilst Elizabeth Poston's descants seldom range above competence, those for Nos. 47, 108 and 109 sound impressive in performance, as does Maurice Jacobson's arrangement of "Leoni", where the varied treatment of several verses builds up a marvellous cumulative effect. Edmund Rubbra's "Lindens" captures effectively the mood of John Gwyneth's sixteenth-century lyric. We may well wonder what "Crimond" is doing among all this (supposed) excellence, but there it is, alongside four other 23rd Psalm paraphrases (but not H. W. Baker's). Bliss (No. 96) and Mellers (No. 95) are strange bedfellows for

No. 94's modulating monstrosity of "St Ethelwald", about which the book's fulsome critics were strangely silent, as they were of the almost unbelievable travesty of the great "Gerontius" theme at No. 89.

We may ask of the special merits of "Compton Scorpion" (No. 63) over the metrically equivalent "Regent Square", which, to quote Ralph Vaughan Williams' famous words, apparently "doesn't enter into the scheme of the book". Neither Berkeley's "Wiveton" (No. 61) nor Howells' "Erwin" (No. 62) have been taken up by other books; one wonders why. Britten's imaginative descants for "Tallis' Canon" and "Melita" are valuable assets; so is the Vaughan Williams' version of "Come my way", adapted from the five Mystical Songs.

Space precludes detailed consideration of the carols, rounds and other material, but the range of style mentioned above shows something of the book's contents and the pleasures in store for an enterprising choir. Elizabeth Poston's "Jesus Christ the apple tree" (No. 111) is, in my view, the gem of the book.

Three North American Hymn Books

Those of us who enjoy examining hymn books have, over the years, developed a degree of unshockability when we turn pages and find that the reactionary and the progressive, the noble and the trivial, the truly great and utterly appalling tunes occur in bewildering succession. In such circumstances, one wonders what the guiding editorial principle is, since those who wallow in mediocrity are clearly unlikely to use the better material, lest by so doing they are shaken out of their complacency. On the other hand, those whose tastes and standards are more worthy may find insufficient material for their needs.

However, no British experience affords us an adequate preparation for an examination of the *Methodist Hymnal*,

1964. The Methodist Church is one of the largest Protestant sects in the U.S.A., with a membership of over 10,000,000, so we can assume that its hymn book enjoys a corresponding usage. What are the chief surprises? Amid the general confused mediocrity of "St Margaret" (Peace) and "Rest" (Maker) facing one another on opposite pages, to see Peter Cutts' "Wylde Green" was certainly the first. This was followed by "King's Weston" (Vaughan Williams) for "At the Name of Jesus", "Let us break bread together", "Herr Jesu Christ" in delightful irregular rhythm, a pre-Bach version of "Wachet auf", and "Hark! the herald angels sing" set to the tune of "Jesus Christ is risen today".

The custom of giving a fresh number to each setting of a hymn is not uncommon, but elsewhere they follow consecutively. Here, the versions of "Bread of the world" occur at No. 320 and No. 322, and "Jesus Christ is risen today" (to "Easter Hymn" and "Llanfair") at No. 439 and No. 443, which denotes some degree of editorial slackness. The tunes usually have the names by which they are known in Britain, but the associations are somewhat different. "Christ, whose glory fills the skies" ("Ratisbon") occurs in the Christmas section. Sparrow Simpson's words "Cross of Jesus" (all of them!) are *not* set to Stainer's tune. "Irish" for "Through all the changing scenes of life", "Innocents" for "Let us with a gladsome mind", "When all thy mercies" to "Winchester Old", "Make me a captive, Lord" to "Diademata", "There is a green hill" to "Windsor" (even though "Horsley" occurs twice elsewhere) are just a few of the "marriages" in the book which seem rather capricious to a Briton. Other shocks include "O worship the King", "Thou whose almighty word", "When I survey the wondrous cross", not set to their familiar tunes, and "Arfon" and "Llangloffan" in *major* key versions!

Yet alongside such trivia as Lowell Mason's tunes we find such desirable items as "Sine Nomine", "Old 107th", "Old 124th" (to "Father Eternal, Ruler of Creation" and "Turn back, O man"), "Down Ampney", "Vater unser", "Christe Sanctorum", "Schmücke dich" (with its irregular rhythm) and

"Dominus regit me". None of the harmonizations of standard tunes seem to be particularly distinguished, and Bach's "Du Friedensfürst, Herr Jesu Christ", set not very happily to "The day is past and over", was one of the few meritorious tunes I found that is not generally known in Britain.

The Hymnal, 1940, is the kind of book *Ancient and Modern Revised* might have been had it emerged ten years earlier. There is a fair amount of worthwhile unfamiliar material. These include items by Tertius Noble, whose brief recruitment into British hymnody in the 1904 *Methodist Hymn Book* was terminated by his departure from these shores soon after. His "New England" (C.M.) and "Mauburn" (irregular) are very agreeable pieces, as are Vincent Gray's "Holy Innocents" (C.M.), W. A. Goldsworthy's "Bouwerie" (C.M.), Percy Coller's "St Joan" (67676666) and Philip James' "Tregaron" (D.C.M.). The latter is set to fine words, "And have the bright immensities", which are also set to a Handel adaptation. But one looks in vain for "Gopsal". Attractive traditional fare includes "Kedron" (L.M.) and "Morning Song" (868686). There are also interesting pre-Bach versions of "Weimar", "Eisenach" and "Herzliebster Jesu". Among older tunes, "Elbing" (8787887) by Peter Sohren in a Chorale style harmonization and J. B. Koenig's "Mentzner "(989888) in a free metrical rhythm have much character.

One wonders how much homesickness John Goss's "Arthur's Seat" will induce in emigré Scots, even though it isn't a very distinctive tune, and it is interesting to discover how "Morning Light", G. J. Webb's tune for "Stand up! stand up for Jesus" acquired its name. Here it is set to "The morning light is breaking". Setting "My God, how wonderful thou art" to "Windsor" rather than to "Westminster" denotes an exchange of rapture for awe. R. R. Terry's fine tune "Newman" for "Praise to the Holiest in the height" has been included in no British hymn book in current use, not even the Catholic ones. I wonder why.

Two "contemporary" favourites, "McKee" and "Kremser" make their appearance here, fully a generation before crossing the Atlantic. The inclusion of Guy Warrack's "Wellington Square" and Martin Shaw's "Riley" indicates a familiarity with *Songs of Praise*, but one is left wondering what there was in these tunes that caught the editors' fancy rather than other and more meritorious ones from the same source. Even more overtly British is Rudyard Kipling's "Non nobis Domine", which has not appeared in any standard book over here. Other *tunes* that could well be imported by us include Leo Sowerby's "Palisades" (L.M.), "Chelsea Square" (C.M.) by H. C. Robbins, Franklin Glynn's "Maxon" for Masefield's "Sing men and angels sing" and "Tysk", a German melody that could prove to be a formidable rival to "Arnsberg" ("Neander") for "God is in His Temple".

W. H. Monk has thirteen tunes included, not a great number by British standards but they include two, "Supplication" (8787D) and "Coronae" (878747), that are unknown in Britain. They may both be described as workmanlike rather than inspired.

The rhythmic freedom when using the L.M. metre of Franklin Glynn's "Woking" shows a clear anticipation of "contemporary" trends. The prayer "for those in peril on the sea" has been adapted from Whiting's original to include the dangers of land and air travel, and set to Dykes's ubiquitous "Melita". Ann Miller's "Vermont" (C.M.) anticipates the harmonic parallelism of later writers, and the textural bareness of Elizabeth Poston.

A book variously entitled *The Hymn Book* and *The Book of Common Praise* for the Anglican Church in Canada also has an *Ancient and Modern* aura surrounding it. There are here some fine plainsong accompaniments to "Veni Creator" and "Vexilla Regis" by Healey Willan. His faux-bourdons for "Richmond" and "Martyrdom" are equally impressive, but his original tunes, apart from "St Osmond" (878747), I found disappointing. Of the hymn tunes in Stainer's *Crucifixion,* only "Cross of Jesus" and "All for Jesus" have found their way into contemporary British hymnody. Here we are given the extremely dubious pleasure of having the others — "Etiam pro nobis", "Adoration" and "Plead for me". Generally tune names and associations are as one would find in Britain. An adaptation of "The heavens are telling" (Haydn) and one from Beethoven's Ninth Symphony (minus the syncopation in line seven — despite the obsession with this rhythmic device in modern hymnody) seem to be very popular in North America.

Other curiosities include a remarkably Victorian sounding tune "Moving Tent" (D.S.M.) by Martin Shaw. Can this *really* be the work of the author of *Principles of Church Music Composition* who could lay down the law so dogmatically, and hurl his envenomed darts at Victoriana and everything associated with it? No wonder he could find no room for it in *Songs of Praise*. We are given no fewer than five tunes for "Through the night of doubt and sorrow" including "Marching", "St Oswald", "Sussex" and a couple of nondescript 8787Ds.

What a world of difference lies between the gospel song rhythms of "Lanier" and Vaughan Williams' deeply imaginative and starkly challenging "Mantegna" (S.P.) for "Into the woods my master went". Of the modern tunes, Ernest Bullock's "Litlyngton" (88887), W. Wells Hewitt's "Stratford-on-Avon" (C.M.), "Qui Tenet" (L.M. irregular) by E. S. Barnes, and "Carroll Street" (6664884) by A. L. Jacob engaged my favourable attention.

Inevitably, in a book of over 800 hymns and a large tune supplement serving a variety of worshipping traditions, there will be quantities of dross, but here, as in *The Hymnal*, there is no lack of fine material which, apart from the exclusive items already mentioned, is listed in the index of the present book.

With One Voice – a hymn book for all the churches
(The Australian Hymn Book)

This collection has enjoyed a favourable critical reception since its publication in 1979 because it forms a beautifully presented book and the motive behind its compilation is wholly admirable. However, when one examines its contents doubts arise. More than 400 of its 579 hymns are provided with fine settings, but because of duplication, the actual number of tunes is less than three-quarters of this figure. Most of the tunes are known by their British titles and are set to words which generally have an existing denominational affiliation in Britain, e.g. "St Helen", "Hyfrydol", "Congleton", "Unde et memores", "Song 1", "Rendez à Dieu", "Dundee", "Wareham" and "Lyngham" (that vulgar eighteenth-century fuguing tune that also appears in *English Praise* — of all places).

The editors appear to have gone out of their way to cast their net as widely as possible, so as to be freed from sectarian partiality. There are melodies of Asiatic origin, negro spirituals, 20th Century Light Music, Gelineau, and responsorial psalm settings which have formed such a significant contribution to contemporary hymnody from the Roman Catholic Church. There are also words and music from M.R.A. song books, contemporary hymns and tunes of the most uncompromising kind, e.g. Thomas Wilson's "Stonelaw" from the *Church Hymnary: Third Edition,* and Adrian Beecham's "Yellow Bittern" from the *Cambridge Hymnal.* Other contemporary tunes include "Michael", "Sharpethorne", "Godmanstone", "Birabus", and carols by Sidney Carter. From American hymnody "Grand Isle" is a worthy recruit.

Alongside these the idioms of the earlier twentieth century from the *English Hymnal* and *Songs of Praise* coexist with a generous selection of Nonconformist favourites such as "Mountain Christians", Peace's "St Margaret", "There's a light upon the mountains", "Edgware", Victorian Gospel hymns and the Anglican tunes of Wesley and Monk. The staple fare of the eighteenth and nineteenth centuries in both words and music appear to be well represented, so what is there to complain about? Personally I have the uneasy feeling that the sense of balance which produced this selection has tried to be all things to all men, with the same consequences as occur in other of life's activities when this principle is applied. Alongside much duplication, particularly in the standard metres, one regrets that no place could be found for "St Bride", "Song 20", "Beulah", "Binchester", "Cheshire", "King's Norton", "Lincoln", "St James", "Cromer", "Illsley", "Kent", "St Venantius", "Simeon" and "Whitehall". A similar exclusion is apparent throughout the other metres.

Finally, there is the new material, including that not found elsewhere, to be taken into account. This includes some striking compositions, of which the following may be recommended:

Irregular	Coelho Psalm 33 (Responsorial setting.)	C. Coelho
10 10 10 10 9 *and refrain*	Cosmic Praise	R. Connolly
C.M.	Belair	H. P. Finnis
7878 *and refrain*	Ruggiero	R. Connolly
C.M.	Joy	D. Britton
S. M. Tern	Pilgrims	L. Rowlands
7777 *and refrain*	Lindfield	R. Connolly
7777	Catherine	R. Connolly
88 10 10 4	Bilaam	Philippine Melody
Irregular	Psalm 122	R. Reboud
76767686	Indonesia	Batak Carol Melody
12 11 12 12	Kremser	Netherlands Folk Melody
Irregular	Aaronic Blessing (So much better than Lowell Mason.)	D. Britton
C.M.	Bramwell	R. K. Boughen
8888	Laura (So much better than "Celeste", which also appears here for "This, this is the God we adore".)	L. F. Bartlett
L.M. *and refrain*	Newtown	R. Connolly
12 12 12 12	Omnipotens	D. Britton
Irregular 11 10 11 10 *and refrain*	New Commandment Love is the fulfilling	Unknown R. Connolly
9 10 *and chorus*	All the earth	L. Deiss
S.M.	Montgomery	D. S. Goodall

During a recent visit to Australia the writer was impressed by the extent to which churches of many different denominations now used the "Australian Hymn Book". This seemed to be a gesture towards nationhood as well as towards ecumenism. Many of those to whom I spoke expressed unease about what seemed to them a disproportionate Methodist influence in the choice of words and also in the harmonizations of standard tunes. No one seemed disposed to admit that the latter could conceivably be better than the ones to which they were used. In general, sentiment towards the book was less favourable than I anticipated.

The (Irish) Church Hymnal

The contents of this book, published in 1960, were excluded from the main index because they are not widely known in Britain. Nevertheless, in addition to the tunes it shares with other collections, which usually also share a common title, it has some interesting features of its own. These include:

7686D	Saints Victorious: Ten thousand times ten thousand	H. A. Chambers
10 10 10 10	Inchigeela: God of our fathers	J. T. Horne
7474746	Jesu meines herzens Freud: Jesu joy of all my heart (A gem, would make a fine choir piece.)	J. S. Bach
S.M.	Combe Martin: Put thou thy trust in God (Rescued from the *Oxford Hymn Book*.)	B. Harwood
386563	Stonethwaite: Day by day dear Lord (St Richard's Prayer—also in *Songs of Praise*.)	A. Somervell
L.M.	Land of our birth: We've no abiding city	K. G. Finlay
7676D	Bohemian Hymn: O Master when Thou callest	Bohemian Brethren
7777D	Clyde Road: For Thy Saints unknown to peace	W. H. V. Barry
7575D	Egerton: Father let me dedicate	G. T. Thalben-Ball

There are also fine versions of "Old 77th" ("Old 81st"), "Vreuchten" and Psalm 68 harmonized by Charles Wood, Luther (from Bach's *Christmas* oratorio), "Werde Munter" (as in "Jesu, joy of man's desiring"), and "Grenoble" harmonized by C. H. Kitson. F. G. Carter's setting of, "What a Friend we have in Jesus", deserves to replace the current tune.

The Supplements

It is, I suppose, a measure of our theological and liturgical uncertainty, together with our strained ecclesiastical finances, that instead of wholesale revisions of the standard hymn books, supplements of roughly a hundred hymns have been published instead. It needs to be borne in mind that each has been compiled to serve a different purpose; some have been used to introduce hymns and tunes that have gained popularity since the publication of the parent book — in the case of *English Hymnal* a period of over fifty years; others, such as the Baptists' *Praise for Today* have concentrated on the twentieth century, even to the extent of introducing material they know to be ephemeral. In their selections, the compilers have reflected the taste and traditions of the parent books, thus *English Praise* reflects the liturgical quality of *English Hymnal*, whilst *Ancient and Modern's* two supplements, *One Hundred Hymns for Today* and *More Hymns for Today*, take what is interesting but not revolutionary from today's material. As has always been the case with *Ancient and Modern* (except 1904's "failure" which sold only 2,000,000 copies) the editors have judged the market to a nicety, and both books have enjoyed phenomenal success.

One has the feeling that the Methodist *Hymns and Songs* has been used as a try-out for material that is under consideration for the next Methodist hymn book, whenever that may appear. *New Church Praise* is designed as the supplement to both the *Church Hymnary* and *Congregational Praise*. It was the most radical of the supplements when it first appeared, in that it covered a wider range of material, including lyrics with their freer rhythms which pushed back the frontier of what we considered to be a hymn. Thus the alleged conservatism and lack of adventure so far as the words are concerned in *Congregational Praise* and *Church Hymnary: Third Edition* has been remedied, and a still more radical compilation *Songs for the Eighties* is promised.

Partners in Praise, a collection that attempted to accommodate both the needs of parents and children, and *Songs of Worship,* Scripture Union's supplement to *Hymns of Faith,* contain little original material that is likely to prove of lasting value. The promised *Broadcast Praise,* the supplement to the *BBC Hymn Book* now thirty years old, has recently appeared, but notwithstanding its having a number of fine tunes, including some specially composed, its comparatively high cost may well restrict its influence.

Reference is made in the index to what the writer considers to be the outstanding musical items. What one would like to see is some consensus among the various editors as to the best tune for each lyric, which may involve them in sacrificing the one *they* have written. As *Ancient and Modern* discovered more than a century ago, much of a hymn's effectiveness, popularity and survival depends upon an appropriate match being made.

17
The future

However widely one interprets the term "mainstream hymnody" there has also been a tributary associated with the Charismatic Movement whose *Sound of Living Waters*, 1974, and its sequel *Fresh Sounds,* 1976, (published by Hodder and Stoughton) have attracted enthusiastic attention. The range of musical styles extends from Handel to "Godspell', and it has influenced, and no doubt been a source of joy to many worshippers particularly among the young. There has clearly been an assault on the whole concept of traditional hymnody, as distinct from specific examples, and this has come from a number of quarters; the *Billy Graham London Crusade Song Book,* school material with foot-tapping melodies and minimal religious content, the 20th Century Light Music Group, and collections of gospel choruses intended for Sunday School use that have been pressed into adult worship.

Much new material, such as that found in *Youth Praise,* has worn thin, and some of the texts in *New Life* would strike most people as being in dubious taste in the context of a service. It is when juxtaposed against traditional fare and material conceived according to some artistic principle, that the shoddiness — whether judged from the standpoint of religious content or art — of much of the newer material is intensified. One might make a plea that those who feel impelled to use it do so either in informal religious meetings, or in services which use this material *and none other*.

The church musician should not reject all this out of hand, because he is prejudiced against its idiom. By displaying such an attitude he is behaving no better than those who are opposed in principle to traditional hymnody, and he should look sympathetically to see what is genuinely worthy of admiration. What is surely needed is a consistency of outlook. This poses real problems. If we object to the secularity of the Dam Busters' March in *Songs of Worship* what must our attitude be to Sydney Nicholson's "Crucifer", *AMR*, which it closely resembles? Whilst I may be accused of casuistry, my own solution to this problem is to state that Nicholson's tune came first and if we use that, we have no need of the Dam Busters. For my part I have found disappointingly little of interest in the books mentioned, and also little that has found its way into more permanent collections. When a piece appears to be meritorious, further examination shows that this is merely because the work which surrounds it is so poor.

Rumours abound of two large-scale Anglican hymn books, one which attempts to relate the language of the hymns to that of the 1980 *Alternative Service Book,* whilst the other regards as its chief priority the provision of hymns to match the two year cycle of lessons that the Series 3 Communion Service provided. Work on a revised *Methodist Hymn Book* is also under way.

A third volume in the *Sound of Living Waters* series called *Cry Hosanna* has appeared recently, as did James Quinn's *New Hymns for All Seasons II.* The latter contains some plainsong melodies, whose words have been adapted to fit the tune, not the other way round as is usually the case. This collection includes Gaelic melodies too, whose specially composed words have a flexibility not found in older Office Hymn translations and biblical paraphrases. So far the work of Quinn has proved to be a most valuable Catholic contribution to ecumenical hymnody.

The consolidation which has been advocated elsewhere in the book is clearly needed where Catholic hymnody is concerned, since none of the three major modern books has made an overwhelming impact; the *Parish Hymn Book* has been considered too staid, and the *New Catholic Hymnal* too radical. Perhaps a revision of the middle-of-the-road *Praise the*

Lord may provide the answer. But we can be sure that alongside this process of consolidation there will be fresh creative efforts in both idiom and content.

Exciting and challenging developments in America are likely to influence British hymnody. These include the removal of sexist language when referring to the Almighty in the *Lutheran Book of Worship* (Augsburg Minneapolis, 1978) and *Ecumenical Praise* (Agape, Carol Stream, 1977) whose musical content includes items by Leonard Bernstein, Benjamin Britten, Duke Ellington, a round in twenty-three parts and a setting of "Sometimes a light surprises" which has thirteen changes of time signature!

What must be our attitude to all this? Should we welcome it as evidence of the Holy Spirit at work in the world? Or should we stick to what we know, what is, at best, the tried and the trusty? I believe we should examine our traditional hymnody very closely and be quite merciless in excluding that which honestly falls short in either words or music in fulfilling today's needs. Such exclusion would make room for new twentieth-century material, some of which is stylistically congruent with the old. And we must make sure that our young people are acquainted with the best of new and old lest the age gap which is such a divisive feature in contemporary life will find even greater expression in the Church. The *avant-garde* material could be used initially at special services of the Hymn Recital kind where the new radical hymns with their unorthodox rhythms and accompaniments could be both rehearsed and sung, a practical instance of "informal worship" that we hear so much about. Such material, some of it experimental in character, could be tried out and a decision taken as to its quality *in performance*, as distinct from its appearance on paper, before it is presented in the context of more formal worship.

Finally, in these days of photo-copying and consequent lawsuits, it would be good to read of copyright holders who were willing to let anyone who wished print their hymns and tunes without penalty, and for the good of all.

18
The indexes

The four indexes were compiled after the main part of the book was written and are intended to embody its general philosophy. It is hoped that readers will not be unduly inconvenienced by this arrangement which was adopted in order that the distinctive character of each set of tunes would be highlighted. Had only one composite index been prepared this distinction would have been obscured.

The purpose of the main index is to list the great tunes, whose durability has been proved over the centuries and to draw attention to the wealth of fine, readily singable material outwith that used by a congregation normally. Ecumenical and other considerations make it desirable for congregations to use tunes whose ethos lies outside their normal worshipping traditions but are no worse for that. Such a tune is "Fulda", which, until the last decade or so, was foreign to the experience of most Anglican congregations. When sung to "We have a Gospel to proclaim" it can sound magnificent. No apology is offered for the omission of the "bad old favourites", but there were a number of other tunes whose exclusion was made only after considerable debate. The determining factors were the presence of a weak line or awkward melodic "bump" and/or the availability of superior tunes in a similar metre or idiom. At the same time there has been no pursuit of austerity or obscurity, nor a desire to retain old tunes whose reputation seems difficult to justify.

It is easier to write a successful hymn tune in some metres than in others. There are very few recommendable 7676 Iambic tunes. On the other hand, almost every collection has its own crop of bright, optimistic, eminently serviceable tunes in 8787 metre that have not been taken up by other hymn books. Clearly there is a limit to the number of such tunes any one congregation can use. No attempt has been made to provide a tune for every metre but a recommendation has been made for almost every standard hymn.

Four categories of tune have been excluded:

1. Those, chiefly of the "Jingle with chorus" type, that would be unsuitable in adult worship. Tunes which could be used only in association with children's hymns have likewise been excluded. Generally speaking children's hymn singing a generation and more ago tended to have a greater "adult content" than is the case today. An examination of the *Methodist School Hymn Book* c. 1953 and *School Worship* of slightly earlier date would confirm this.

2. Plainsong tunes because problems of critical selection do not arise.

3. Christmas hymns and Carols. There is now so much material available for this season, and only a small quantity of it is unworthy.

4. Tunes with well-known secular associations, e.g. "Londonderry Air", "Ar hyd y nos", etc. I believe strongly against the use of such tunes. A number of tunes, e.g. "Shipston" are included which have a secular origin, but since this is not known to the average worshipper, no harm can result.

The aim has been to include a tune only once, and in its most suitable metre. There are, of course, occasions when it is desirable to use a well-known tune with another association, as for instance when only a small congregation is assembled, or when a particular Saint's Day is commemorated. The ideal of one tune per hymn, and vice versa, ensures that the danger of over-exposure is greatly reduced. Another exception that comes to mind is "Slane" which is often sung to "Be thou my Vision" and "Lord of all hopefulness". The latter is well provided for by "Miniver" (for which other words have also been written) but it would be churlish to discount "Slane" since this is the tune Jan Struther had in mind when she wrote the words.

A tune has been *listed under the name by which it is best known,* but the chief variants are also listed. If difficulty is found in locating a tune, it is suggested that the sol-fa index be explored.

The index has been divided into *Main and Supplementary lists* under one metrical scheme. The Supplementary list designated *See also* includes tunes that are either less meritorious or less well-known. In a few instances a tune of marginal quality (but eminently usable) has been included to represent an obscure metre. The inclusion of a tune in one or more of the six chief denominational hymn books is indicated, and a few minutes' comparison of this with the indexes of other hymn books will enable ticks to be written in, alongside a tune's name. Some fifteen per cent of the tunes recommended are in none of the six books. In these instances, *all* the sources are named in bold type. "2" in the CH3 column shows that the tune is in the *Church Hymnary: Second Edition* but not in the *Church Hymnary: Third Edition;* "S" in the AMR column shows that the tune is in *Hymns Ancient and Modern Standard Edition* only.

The name given under *Composer* is for identification only, since considerations of space preclude more precise attributions.

The extent to which tunes vary from one book to another in respect of rhythm, metre, melody and harmony is enormous, and to have listed all these would have needed a book of much greater size without corresponding usefulness. I have tried therefore to draw attention to musically valuable faux-bourdons (fa-b), harmonies (h), descants (d), melodic variants (m), rhythmic variants (r), unison (u) and harmony (h) versions. References to other treatments are self-explanatory. Variants of no musical importance — both in respect of normal melody and harmony and in varied treatments — have been ignored. The versions in *Oxford Hymn Book* (O) and *Songs of Syon* (SS) are usually of harmonies and faux-bourdons of older vintage and greater musical elaboration than those found in newer hymn books. Whilst editions of these are not easy to obtain, copies are obtainable on loan from most public libraries. Some books, notably the *Cambridge Hymnal* and *Hymns for Church and School,* have two or three varied treatments for some tunes and these are listed (var). The *Anglican Hymn Book* contains a number of elaborate choir versions (ch) intended for use with congregational singing of the tune. These are of the type popularized by Sir David Willcocks in his *Hymns for Choirs* (OUP) to which the reader is referred. A colon separates the various versions.

In a few instances, tunes of peculiar metre are quoted which may enjoy a well-deserved denominational popularity in association with a particular hymn (see also), which it would be unwise to end. These tunes are however inferior to the recommended tune. Compare for example "Doxford" and "Milton Abbas" for "Christ for the world we sing".

The standard tunes are well-represented in the Supplements, and all such instances are cited. A bracket around the source indicates that this is set to an older hymn. Not every contemporary hymn is better served by a modern tune than an older one. Some tunes dating from the earlier part of this century are clearly of better quality than some of the newer ones, and should not be driven out by the latter.

Amidst all the variants, occasionally one can recommend a harmonization of a tune that is clearly superior to others. Regrettably, in other instances, there is one version that is significantly worse than the others. It should be mentioned that the musical editors of *Ancient and Modern Revised* have seen fit to provide a number of simplified Chorale harmonizations as a matter of policy, because in this form they believe them to be more suitable for use in congregational singing. Others claim to use Bach's harmonies when such is not wholly true. However, the beauty of a Bach Chorale consists not only in the interplay of the vocal lines (which can be learnt if choirs are willing to practise them) but in the richness of the resultant harmonies which can be experienced even when no choir is present, and are audible only in the organ accompaniment. The recommended "Best version" is therefore the one which yields the greatest musical satisfaction in terms of rhythm, melodic contour and harmonic progression. This will not necessarily be the earliest nor the most authentic version. The doctrinaire pursuit of a narrow academicism or historicity is inimical to the vital hymn singing in our churches which should be our aim.

In the majority of cases, a clear-cut preference cannot be given: in others an amalgam of the best features of several versions would be desirable, e.g. "Song 13" where *Ancient and Modern Revised's* beautiful harmonies at the end of line two could be combined with the version in *Hymns for Church and School*.

The presence or absence of gathering notes in Psalter and similar tunes is ignored when making comparisons or critical evaluations between one version and another. Gathering notes are used consistently in the *English Hymnal* and *Songs of Praise*, but in the other books no such consistency is to be found. Psalter tunes which are well-known tend to be printed without gathering notes, and those that are less familiar with them. Transpositions for the purpose of comparison are ignored.

Thematic Index

The thematic index has been compiled to assist those who have no knowledge of staff notation in identifying a particular tune. A keyboard diagram will enable a tune to be played in C major or A minor by those with no knowledge of sol-fa for singing purposes. But it must be pointed out that in comparatively few instances will this be the actual singing pitch.

Vertical lines denote bar lines and the following note will carry an accent.

Notes joined by a curved line are each of half a beat's duration. They are not necessarily to be sung to one syllable.

Dotted rhythms are ignored.

A horizontal line(s) after a note indicates its prolongation for additional beat(s).

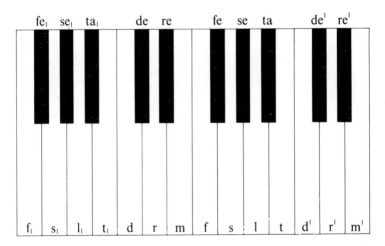

METRE—TITLE—COMPOSER	BHB	CH3	CP	MHB	AMR	EH	SUPPLEMENTS
S.M.							
Bethlehem (Doncaster) *S. Wesley*	√	2	√	√	√		BP = HHT
Cambridge (Camberwell) *R. Harrison*	√	2	√	√			
Carlisle *C. Lockhart*	√	√	√	√	√	√	WOV, (EP)
Dominica *H. S. Oakeley*		2		√	√		(EP)
Egham *S. Turner*			√	√			HS, PP
Falcon Street (Silver Street) *I. Williams*	√			√			EP, (HHT)
Franconia *König's Gesangbuch*	√	√	√	√	√	√	SW, (HS), PP, SW, WOV, NCP
Mount Ephraim *B. Milgrove*	√	2			√	√	HHT
Narenza *Cologne Kirchengesang*	√	√	√	√	√	√	
St Bride *S. Howard*	√	√	√	√	√	√	(BP = HS)
St Ethelwald *W. H. Monk*	√	2	√	√	√	√	NCP
St George (St Olave) *H. J. Gauntlett*	√	2	√	√	√	√	
St Michael (Old 134) *Genevan Psalter 1551*	√	√	√	√	√	√	HHT
St Thomas *Williams' Psalmody*	√		√	√	√	√	HHT
Shere *E. H. Thiman*	√		√				
Song 20 *O. Gibbons*		2	√	√		√	(NCP)
Southwell *Damon Psalms*	√	√	√	√	√	√	(BP)
Windermere *A. Somervell*	√			√		√	(MHT), AHB
See also **Corinne** *J. T. Williams*			PP				
D.S.M.							
Corona *C. H. Stewart*	√				√	√	
Diademata *G. J. Elvey*	√	√	√	√	√		
From strength to strength *E. W. Naylor*	√	√	√	√			

VARIED TREATMENTS	BEST PLAIN VERSION	THEMATIC INDEX
	MHB = CP = BHB	s | d'mfl | s - -
	CH2	d | mr͡dr͡dt₁ | d - -
ChP = AHB = CP = SP (d): O (h)	CH3 = EH = CP	d | sdm͡rd͡t₁ | d - -
		s₁s₁s₁ d͡r | m͘ - -
O(h)		m | rdfm | l - -
EP (m + r)	SP = BBC	d' | s͡s ms | d' - -
Camb. (tune in bass)	AMR = EH = MHB	d | rmfs | m - -
		d | mrd | s͡fmr | d -
PTL (d)		d' | tslt | d' - -
SP (fa − b): SS	CH3 or EH	l | mld't | l - -
		s | fmrm͡f | m - -
		m | flsf | m - -
SP (fa − b): O (h)	EH = SP	s₁ | dmrr | d - -
	BBC	s₁ | ddmr͡d | r - -
		dmsd' - r' | m' - - - -
	EH	d | drmf | s - -
PTL: SP (fa − b); Camb. (d): SS (h + fa − b): O (h)	EH = SP	l | d'd'tt | l - -
		s | lsf s͡l | s - -
		d͡r | mrmf | s - -
See PTL for other words, but the tune's rhythm is mutilated		d' -ss | ls͡fs -
AHB (2 versions)		dd͡dmm | l - -
		ds͡₁s₁ d͡r | m

METRE—TITLE—COMPOSER	BHB	CH3	CP	MHB	AMR	EH	SUPPLEMENTS
Ich halte treulich still (c) *J. S. Bach*	✓	✓	✓	✓	✓	✓	
Ishmael *C. Vincent*	✓			✓			
Llanllyfni *J. Jones*	✓	2	✓	✓		✓	
Old 25 *Genevan Psalter*		2			✓	✓	
Ridge *S. Wesley*				✓			
See also **Dinbych** *J. Parry*				✓			
C.M. **Abbey** *Scottish Psalter*		✓	✓	✓			
Aberdeen (St Paul) *Chalmer's Collection*	✓	✓	✓	✓	✓	✓	
Abridge (St Stephen) *I. Smith*	✓	✓	✓	✓	✓	✓	SW
Albano *V. Novello*	✓	2	✓	✓	✓	✓	
Amazing Grace *Early American*	CH	CW	HF	PP	WOV		PP
Arden *G. T. Thalben-Ball*	✓	✓					
Bangor *W. Tans'ur*	✓	✓	✓	✓	✓	✓	HS = MHT: CH3
Bedford (Leicester) *W. Weale*	✓	2	✓	✓	✓	✓	
Belgrave *W. Horsley*	✓	2	✓	✓	✓	✓	
Beulah *G. M. Garrett*				✓	✓		
Billing *R. R. Terry*	✓						(MHT), WOV, (EP)
Binchester *W. Croft*	✓	✓	✓	✓	✓	✓	
Bishopthorpe (St Paul's) *J. Clarke*	✓	✓	✓	✓	✓	✓	
Bristol *Ravenscroft's Psalter*	✓	✓	✓	✓	✓	✓	
Bromsgrove (Evangelica) *Psalmodia Evangelica*		2	✓		S	✓	
Burford *Chetham's Psalmody*	✓	2		✓	✓	✓	

VARIED TREATMENTS	BEST PLAIN VERSION	THEMATIC INDEX
SS: Tune equally good for robust or gentle treatment	SS	s | m r͡d s l͡s | s - -
		s | d'tlt | s - -
		l₁ | m͡m r d | t₁ -
SS (h, r, fa − b): O (h + r)	EH	d | m r m f | s - -
		d | d t₁l₁s₁m | r - -
		l₁ | m m m r͡d | t₁ - -
BBC (rhythm)	CH3; BBC	d | d m r d | d t₁ d
	BHB; CP; CH3	d | r m s₁d | r t₁d
SP (fa − b)	EH	d | s − d' | d'tl | sfm | m r
		m | sfmr | d r t₁
PP (u) WOV (h)	WOV	s₁ | d - m͡d | m - r | d - l₁ | s -
		d m d | s - m | f m r | m -
	EH = SP	m - d t₁ | l₁m l s͡f | m -
SP (fa − b)	EH	s | m - d | l - s | f - m | r -
Camb. (d)	AMR	s | m - s | d' - m | f s l | r -
Would be better with an A ♮ tenor in line 4		m | r m d s | f s m
PTL (d)		d m s | d' - l | s - r | m -
	EH = CP	m r d | t₁ - - | s f m | r -
	AMR = EH	s͡f | m r d | t₁l₁f | m d t₁ | d -
AMR = CH2 = EH = SP (fa − b): SS (h)	EH = SP = CP = CH3	s - | f r m d | r r d
	CP = EH	d - d s₁ | l₁t₁df | m r d t₁ | d -
	AMR = MHB	l | l - t | d' - m' | m'r'd' | t -

METRE—TITLE—COMPOSER	BHB	CH3	CP	MHB	AMR	EH	SUPPLEMENTS
Caithness *Scottish Psalter*	√	√	√		√	√	MHT
Cheshire *Este's Psalter*		√		√	√	√	
Chorus Angelorum *A. Somervell*	√	√	√		√		(BP, HS)
Cornhill *H. Darke*			√			√	
Crediton *T. Clark*		√	√	√	S	√	MHT
Crucis Victoria *M. B. Foster*				√	√		HHT, MHT, WOV
Daymer *R. Sheldon*			**AHB**				
Dorking *English Traditional Melody*	√			√	√		
Dublin *S. Howard*		√	√	√			
Dundee (French) *Scottish Psalter 1615*	√	√	√	√	√	√	PP, WOV
Dunfermline *Scottish Psalter 1615*	√	√	√	√	√	√	HHT
Durham *Ravenscroft's Psalter*		2	√				
Epworth *C. Wesley*		2	√	√			MHT, (EP)
Farrant *J. Hilton*	√	√	√			√	
Gerontius *J. B. Dykes*	√	√	√	√	√		(EP)
Glasgow *Moore's Companion*	√	√	√	√			MHT
Glenluce *Scottish Psalter 1635*			√				
Haresfield *J. Dykes Bower*		**BP HCS HS MHT**					
Harington (Retirement) *H. Harington*	√	√	√	√		√	
Hermon (Hannah, If Angels sing) *J. Clarke*			√		S		BP = MHT, NCP
Horsley *W. Horsley*	√	√	√	√	√	√	
Irish *Irish Collection*	√	√	√	√	√	√	
Jackson (Byzantium) *T. Jackson*	√	√	√	√	S	√	MHT

VARIED TREATMENTS	BEST PLAIN VERSION	THEMATIC INDEX
		d - | mfsd | t₁dr
O (h): SP (fa − b): HCS (h − Wood): SS	EH = SP	l₁ - l₁t₁ | ddt₁t₁ | l₁ -
		drm | f - m | l - s | d' - t
		s | l - s | m - d | rmd | r -
	EH = SP	s | d'td's | lsᴙ m
HCS (d)		d | mfsm | fsl
		d'ts | l - f - sm | r -
		s₁ | ds₁ds₁ | d̂r m̂f s₁
	CP	m | msf | mrd | rl₁t₁ | d -
AHB = CH2 = EH = SP (fa − b); HCS (d): Camb. (d); O (h)	EH = CP = CH3	d - | mfsd | rmf
BBC (rhythm); SP (d)	BBC	d - dr | mfss | m -
Camb. (d)		d - sm | lsmd | r -
	SP	d | msd'm | r̂lsᴙm
SP (fa − b)	MHB	d | drmr | dfr
HCS (d); BHB (d)		mmr | d - s₁ | d - m | s -
	Not CP	s₁ | d - r | m̂rdm | sᴙsf | m -
		d - mf | slsf | m -
		d | mfs - l - | drm - -
		s | d'tl | sfm | fsl | s -
	Not CP	m | ltd't | ltᴙse
SP (fa − b)		d | rmfm | sf̂mr
O (h)	EH = AMR	d | d - s₁ | drm | fmr | m -
	CH3	s | sd̂tls | f sᴙm

F

METRE—TITLE—COMPOSER	BHB	CH3	CP	MHB	AMR	EH	SUPPLEMENTS
Kilmarnock *N. Dougall*	✓	✓	✓	✓	✓	✓	(HHT), WOV
King's Norton (c) *J. Clarke*						✓	
Lincoln *Ravenscroft Psalter*			✓	✓	✓	✓	
London New *Scottish Psalter 1635*	✓	✓	✓	✓	✓	✓	MHT
Maisemore *J. Dykes Bower*			MHT				
Manchester (New) *R. Wainwright*		2	✓	✓	✓	✓	
Martyrdom *H. Wilson*	✓	✓	✓	✓	✓	✓	
Martyrs *Scottish Psalter 1615*	✓	✓	✓		✓	✓	CH3
Metzler's Redhead (Waveney) *R. Redhead*	✓	✓	✓	✓	✓	✓	
Miles Lane *W. Shrubsole*	✓	✓	✓	✓	✓	✓	
Nativity (New) *H. Lahee*	✓	✓	✓	✓	✓	✓	PP
Nun danket all (Gräfenburg) (c) *Praxis Pietatis*	✓	✓	✓	✓	✓	✓	(MHT)
Oswald's Tree (c) *H. Walford Davies*					✓		
Oxford (New) *J. M. Coombes*			✓		✓		
Praetorius *Görlitz Gesangbuch*		✓	✓			✓	
Richmond *T. Haweis*	✓	✓	✓	✓	✓	✓	
Rochester *C. Hylton Stewart*		2	✓				
Rodmell *English Traditional Melody*	✓	✓		✓		✓	MHT
St Anne *W. Croft*	✓	✓	✓	✓	✓	✓	
St Bernard *Tochter Sion 1741*	✓	✓	✓	✓	✓	✓	HS = PP
St Botolph *G. Slater*	✓	✓			✓	✓	HHT, (HS), AHB, MHT
(St) Flavian (Old 132nd) *Day's Psalter*	✓	✓	✓	✓	✓	✓	(BP)
St Fulbert *H. J. Gauntlett*	✓	✓	✓	✓	✓	✓	MHT

VARIED TREATMENTS	BEST PLAIN VERSION	THEMATIC INDEX
CH2 (fa − b)	CH3	d $\mid$ msl$\widehat{sm}$ $\mid$ mrd
O (h)		d'tl $\mid$ se - m $\mid$ $\widehat{\text{lt}}$d'r' $\mid$ m' - -
AMR; EH = SP (fa − b); SS	EH = SP	d $\mid$ rmrd $\mid$ dt₁d -
CH2 = SP (fa − b): Camb. (d) + (fa − b)	EH = CP = CH3	d $\mid$ smd's $\mid$ ld't
		mfs $\mid$ l - s $\mid$ d - r $\mid$ m
Some melodic differences		d $\mid$ m - r $\mid$ d - d' $\mid$ lsf $\mid$ m -
Camb. (d): SP (fa − b)	Not CH3	s₁ $\mid$ d - l₁ $\mid$ s₁ - $\widehat{dr}$ $\mid$ m - r $\mid$ d -
CH2 = BHB = SP (u); SS; CH2 (h); SP (d); BBC (u)	Not AMR	l₁ - dl₁m - d - t₁l₁m -
	CP	m $\mid$ rdd's $\mid$ lls
SP (d)	CP	s₁ $\mid$ dddr $\mid$ m$\widehat{rd}$ r
Camb. (d)		m$\widehat{mm}$ ss $\mid$ d'd'm'
Camb. (u)	EH	d' - ls $\mid$ d' - r' - $\mid$ m'm'r'
		s $\mid$ sls $\mid$ tls $\mid$ d'tl $\mid$ sm
	BBC	d's$\widehat{dt}$ $\mid$ ltd' $\mid$ r'm'r' $\mid$ d' -
Needs a slow tempo	EH	d $\mid$ ssls $\mid$ sfm
AHB = BHB = CH2 = ChP = SP (fa − b): AHB (Ch): HCS (d)	CH3 = EH	s₁dm $\mid$ s - f $\mid$ mfr $\mid$ d -
		d $\mid$ drm $\mid$ fmr $\mid$ d - r $\mid$ m -
		s $\mid$ d'tlr' $\mid$ $\widehat{d't}$ $\widehat{lt}$ s
AMR (d) CH2 (fa − b; extd org. version): SP (fa − b): Camb. (var): HCS (var)		s $\mid$ mlsd' $\mid$ d'td'
		s $\mid$ drm$\widehat{rd}$ $\mid$ fmr
		d $\mid$ m - d $\mid$ s - m $\mid$ rdt₁ $\mid$ d -
AMR = SP = EH = BP (fa − b): CP (d)		d $\mid$ dt₁dm $\mid$ rrd
AMR (Alleluia): SP (fa − b)		s $\mid$ sdrl $\mid$ sfm

METRE—TITLE—COMPOSER	BHB	CH3	CP	MHB	AMR	EH	SUPPLEMENTS
St James *R. Courteville*	✓	✓	✓	✓	✓	✓	
St Leonard *H. Smart*	✓	✓	✓	✓	✓		
St Magnus (Nottingham) *J. Clarke*	✓	✓	✓	✓	✓	✓	CH3
St Mary *Pry's Psalter*	✓	✓	✓	✓	✓	✓	WOV, MHT
St Matthias (Song 67, Song 47) *O. Gibbons*	✓	✓	✓	✓	✓	✓	
St Nicholas *Holdroyd's Companion*	✓	✓	✓			✓	MHT, WOV
St Peter *A. Reinagle*	✓	✓	✓	✓	✓	✓	
St Stephen (Newington) *W. Jones*	✓	✓	✓	✓	✓	✓	
St Swithun *S. Watson*			HCS				
Salisbury *Ravenscroft's Psalter 1621*	✓	✓			S		
Salzburg *J. M. Haydn*	✓	✓	✓				(MHT)
Sennan Cove *W. H. Harris*	✓				✓		(BP, HS)
Southwell *H. S. Irons*	✓	2	✓	✓	✓		
Stracathro *C. Hutcheson*	✓	2	✓	✓	✓	✓	(HHT)
Stroudwater *Williams Psalmody*		✓	✓			✓	WOV
Tallis Ordinal (Tallis, 9th Tune) (C—Camb.) *T. Tallis*	✓	✓	✓	✓	✓	✓	
Tiverton *— Grigg*	✓	2	✓	✓	S		
University *J. Collignon*	✓	✓	✓	✓	✓	✓	
Walsall *Anchor's Psalmody*	✓	2	✓	✓	✓	✓	
Warwick *S. Stanley*	✓	✓	✓	✓			
Westburn *K. G. Finlay*			AHB				
Westminster (Birmingham, St Margaret) *J. Turle*	✓	✓	✓	✓	✓	✓	SW
Wetherby *S. S. Wesley*		2	✓	✓			(BP)

VARIED TREATMENTS	BEST PLAIN VERSION	THEMATIC INDEX
SP (fa − b)		s_1 ∣ drmd ∣ rfm
		s ∣ smls ∣ ltd'
CH2 = SP (fa − b); Camb. (d)	BBC	s_1 ∣ drt$_1$s$_1$ ∣ drm
O (h)		l_1 ∣ dt$_1$l$_1$l ∣ sfm
Camb. (d) (2 versions)		d - ∣ smfs ∣ lls
BBC (rhythm)	Not EH	l_1 ∣ d - m ∣ l - m ∣ fm͡rd ∣ t$_1$ -
SP (fa − b)		s ∣ d'tls ∣ sfm
SP (fa − b)	BBC	d ∣ smd͡rd ∣ t$_1$dr
		m ∣ rdsm ∣ r͡drm
		d - ∣ rfms ∣ sfe s
	CH3	d ∣ m - s ∣ sfm ∣ m - r ∣ d -
		smd ∣ f - r ∣ drt$_1$ ∣ d -
		d ∣ mmsd ∣ dls
	CP	d ∣ m - r ∣ d - r ∣ md't ∣ l -
	CP	d ∣ s$_1$ - d ∣ s - m ∣ fmr ∣ d -
Camb. (var): SP (fa − b): PTL (var)	EH = SP (not CP)	d ∣ mfss ∣ lls
Camb. (d)	CH2 = SP	s_1 ∣ drmd͡it$_1$ ∣ l$_1$t$_1$d
SP (fa − b): Camb. (var)	EH = SP	s ∣ f͡m r͡dd'r͡m' ∣ sfm
O (h)	AMR = EH	l ∣ d'ti͡lmm' ∣ r͡'d' tl
	CP = SP	d ∣ m͡sd'͡lsf͡l ∣ s͡mrd
		d'r'm' ∣ t - d' ∣ lsf ∣ m -
AHB (d)		m ∣ ssdd' ∣ tls
Camb. (d)		m ∣ s - m͡r ∣ d - s ∣ l - l ∣ s -

METRE—TITLE—COMPOSER	BHB	CH3	CP	MHB	AMR	EH	SUPPLEMENTS
Wiltshire *G. Smart*	✓	✓	✓	✓	✓	✓	
Windsor *Damon's Psalter*		✓		✓	✓	✓	(BP)
York (The Stilt) *Scottish Psalter 1615*		✓	✓	✓	✓	✓	(HS)
See also **Belmont** *Gardiner's Sacred Melodies*	✓	✓	✓	✓	✓		
Blackbourne *Harrison's Sacred Harmony*		2		✓		✓	
Bon Accord *Aberdeen Psalter 1625*			BBC				
Clifton *J. C. Clifton*		2					
Crimond *J. S. Irvine*	✓	✓	✓				(HHT, HS)
Eatington *W. Croft*					✓	✓	
St Andrew *Tans'ur's Harmony*		✓	✓				WOV
St David *Ravenscroft's Psalter*		✓		✓	✓	✓	
St Enodoc *C. S. Lang*			AHB				HS
St Francis Xavier *J. Stainer*	✓			✓	✓		
St Gregory *R. Wainwright*			✓				
D.C.M. **Ladywell** *W. H. Ferguson*	✓	2	✓		✓		
Old 107th *Scottish Psalter 1635*		✓	✓			✓	
St Matthew *W. Croft*	✓	✓	✓	✓	✓	✓	
Soll's Sein (c) *Corner's Gesangbuch*	✓			✓	✓		✓	(MHT = BP), WOV
Third Mode Melody (c) *T. Tallis*	✓	✓				✓	MHT: Camb.
See also **St George's Edinburgh** *A. M. Thomson*	✓	✓	✓				
Tana *Kenya Melody*			PP				

VARIED TREATMENTS	BEST PLAIN VERSION	THEMATIC INDEX
SP (d)	SP = EH	s $\mid$ msd' $\mid$ d'td' $\mid$ f'm'r' $\mid$ r'm'
O (rhythm): SP (d)	SP = EH	l $\mid$ ltd't $\mid$ llse
Camb. (d + fa − b): SP (fa − b): SS	AMR = EH = SP	d $\mid$ msfl $\mid$ msr
	CH3 = CP	s_1 $\mid$ m - r $\mid$ d - t_1 $\mid$ $t_1 l_1$d $\mid$ s_1 -
	CH2	l - $\mid$ mrdr $\mid$ d$t_1 l_1$ -
In "reports"		s $\mid$ sdt_1d $\mid$ rmr
	BBC	d $\mid$ m - r $\mid$ dt_1d $\mid$ rm - $\mid$ f
Camb. (d + fa; b)	Not Camb.	s_1 $\mid$ m -$\widehat{\text{fr}}$ $\mid$ s -$\widehat{\text{fr}}$ $\mid$ d - t_1 $\mid$ d -
		d $\mid$ mfrt_1 $\mid$ drm
		d $\mid$ m - m $\mid$ r - m $\mid$ d - t_1 $\mid$ d
SP (fa − b): O (h)		d - $\mid$ sd'ms $\mid$ fmr
		l_1dt_1 $\mid$ l_1 - l $\mid$ r - t_1 $\mid$ m - -
		d $\mid$ rmls $\mid$ fsm
		d $\mid$ m - $\widehat{\text{rm}}$ $\mid$ f - m $\mid$ rdt_1 $\mid$ d -
Full vers: AHB, BBC, BHB, CH2		s_1 $\mid$ drms $\mid$ fmr
Camb. (d): SS		l_1 - l_1 - mmllssm -
		s $\mid$ m - s $\mid$ d' - m' $\mid$ r'd't $\mid$ d' -
		msf $\mid$ m - r $\mid$ d - r $\mid$ t_1 -
SP = EH (fa − b)		$l_1$dd $\mid$ d - - drr $\mid$ m
		d - $\mid$ drmf $\mid$ s - s - $\mid$ s - -
		m $\mid$ sms$\widehat{\text{f}}$ $\widehat{\text{mr}}$ $\mid$ d m r

METRE—TITLE—COMPOSER	BHB	CH3	CP	MHB	AMR	EH	SUPPLEMENTS
L.M.							
Agincourt (Agincourt Song, Deo Gracias) *English 15th c.*		2			√	√	HHT, WOV (2)
Andernach *Andernach Gesangbuch*	√	2	√			√	Needs slow tempo
Anglorum Apostolus *A. G. Murray*	√						
Bow Brickhill *S. H. Nicholson*	√		√		√		BP, (HS)
Breslau (Ach Gott wie manches; Herr Jesu Christ) *Hymnodus Sacer 1625*	√	√	√	√	√	√	HHT
Brockham (Confidence, Gillingham) *J. Clarke*	√	2	√	√	√	√	(BP), HHT, WOV
Bromley (c) *J. Clarke*		2	√				
Cameronian Midnight Hymn *Scottish Hymn Melody*			√			√	
Cannock *W. K. Stanton*	√	√					
Cannons *G. F. Handel*					√	√	HHT
Cerne Abbas *C. V. Taylor*			HHT				
Church Triumphant *J. W. Elliott*	√	√	√	√	√		SW
Cromer *J. A. Lloyd*	√					√	
Das neugeborne Kindelein (c) (Jena) *J. S. Bach*		√	√	√	√	√	888888 in AMR
Das Walt' Gott (Vetter) *J. S. Bach*		√			√	√	CH3
Deus Tuorum militum (Grenoble) *Grenoble Melody*	√	√	√	√	√	√	HHT
Duke Street *J. L. Hatton*	√	√	√	√	√	√	MHT = SW
Eltham *Harmonia Perfecta*		√					
Erhalt uns Herr (Wittenburg) *J. S. Bach*			√	√		√	
Finnart *K. G. Finlay*	√	√			√		
Fulda (Walton) *Gardiner's Sacred Melodies*	√	√	√	√			WOV = BP = HHT = SW: PP
Galilee *P. Armes*	√	2	√	√	√		Fits words better than Truro in Jesus shall reign
Gonfalon Royal *P. C. Buck*	√	√	√	√		√	EP, HHT, (HS), SW

VARIED TREATMENTS	BEST PLAIN VERSION	THEMATIC INDEX
SS	EH	$rrd \mid r - d \mid dt_i - \mid l_i -$
CH3 (h); EH (u)		$d' - d'd' \mid tsl - t - \mid d' -$
		$d \mid mfs \mid l - s \mid fmr \mid m -$
		$d' \mid tld' \mid s - l \mid mfr \mid d -$
SP (fa − b), O (bach)	EH = CH3	$d \mid ddl_i d \mid rt_i l_i$
	EH = SP	$s_i \mid drmt_i \mid drt_i$
		$d \mid m - \widehat{fr} \mid dms \mid sls\widehat{f} \mid fm$
		$s_i \mid d\widehat{mr}ds_i \mid l_i dr$
		$mdr \mid s_i - d \mid fmr \mid m -$
		$l\widehat{m}selt \mid d'r't -$
		$s_i \mid d - s_i \mid l_i t_i d \mid frd \mid t_i l_i$
	AMR	$s_i \mid ds_i mr \mid dl_i s_i$
	EH = SP	$s_i \mid dml_i\widehat{fr} \mid dt_i d$
Camb. (var.)	AMR	$l_i l_i l_i \mid mrd \mid mrd \mid t_i - -$
		$d \mid mssm \mid drm$
u = CH3; EH; CP h = AMR; CP: BHB	BBC or EH	$d \mid m - s \mid d' - s \mid fmr \mid d -$
CP (d): SP (d)		$dm\widehat{l}s\widehat{l}t \mid d'\widehat{t}ls -$
		$l \mid md'tm' \mid rdt$
	EH	$\widehat{l}t \mid d'\widehat{t}l se\widehat{l}t \mid d'tl$
		$d \mid mrd \mid s - l \mid d - r \mid m -$
Many musical variants		$sd't \mid d' - r' \mid slt \mid d' - -$
Camb. (d)		$sm\underset{\cdot}{r} \mid d - d \mid l - l \mid s -$
		$s_i l_i d \mid f\widehat{m}rmd \mid l_i - -$

METRE—TITLE—COMPOSER	BHB	CH3	CP	MHB	AMR	EH	SUPPLEMENTS
Hawkhurst *H. J. Gauntlett*	✓				✓		
Hereford *S. S. Wesley*	✓	✓	✓		✓		(EP, HS) Simpler part arrangement in BBC
Herr Jesu Christ *J. S. Bach*		2			·	✓	SS (pre-Bach), PP (pre-Bach versi
Hymnus Eucharisticus (c) (Magdalen Tower Hymn) *B. Rogers*		2				✓	
Illsley *J. Bishop*	✓			✓	✓	✓	NCP
Invitation (Kent, Devonshire) *J. F. Lampe*	✓	2		✓	✓	✓	HS (earlier version also)
Lansdowne *E. N. Greenwood*				HCS	HS		
Leighton (c) *W. Leighton*						✓	
Melcombe *S. Webbe*	✓	✓	✓	✓	✓	✓	
Montgomery *Magdalen Hospital*					✓	✓	
Morning Hymn *F. H. Barthélémon*	✓	✓	✓	✓	✓	✓	
Mylor *W. K. Stanton*				AHB	BBC		
O Amor quam exstaticus *Old French Melody*		✓		✓		✓	CH3
Old 100th *Genevan Psalter*	✓	✓	✓	✓	✓	✓	
Philippine *R. E. Roberts*	✓			✓			BHB
Plaistow *Magdalen Chapel*		2		✓		✓	
Rockingham (Caton, Communion) *E. Miller*	✓	✓	✓	✓	✓	✓	
Rouen *Rouen Church Melody*						✓	
Rushford *H. G. Ley*	✓	✓					
St Bartholomew *H. Duncalf*	✓	2		✓		✓	HS
St Venantius *Paris Antiphoner*		✓	✓	✓		✓	
St Cross *J. B. Dykes*	✓	✓	✓	✓	✓	✓	
Simeon *S. Stanley*	✓		✓	✓		✓	

VARIED TREATMENTS	BEST PLAIN VERSION	THEMATIC INDEX
		m | fmrr | sfm
		m | mrd | rfm | m͡rdr | rm
		d | msmr | mfes
		l₁l₁l₁ | drm | r͡dt₁l₁ | l₁se₁
SP (fa − b)	AMR = BHB	d | ds₁d͡rm | f͡mrd
	EH = SP	s | mt₁dl | sfm
		d | s - - f | mr͡drl₁ | s₁ - -
		d | r - m | f - m | rdr | m - -
SP (fa − b)	Not EH = SP	s | sfmr | dls
		d' | d'sl | lsf | mrd | s -
AMR (d): SP (d)	CP	d͡r | mmmf͡m | rrr
		l͡₁t₁ | dmrd | t₁t₁t₁
	CH3 = EH	l₁ | m - r | dt₁l₁ | d - r | m -
AHB = CH2 = AMR (fa − b): HCS = SP (2fa − b): PTL (d): O (Bach in 3/4): SS (h + fa − b)	CP	d' - | d'tls | d' - r' - | m' -
		m | mrd | s - m | rdr | m -
		l₁ | mt₁dl₁ | r͡mfm
CH2 = SP (fa − b): AMR (d): Camb. (d): EH (h): HCS (h)	EH; CP	d | mfr | d - m | s - l | s -
		l | d' - t | lsl | m - l | l -
		d - dr | msd'l | s -
NCP (d)		s | d' - s | r' - s | m'r'd' | r' -
BBC (u)		d | msf | mrm | d - r | m -
	EH	d - dr | m - - l | s - f - | m - - -
		ss͡fmf | mrd

METRE—TITLE—COMPOSER	BHB	CH3	CP	MHB	AMR	EH	SUPPLEMENTS
Solemnis haec festivitas *Angers Church Melody*	√	√	√			√	EP, (HS)
Song 5 *O. Gibbons*		√		√	√	√	
Song 34 (Angels, Angels' Song) *O. Gibbons*	√	√	√	√	√	√	
Swanmore *A. K. Blackhall*					√		
Tallis Canon (Canon) *T. Tallis*	√	√	√	√	√	√	
Truro *Psalmodia Evangelica*	√	√	√	√	√	√	HS, (MHT), PP
Uffingham *J. Clarke*	√	2	√	√	√	√	
Vernham Dean *A. Alleyne*					√		
Wareham *W. Knapp*	√	√	√	√	√	√	
Warrington *R. Harrison*	√	√	√	√	√	√	(HS), MHT
Whitehall (Sandys Psalm 8) *H. Lawes*		√	√	√	√	√	BP
Wilderness *R. S. Thatcher*		AHB	HCS				
Winchester New (Crasselius) *German 17th c.*	√	√	√	√	√	√	(HS)
See also **Ivyhatch** *B. L. Selby*					√		PFT
Montesano *J. Law*						√	
Rex Gloriose Martyrum *Andernacher Gesangbuch*					√	√	(BP)
The King's Majesty *G. George*		BBC	HCS				
L.M. and Alleluias **Erschienen ist** (Hermann) (c) *N. Hermann*		√	√	√	√		
God is ascended (c) *German Carol*			√	√			
Ilfracombe *J. Gardner*	HCS	HS	NCP	PTL			
Lasst uns erfreuen (Cologne, Easter Song, etc.) *German 17th c.*	√	√	√	√	√	√	(EP, MHT)

VARIED TREATMENTS	BEST PLAIN VERSION	THEMATIC INDEX
BBC (u): CP = BHB: EH (extd.)	BBC	d | m - f | s - s | lsf | s -
	AMR	mmm | f - r | m - d | t₁ -
SP (d): Camb. (d): SS: O (extension)	Not MHB	d - dd | r - m - fr | s -
		m | s - l | msm | d - r | m -
CH2 (full version): SP (fa − b): Camb. (arr. Britten)		d | dt₁dd | rrm
SP (fa − b): Camb. (d)	Not MHB	d͡mfss | ltd'
Camb. (d)		l͡isf | m - t | d'tl | se -
		s | m - r | d - s | ltd' | t
AMR (d): AHB (f − b): SP (d)	CP	d' | d'tl | s - d' | r'd't | d' -
HCS (d)		ssf | msd' | d'r't | d' -
O (h)		d'tl | d'mfl | s -
		ld'l | m' - - m'lt | d' - -
SP (d)		s | d'sll | sfm
		m͡f | ssmd | r͡mfm
		lsl | m - l | r'd't | l -
BP (2 versions)		d - mf | sslt | d' -
		l₁ | drf m | l₁d͡rd t₁ | l - -
MHB = SP (Bach); SS		rrr | l - t | d'tl | s -
		m | m - l | selt | lsf | m -
		dms | d' - m | l - d' | m' - r'
SS: AHB (Ch): AMR (Ch − rhythm can be adjusted if necessary)	Not AMR	d - dr | mdmf | s -

METRE—TITLE—COMPOSER	BHB	CH3	CP	MHB	AMR	EH	SUPPLEMENTS
D.L.M.							
Dies Irae (Merthyr Tydfil) *J. Parry*	✓		✓	✓			
Jerusalem *C. H. H. Parry*		✓	✓		✓		SW, (EP)
Kettering (London, Addison's) *J. Sheels*			✓		✓	✓	
St Patrick's Breastplate *Irish Melody*	✓	✓	✓	✓	✓	✓	
Schmücke dich (8888D) (c) *J. Crüger*	✓	✓	✓		✓	✓	
See also **Cantate Domino** *J. Barnby*		2				✓	
Clonmachnoise (8888D) *Irish Melody*		✓	✓				
Trewen (888DD) *D. E. Evans*	✓	✓	✓				
Litte Venice (4545D) *G. H. Knight*			**MHT**				
4 10 10 10 4 **Salonica** *J. S. Scott*			✓				
5554D **Bunessan** *Gaelic Melody*	✓	✓	✓				EP, HHT = NCP = PP, SW (2), WO (PFT)
See also **Gun Hill** (55658787) (c) *M. Shaw*			**SP**				
55556565 **Laudate Dominum** (Gauntlett) *H. J. Gauntlett*	✓		✓	✓	✓		
Laudate Dominum (Parry) *C. H. H. Parry*	✓	✓	✓	✓	✓		(EP)
55511 **Sutton Courtenay** *E. Routley*	✓		✓				
558855 **Arnstadt** (Seelen bräutigam, Spire, Thuringia) (c) *A. Drese*	✓	✓	✓	✓	✓	✓	(MHT)
6464 **Bread of Life** (also listed as 10 10) *E. H. Thiman*		✓	✓				
6464664 **Anniesland** *K. G. Finlay*			**AHB**				

VARIED TREATMENTS	BEST PLAIN VERSION	THEMATIC INDEX
AMR = BBC = SW = CP (org. version by Thalben-Ball) *See also* Sirius (BBC) SP = EH (good 1st line) SS (Bach version) *See also* for central portion of St Patrick Deidre (EH and MHB)	AMR = AHB, MHB Not CH3	mlse | l - m | s - r | m dms | l - -d'lsĩ | s - d | mmrs | f͡m r͡d r m | l - l | sms | d'm'r' | d' m - r - | drms | f - m - m | slsm͡r | drm m͡s | l l s͡l | d'r' l | d' - t l | se - l t | l - - mm - r | d - - - | l₁t͡₁dr - s₁ -
See also Qui laborat orat AHB, AMR (c)		d'sl | r - - d | rsrd | l₁t₁d
Wears thin after a time	CP = SP	dms | d' - - r' - - | t l s | l - s - s͡l srr͡m
AMR = CH2 = HCS (u)		m | smr | d - s₁ | mdr | s₁ -
		s | l d' t | d' -
SS (r + h)		dd | t₁ - d - | r -
Vastly superior to other settings		m | drmm | s
		mrd | s - f | m - -

METRE—TITLE—COMPOSER	BHB	CH3	CP	MHB	AMR	EH	SUPPLEMENTS
Wilmington *E. Routley*		√	√				
See also **Watchman** (64646664) (c) *T. H. Ingham*	√						
6466 **St Columba** *H. S. Irons*		√	√	√	√	√	
6565 **Caswall** (Bemerton, Derby, Filitz Wem in Leidenstagen) *F. Filitz*	√	√	√	√	√	√	SW
Glenfinlas *K. G. Finlay*	√	√	√	√	√		EP
Linton (c) *W. K. Stanton*	√						
Pastor Pastorum (Gott ein Vater, Silcher) *F. Silcher*	√	2			√	√	EP = MHT
See also **Eudoxia** *S. Baring-Gould*	√	√	√	√	√	√	
6565D **Cuddesdon** *W. H. Ferguson*	√	√					
Evelyns *W. H. Monk*	√	2	√	√	√		PP
Kings Weston *R. Vaughan Williams*		√				√	
Lyle Road *K. G. Finlay*			√				
See also **Nous allons** (c) *French Carol*		√				√	
Sparsholt (c) *W. K. Stanton*			BBC				
Sutton Trinity *F. P. Green*			HS PFT SW				
6565D and chorus **St Gertrude** *A. S. Sullivan*	√	√	√	√	√	√	
65656665 **Elton** *J. Dykes Bower*					√		
Monk's Gate *English Traditional Melody*	√	√	√	√		√	

VARIED TREATMENTS	BEST PLAIN VERSION	THEMATIC INDEX
Easily best available tune for these words		d - rm | lsd - -
		mrd | rmr
BBC = CH3 (r)	CH3	s | fmrr | d - -
CH3 = SP unison; others in harmony	AMR	mmrr | d - t₁ -
		s₁drm | rdl₁ -
		mdf͡mr | s - d -
		slsf | m - r -
		mmff | s - m -
HCS (h + d)		sltd' | f' - f' -
		msls | d' - s -
		l͡t d't | l - s
		drfm | r - d -
		dmf | s - l | s - f
		l₁t₁dm | l - m -
Words and music both by F. Pratt Green		dddr | m - l -
See also St Dunstan HF		ssss | sls -
(See also Bunyan AMR, AHB gives other words)		d | r - m | sls
		dr | md͡mfs | l -

METRE—TITLE—COMPOSER	BHB	CH3	CP	MHB	AMR	EH	SUPPLEMENTS
See also **Moab** *I. Gwyllt*		√	√	√			
6646664 **Milton Abbas** *E. H. Thiman*	√	√	√				(HHT = HS)
Moscow *Giardini* (adapted)	√	√	√	√	√	√	EP
See also **Denbigh** *Welsh Melody*		√				√	
Wigan (6664884) *S. S. Wesley*					√		
6666 **Kingsland** (Iambic) *W. Boyce*				√		√	
Quam Dilecta (Iambic) *H. L. Jenner*	√	√	√	√	√	√	(BP)
Ravenshaw (Trochaic) *Weisse Gesangbuch*	√	√	√	√	√	√	
St Cecilia (Iambic) *L. G. Hayne*	√	√	√	√	√	√	
Swabia (Iambic) *Spiess Gesangbuch*	√	√	√	√	S		
See also **Eccles** (Iambic) *B. L. Selby*					√		
66666 and chorus **Personent Hodie** (Theodoric) *Piae Cantiones 1582*		√					
666666 **Frilford** *W. H. Ferguson*				√			
Laudes Domini *J. Barnby*	√	2	√	√	√		(BP)
Ludgate (666D) *J. Dykes Bower*	BP	HCS		MHT			
Old 120th *Este's Psalter 1592*	√			√	√	√	√
Waltham *W. H. Monk*	√					√	(BP)
6666D **Annue Christe** (c) *La Feillée's Method*	√	√	√	√	√	√	HHT = BHB = AHB

VARIED TREATMENTS	BEST PLAIN VERSION	THEMATIC INDEX
6666D in MHB	CH3	l | ld't1 | s - - l | d'd't - | t - -
See also Doxford BHB, MHB AHB (d): SP (d)	˙EH = SP	d - dd | s - - l | m - smd | r - t₁ | d - -
	EH = SP	l - lt | d't1 - l | d'tr'd' | t - -
SP (fa – b): SS (complete version of tune) Suits this metre better than S.M.		s | d' - s | lsf | m - m | fmmr | d - - ddmf | s - s - s | fmmr | d - - s | mfrr | d - - l | seltt | d' - -
Holst: NCH, NCP, PFT, PP, PTL, SP, SW Harmony: CH3, EP, MHT	Not (h)	rrl - | ssl -
AHB = HCS (d). *See also* Old 122 (Psalm 3 O Seigneur) fine but exhausting SS: EH = BHB Combine in "Hail to the Lord" BP (*v. 2 Sops v. 4 Full*)	CP = EH = MHB	m | lsmr | d - - m | fsld' | t - l d | rmsl | m - - d - | mfsl | s - m | mr͡mfs | m - -
CH2; CH3 (u); AMR: CP (h): O(u)	SP = CH2 = MHB	ddrmmm

METRE—TITLE—COMPOSER	BHB	CH3	CP	MHB	AMR	EH	SUPPLEMENTS
666688 (*aslo* **6666 4444**)							
Christchurch *C. Steggall*	√	√	√	√	√	√	EP = HHT, (HS), CH3 = AHB
Croft's 136th (Croft's 148th) *W. Croft*	√	√	√	√	√	√	(HS), (MHT), PP, AHB
Darwall's 148th *J. Darwall*	√	√	√	√	√	√	
Eastview *V. Lee*	√		√				(BP)
Gopsal *G. F. Handel*	√	√	√	√	√	√	
Harewood *S. S. Wesley*	√	2	√	√	√		EP, HHT, WOV
Little Cornard *M. Shaw*	√	2	√	√	√		EP = MHT are based on original words but are more consistent with contemporary thought. HCS a more conservative revision. SW.
Love unknown (c) *J. Ireland*		√	√	√	√		(BP), (EP), HHT
See also **Adoration** (St John) *W. H. Havergal*	√	√		√			
Hembriggs *L. Blake*			HCS				
Latchford *W. Statham*			√		S		BP
Lawes Psalm 47 *H. Lawes*	√		√				BP = HHT, HS
Linnington *G. L. Barnes*			PFT				
Pro Patria *J. Armistead*					√		
Warsaw *T. Clark*		2		√		√	
667D							
Nunc Dimittis (c) *Genevan Psalter*	√	√	√			√	
See also **Fulneck** (667777) *C. Latrobe*			√				
6684							
Temple (c) *H. Walford Davies*					√		
Totteridge *S. H. Nicholson*				√			

VARIED TREATMENTS	BEST PLAIN VERSION	THEMATIC INDEX
SP (d)	Not MHB	d - ms $\mid$ d'r's -
SP (fa − b): O (h): SS		s - $\mid$ d't d's $\mid$ l -
AHB = Ch P = SP (fa − b): AMR (d): Camb. (d): HCS (d): CP (d)		d $\mid$ mdsm $\mid$ d' - -
		m $\mid$ smdr $\mid$ s₁ - -
HCS (original postlude): PTL (ditto): PSHB (d)		s $\mid$ lsmfe $\mid$ s - -
CH2 = BBC (rhythm): O (original version)		s $\mid$ ltd'r' $\mid$ d't
EP, CH2, MHB (u), AMR (u and h)		l₁d̂r mm $\mid$ l -
AMR (h): AHB (complicated choir setting)		m - sl $\mid$ m - r - $\mid$ d - -
		d $\mid$ mmss $\mid$ d' - -
		sld' $\mid$ r'd't $\mid$ l - -
		s $\mid$ mdl₁d $\mid$ s₁ - -
	BBC	m - $\mid$ rsdr $\mid$ m - -
		mr̂d $\mid$ t₁l₁s₁ -
		m $\mid$ sdfm̂r $\mid$ m - -
	SP = EH	d'ŝfmd $\mid$ s - -
SS (h). *See* Brindley MHB, a simpler tune		s - ls $\mid$ f - m - $\mid$ r - - -
		d $\mid$ s₁dr̂mf $\mid$ m - -
See also Corrow Bothy CP, CW and Amen Court AMR, ICH, AHB, HÇS		d $\mid$ sslm $\mid$ s - -
		mfs $\mid$ l - d' $\mid$ r' -

METRE—TITLE—COMPOSER	BHB	CH3	CP	MHB	AMR	EH	SUPPLEMENTS
6684D **Leoni** *Adapted from Hebrew Melody*	✓	✓	✓	✓	✓	✓	
See also **Ascalon** (Schönster Herr Jesu, St Elizabeth) (668D) *Silesian Melody*	✓	✓	✓	✓			
668D 3366 **Gröningen** (Arnsberg) *J. Neander*	✓	✓	✓				WOV
66 11D **Down Ampney** *R. Vaughan Williams*	✓	✓	✓	✓		✓	SW
67676666 **Darmstadt** (O Gott, du frommer Gott) (c) *J. S. Bach*	⎸EP	HCS	HHT	SP⎸			
Nun danket alle Gott *J. Crüger*	✓	✓	✓	✓	✓	✓	
Rinkart (c) *J. S. Bach*	✓	✓	✓				
6767D **Vreuchten** (c) *Dutch Carol*		✓	✓				(PP), (PFT)
See also **Christ ist erstanden** (67777 + Alleluia) *12th c. Melody*		2			✓	✓	EP 7878 + Alleluias (c) (arr. Woodward)
Crosby (68888) *E. Shave*			✓				
7474D **Gwalchmai** *J. D. Jones*	✓	✓	✓	✓	✓	✓	
See also **Jouissance** (c) (747477) *P. Bonnet*		✓					
St Aidan (7575) *H. Popple*		✓					
Dedication (7575D) *G. A. Macfarren*	✓			✓	✓		Line 2 in some versions is "All my times to Thee", thus making the hymn useful throughout the year
Heaven (757577) *B. L. Selby*				✓	S		
7676 **Christus der ist mein leben** (Pastor, Bremen, Vulpius) *J. S. Bach*	✓	✓	✓	✓	✓	✓	
St Alphege *H. J. Gauntlett*	✓	2	✓	✓	✓	✓	
See also **Farmington** (767674) *G. L. Barnes*			PFT				

VARIED TREATMENTS	BEST PLAIN VERSION	THEMATIC INDEX
PSHB (d): Camb. = Clarendon, extended version	SP = EH	m | l t d' r' | m' - -
Also irreg.: CH3 (u): BBC, CP, WOV (h)	WOV	d - dd | rt,d -
	CH3	mmmm | r - r -
See also North Petherton, AMR, HCS		d - rm | s - l - | s
PTL: SS (m + h) BHB, CH3, CP (h): AHB, HS, SP, WOV (u)		s | m r̂d s s | l - - s | s s l l | s - - s | m r d d' t l | s
PTL (poor): CH3 = EP (Wood): CP (Shaw) SS. *See also* 78784 in EH, CH2, SP (less good)		s, | d r m f | s - - m - rm | s l m - d - d | dt,d | r - m | d
Camb. (d). *See also* Bemberton HCS		ms | d r̂m | fm | r - d r̂m f s m | l ŝf m - s f̂m s d' | r' d' t l - smfs | l l l - sfms | d' t l -
		d | m r m f | s - m d | m f s d | t, - d - s m̂r d r | t,s, - -

METRE—TITLE—COMPOSER	BHB	CH3	CP	MHB	AMR	EH	SUPPLEMENTS
7676D							
Ave virgo virginum (Gaudeamus pariter) (c) *Leisentritt's Gesangbuch*	√	√	√		√	√	NCP = MHT
Crüger (Herrnhut) *J. Crüger*	√	√	√	√	√	√	WOV, PP, CH3
Ellacombe *Mainz Gesangbuch*	√	√	√	√	√	√	
Ewing *A. Ewing*	√	√	√	√	√	√	
Harvest Song *J. L. Thomas*	√						
Herzlich thut mich verlangen (Passion Chorale) (c) (O Haupt voll Blut) *J. S. Bach*	√	√	√	√	√	√	
King's Lynn *English Melody*			√			√	(HS), PFT
Komm Seele *J. W. Franck*		2	√	√		√	
Llangloffan *Welsh Hymn Melody*	√	2	√	√		√	BP, HHT
Morning Light (Stand up for Jesus) *G. J. Webb*	√	√	√	√	√	√	
St John Damascene (Trochaic) *A. H. Brown*					√		
St Theodulph (Valet will ich dir geben) *M. Teschner*	√	√	√	√	√	√	
Stokesay Castle *E. H. Thiman*	√		√				
Thornbury *B. Harwood*	√	√	√		√	√	(HS), PP
Wolvercote *W. H. Ferguson*	√	2	√	√	√		MHT, SW
See also							
Ach Gott vom Himmelreiche *M. Praetorius*					√	√	
Au fort de ma détresse *Genevan Psalter*			√			√	
Erfreut Euch *German Melody*					√		
Golden Grove *G. Cooke*					√		
Helder (Wohlauf thut nicht versagen) *B. Helder*		√				√	
Ist Gott für Mich *Augsburg Gesangbuch*		√					
Loughborough College *G. W. Briggs*				√			

VARIED TREATMENTS	BEST PLAIN VERSION	THEMATIC INDEX
AMS in plain rhythm. SS		dds₁s₁ | drm -
		s | lsfm | r - m
DCM in BHB, CP		s | d'tīsd' | mfs
		d | rdfm | r -d
		l | ltd't | l - s
2 Bach versions in EH, SP, HCS, CH2, CP: A 3rd version in BBC: MHB, AMR non Bach		m | lsfm | r - m
		m | rml₁t₁ | drs
		s | d'slsf̂ | m -m
	CH2, MHB	m | lltt | d'tl
AHB (d) *See also* Stand up AHB		s₁ | ddmd | d - l₁
		s₁l₁dd | drm -
AHB = EH (Bach): HCS (2 versions): SS (m + h)		d | sslt | d' - d'
See also Tanworth (BBC)		s | d'd'd̂r̂m̂f̂ | s - m
AHB (d): EH (u—only)		s | mt₁dl | d - t₁
BBC (h)	BBC	s₁ | dfmr̂m̂ | dl₁s₁
	EH	s₁ | d - dr - f | mrmr -
	EH	m' - | ltd't | l - s
3 Bach versions extant, "Ich dank dir lieber Herre"		d | dt₁dr | t₁l₁s₁
		m̂f̂ | sm̂r̂dm | l - s
CH3 is 76868686		d | mmrd | f - m
		rllr' | d' - l -
		m | fmrl₁ | t₁ - d

METRE—TITLE—COMPOSER	BHB	CH3	CP	MHB	AMR	EH	SUPPLEMENTS
Munich (Bremen) *Meiningen Gesangbuch*	√	2	√	√		√	
Nyland *Finnish Melody*	√	2		√			
Tyrolese *Tyrolese Carol*	√	√					HHT, SW
Weimar (Jesu, Leiden, Pein und Tod) (Trochaic) *M. Vulpius*						√	
7676D and chorus **Wir pflügen** (Schulz, Arator, Dresden) *J. A. P. Schulz*	√	√	√	√	√	√	
See also **Varndean** (767677) *E. Routley*			AHB				
Carrick (76767776) *K. G. Finlay*			AHB ChP				
Wytham *S. Watson*			AHB HS				
Eastham (7686D) *F. A. G. Ouseley*			HF				
Dying Stephen (77447D) *J. F. Lampe*				√	S		
Hosanna in Excelsis *S. H. Nicholson*					√		
776778 **Innsbruck** (c) (O Welt, ich muss dich lassen) *J. S. Bach*	√	√	√	√	√	√	
777 **Weston** *S. S. Wesley*		2					
See also **Heiliger Geist** (c) *J. Crüger*		2				√	PP
Tyholland *German Carol Melody*	√	2		√			
7773 **Beeding** *E. H. Thiman*			√				
Morgenglanz der Ewigkeit *J. A. Freylinghausen*		2				√	
7775 **Capetown** (Morgenglanz der Ewigkeit) *F. Filitz*	√	√	√	√	√	√	
Charity *J. Stainer*	√	2	√	√	√		SW, (BP)
Huddersfield *W. Parratt*	√	2		√		√	BHB, MHT

VARIED TREATMENTS	BEST PLAIN VERSION	THEMATIC INDEX
cf. Cast thy burden (Elijah) (Mendelssohn)	SP = EH BBC	$\widehat{dr} \mid mlsf \mid m - m$ $s \mid mrd\widehat{rd} \mid l_1 - s_1$ $s_1 \mid ddmd \mid t_1\widehat{rt}_1s_1$ $mrdr \mid mfs -$
		$s_1 \mid dds_1s_1 \mid m - d$ $d'sms \mid lls -$ $mdrr \mid t_1s_1l_1 -$ $d'ssl \mid d'r'm'$ $s_1 \mid drmf \mid s - m$ $d\widehat{ml} sf \mid m - r -$ $s \mid d'smf \mid slt$
BBC (Isaac 7767710). There are also 2 versions 776778. AMR not Bach		$m \mid dr\widehat{ml} s \mid f - m$
These tunes are quoted for the benefit of those churches who require a number of settings for their weekly Lenten litany		$ltd'\widehat{tl} \mid tsel -$ $l - d' \mid t - de' \mid r' - d' \mid t$ $d - m \mid s - l \mid sfm \mid s - -$
SP787873: SS (m + h)		$msdr \mid mrd$ $m\widehat{rd}sl \mid sfm$
SP (fa − b)	EH	$smls \mid ffm -$ $dfmr \mid drs_1 -$ $msfm \mid rmdr$

METRE – TITLE – COMPOSER	BHB	CH3	CP	MHB	AMR	EH	SUPPLEMENTS
7777							
Bonn (Festus) *Freylinghausen's Gesangbuch*	✓	2	✓	✓			
Buckland *L. G. Hayne*	✓	✓	✓	✓	✓	✓	HHT
Crucis Milites *M. B. Foster*	✓		✓		✓		
Galliard *J. Dowland adapt.*		✓				✓	
Harts (Hartford) *B. Milgrove*	✓	✓	✓	✓	✓	✓	
Heinlein (Aus der Tiefe) *M. Herbst*	✓	✓	✓	✓	✓	✓	
Melling *J. Fawcett*	✓	2		✓		✓	HHT
Monkland *J. Wilkes*	✓	✓	✓	✓	✓	✓	(EP)
Newington *Archbishop Maclaglan*	✓		✓	✓	✓		(BP)
Northampton *C. J. King*					✓		(BP, HS)
Nun komm der heiden heiland *J. S. Bach*		2			✓	✓	
Orientis Partibus (St Martin) *French Medieval*	✓	✓		✓	✓		
Savannah (Herrnhut) *Foundery Collection*		2	✓	✓	✓	✓	(BP), HHT
Song 13 (Canterbury, Simplicity) *O. Gibbons*	✓	✓	✓	✓	✓	✓	MHT
University College *H. J. Gauntlett*	✓	✓	✓	✓	✓	✓	
Vienna (Ravenna) *J. H. Knecht*	✓	2	✓	✓	✓	✓	(HHT)
See also							
Bewdley *F. A. G. Ouseley*					✓		(BP)
Corbeil *13th century*					✓		
Da Christus geboren was *J. F. Doles*		2	✓			✓	EP
Freuen wir uns *M. Weisse*						✓	
Hamilton *K. G. Finlay*			AHB	BP			
Keine Schönheit *G. Joseph's Seelenlust*	✓	✓			✓	✓	

VARIED TREATMENTS	BEST PLAIN VERSION	THEMATIC INDEX
AHB, BHB, CP, MHB set as L.M.		d'$\widehat{\text{tl}}$sl | rfm -
		smrd | rrm -
		smrd | fls -
Full version in SS		m - rd - t₁ | l₁ - dr - -
AHB = CP (harmonic and melodic differences in other versions)	EH, SP, BBC	s₁s₁dd | rrm -
SP (fa − b)	EH	mml₁t₁ | drm -
		ds₁$\widehat{\text{drm}}$f | mrd
SP (d)		dmsm | $\widehat{\text{fs}}$$\widehat{\text{lt}}$d' -
		mmfr | l₁t₁d -
		mrfm | rl₁t₁ -
AMR not Bach: SS (h)		llsd' | $\widehat{\text{tl}}$tl -
Should be performed quickly EH = SP (u) 3/4: CP (h) 3/4: AMR (h) 4/4: SS (hm 3/4) With Alleluia: EH, BHB, CP, NCP	EH = SP	d - r | m - d | r - t₁ | d - -
CP (d): SP (fa − b)		ss$\widehat{\text{f}}$mr | $\widehat{\text{dr}}$mr -
CP; EH; SP; Camb. correct melody; AMR better (h)	AMR	m - f | slrd | m -
	AMR, BHB, CP	mdls | fmr -
	EH	mrdm | sfm
		sslr' | td'r' -
		llll | sfem
		$\widehat{\text{drm}}$f sl | f$\widehat{\text{sf}}$ m -
SS		l - t - | d'tls | l - - -
		s₁s₁ld | rdrm
SS (h)	AMR	mfs | f - m | r - r | d - -

METRE—TITLE—COMPOSER	BHB	CH3	CP	MHB	AMR	EH	SUPPLEMENTS
Louez Dieu (Psalm 136) *Psalm 136 Genevan Psalter*		✓				✓	
Petersfield *W. H. Harris*			HCS	HS	NCP		
Tres magi de gentibus (c) *C. S. Lang*				HCS			
Tunbridge *J. Clarke*					✓	✓	(EP), (NCP)
Xavier *F. Champneys*					✓		
7777 and Alleluias **Ascension** *W. H. Monk*	✓		✓	✓	✓		
Chislehurst *S. H. Nicholson*					✓		
Easter Day (Easter Hymn) *Lyra Davidica*	✓	✓	✓	✓	✓	✓	
Llanfair *Welsh Hymn Melody*	✓	✓	✓	✓	✓	✓	
77774 **Würtemburg** (Nassau) *J. Rosenmüller*	✓	✓	✓	✓	✓	✓	CH3
777777 **Arfon** *Welsh Melody*	✓	2	✓	✓		✓	(HS)
Dix (Treuer Heiland) *C. Kocher*	✓	✓	✓	✓	✓	✓	
England's Lane *English Melody*	✓		✓			✓	MHT
Heathlands *H. Smart*	✓	✓	✓	✓	✓	✓	
Jesu, meine Zuversicht (Ratisbon) (c) *J. Crüger*		2		✓	'	✓	
Ministres de l'éternal (Genevan Psalm 135) *French Psalter 1562*		✓				✓	
Nicht so traurig (c) *J. S. Bach*	✓	2		✓	✓	✓	(BP)
Petra (Redhead No. 76 Ajalon) *R. Redhead*	✓	✓	✓	✓	✓	✓	
Veni Sancte Spiritus (777D) *S. Webbe*	✓	2	✓		✓	✓	WOV
See also **Croydon** *H. J. Foss*	✓						
Jesu, Jesu die mein Hirt (The Good Shepherd) *P. Henlein*					✓	✓	

VARIED TREATMENTS	BEST PLAIN VERSION	THEMATIC INDEX
SS (h)	EH	s_l - s_l - | d r m f | s -
		d - d r - d | dl_lt_ld - -
Has fine choral ending		l_ll_lmm | f s m -
Camb. (d)		l d' t m | f r m -
		d' s l f | r s m -
AMR (d) = AHB	Not CP	m s d d | r f m -
		$\widehat{mr}$ d s_l | $\widehat{l_l}$ d r -
EH = SP (2 versions): AMR (d) = AHB: SS	BBC = EH = SP	d m s d | f l l s
Camb. (d)		d d m m | s $\widehat{fm}$ r -
SS	Not MHB	m m s s | d r m -
8787D. HS HCS (elaborate last verse)		m l l $\widehat{se}$ f $\widehat{em}$ | l t d' -
PTL (d): SS: AMR (d) = HCS = AHB		d $\widehat{t_ld}$ r d | f f m -
		d' $\widehat{m_l}$ r d' s | m d s -
	CP	s d' t s | l l s -
Used for extended version of "Jesus lives" in HCS	EH = MHB	s $\widehat{fm}$ l t | d' d' t -
		d' - l - | s s l t | d' - - -
		d' $\widehat{t_l}$ m' r $\widehat{d'}$ | t d' $\widehat{r'}$ se -
		d d r m | f f m -
	AMR	d d d r | m r d -
		d' s l $\widehat{sf}$ | m r m -
SS	AMR	m m l s | f f m -

METRE—TITLE—COMPOSER	BHB	CH3	CP	MHB	AMR	EH	SUPPLEMENTS
Lucerna Laudoniae *D. Evans*		✓					(HS)
Noricum *F. James*	✓			✓			
Te Laudant Omnia *J. F. Swift*	✓			✓			
7777D **Aberystwyth** *J. Parry*	✓	✓	✓	✓	✓	✓	
St Edmund *C. Steggall*					✓	✓	
St George's Windsor *G. J. Elvey*	✓	✓	✓	✓	✓	✓	
See also **Loughborough College** *G. W. Briggs*				✓			
Naphill (Iambic) *H. E. Darke*	✓				✓		(NCP)
St Hilary (7777D) *J. Goss*				S			
Salzburg (Alle Menschen) *J. S. Bach*	✓	2	✓	✓	✓	✓	
Noddfa (Refuge) (7787D) *J. D. Jones*			✓				
7878 and Alleluias **Feniton** *S. H. Nicholson*					✓		MHT
78784 **St Albinus** *H. J. Gauntlett*	✓	✓	✓	✓	✓	✓	
787888 **Liebster Jesu** (Dessau, St Mark) (c) *J.R. Ahle*	✓	✓		✓	✓	✓	EP
8336D **Benifold** *F. Westbrook*			HS	MHT			
847D **Meine Armuth** *J. A. Freylinghausen*	✓			✓			
See also **Langham Place** *B. Rose*			BP				
848484 **Severn** (c) *H. Howells*		✓					
See also **Bushmead** (8583) *C. V. Taylor*				BBC			

VARIED TREATMENTS	BEST PLAIN VERSION	THEMATIC INDEX
		$\widehat{ss}$| m'd'r'$\widehat{m}$' | l -
		ddd$\widehat{t_1l_1}$ | s₁fm -
		msdr | dt₁d -
SP (d)		l$\widehat{l}$t$\widehat{d'r'}$m' | d'tl -
		msrm | dl₁s₁ -
Camb. (d)		mmsm | drm -
		dmsd | rt₁d -
See also Fortem virili pectore (SP) and Wood End BBC		s₁ | drmf | r - r
		dmsd' | tls -
SP (fa – b): AMR (not Bach): MHB has original metre 87877777 plain: SS		sd'sl | sfm -
		s₁ | s₁ddr | mrd
		dl₁dr | mss -
		mdsm | lls -
BHB, CH3, SP, EH (Bach); AMR (another Bach variant) SS	Not MHB	m$\widehat{rd}$rs | mdr -
		s₁s₁dd | $\widehat{rm}$ $\widehat{fs}$md
See also Warwick CP		$\widehat{drm}$fsm | ls$\widehat{f}$md
		s₁drm | slmr
		d | s - - $\widehat{fm}$ | fsdd | r
		mfls | drfm

METRE—TITLE—COMPOSER	BHB	CH3	CP	MHB	AMR	EH	SUPPLEMENTS
8585843 **Angel voices** *E. G. Monk*	√	√	√	√	√		PP
See also **Arthog** *G. T. Thalben-Ball*		√					
85858885 **Carolyn** *H. Murrill*	**BBC**	**EP**	**HCS**	**HHT**			
8684 **Shrewsbury** *J. E. Hunt*					√		
See also **Brunswick** (868686) *G. F. Händel*						√	
Auch jetzt macht Gott (868688) *Koch's Choralbuch*						√	
Conquest *D. S. Barrows*	√		√				
Emaim Macha *C. Wood*		√					
O Jesu *J. B. Reimann*						√	
86886 **Binneys** *E. H. Thiman*			√				
Nicolaus (Hermann, Lobt Gott) (c) *N. Hermann*	√	√		√			
Repton (c) *C. H. H. Parry*	√	√	√		√	√	(HS)
See also **Gatescarth** *N. Micklem*			**BP**	**NCP**			
Henwood (87348) (c) *G. T. Thalben-Ball*			**BBC**				
Nonington (8783) *D. Grundy*				**AHB**			
St Leonard's (8785) *A. C. Barham Gould*	√						
8787 **Ach Gott und Herr** (Beccles) (c) *J. S. Bach*	√	√	√		√	√	(HHT), PP, NCP
Adoration *J. E. Hunt*			**Ch**	**P**			
Cross of Jesus *J. Stainer*	√				√	√	(EP), SW (2)

METRE—TITLE—COMPOSER	BHB	CH3	CP	MHB	AMR	EH	SUPPLEMENTS
Dominus Regit Me *J. B. Dykes*	√	√	√	√	√		(EP)
Gott will's machen *J. L. Steiner*	√				√	√	HHT
Halton Holgate (Sharon) *W. Boyce*	√	2	√	√	√	√	(MHT), (BP), (EP), (HS)
Laus Deo (Redhead 46, Dresden) *R. Redhead*	√	√	√	√	√	√	CH3
Marching *M. Shaw*	√	√	√	√	√	√	WOV
Merton *W. H. Monk*	√				√	√	
Ottery St Mary *H. G. Ley*		√					
St Columba (Erin) *Irish Traditional Melody*	√	√	√	√	(√)	√	WOV
Shipston *English Traditional*	√	√	√	√		√	HS = PP = BBC = WOV = BHB
Stuttgart *C. H. Dretzel*	√	√	√	√	√	√	PP, BHB
Sussex *English Traditional*	√	√	√	√		√	MHT, NCP
Waltham (Gott des Himmels) (c) *H. Albert*	√	√			√		(HS)
See also **Hartley Wintney** *G. L. Barnes*			PFT				
Jacob's Well (Iambic) *B. Rose*			BP				
May Hill *S. Watson*			AHB HS SW				
Wilford *G. Gardner*			HHT				
Wraysbury *E. J. Hopkins*	√						MHT
8787337 **Meine Hoffnung** *Neander's Collection*	√	√	√	√			
Michael *H. Howells*		√					(HS = BP = HHT)
878766667 **Ein' feste Burg** (A stronghold sure) *M. Luther*	√	√	√	√	√	√	
87877778 **Genevan Psalm 42** (c) *Genevan Psalter*		√			√	√	PP

VARIED TREATMENTS	BEST PLAIN VERSION	THEMATIC INDEX
AHB (Choral): AMR (d)		m｜sfmm｜rrd
CP extd. by Walford Davies: SS (2 versions—h)	Not BBC 9898:	dm r͡s₁ s₁｜dm r͡s₁ s₁
CP (poor): HCS (d): Camb. (d) EH (poor 7777)	AMR	mdsd｜r͡m ffm
AHB = AMR (d): HCS (d): SP (d)	AMR	dt₁dm｜rddt₁
HCS (fa − b and u)		mfss｜ltd't
		dmss｜flls
HCS = HS (d)		llll｜ttd'l
HCS (d + h): MHB (CM, Stanford h)	EH: AMR (poor)	d͡r｜m -f｜s -f͡s｜m -r｜d -
		dmsl｜s͡fm͡rm d
HCS (d): SP (d): SS	Not CH2 + 3 EH = SP	s₁s₁dd｜rrmd
		m m m r｜d͡r m͡r dl₁
EP (Steggall and Bach). Several compromises with Bach in other versions		dr͡mfs｜dt₁l₁s₁
		smrd｜r͡m fmd
		m｜rms₁s₁｜l₁ds₁
		m m s m｜d r m f
		d｜mrms｜lsm
		mrdm｜rs͡mrd
	SP	lselt｜d'd'tm
EP (d)—difficult		ssms｜f͡m r͡d r - d
Bach: EH, SP, BBC, CH3: Part-Bach MHB: Plain: BBC, CP, AMR	Not AMR	d'｜d'd's͡lt｜d͡'t ls
F♮ in line 6 in EH a master stroke: SS (h and fa − b)	AMR	d - rm - r｜dt₁l₁ - s₁ -

G[✳]

METRE—TITLE—COMPOSER	BHB	CH3	CP	MHB	AMR	EH	SUPPLEMENTS
8787 4/8 7							
Cwm Rhondda *J. Hughes*	✓	✓	✓	✓	✓		
Grafton (Tantum Ergo) *French Church Melody*	✓	✓	✓	✓	✓	✓	SW
Helmsley *T. Olivers*	✓	✓	✓	✓	✓	✓	
Kingley Vale *H. P. Allen*	✓						BP = HHT
Neander (Unser Herrscher) *J. Neander*	✓	✓	✓	✓	✓	✓	PP
Oriel *C. Ett*	✓	✓	✓	✓	✓	✓	MHT
Picardy (French Carol) *French Melody*	✓	✓	✓		✓	✓	(HS), (PP)
Praise my soul *J. Goss*	✓	✓	✓	✓	✓	✓	
Regent Square *H. Smart*	✓	✓	✓	✓	✓	✓	HHT, SW
Rhuddlan *Welsh Melody*	✓	✓	✓	✓	✓	✓	BHB, WOV
St Helen *G. C. Martin*					✓		EP
Tantum Ergo (Corinth, Alleluia Dulce Carmen, Bithynia) *S. Webbe*	✓	✓	✓	✓	✓	✓	HHT, MHT
Westminster Abbey (Belville) *H. Purcell*	✓	✓	✓		✓		BHB, EP, (HS)
See also **Bryn Calfaria** *W. Owen*			✓	✓		✓	
Lingwood *C. A. Gibbs*	AHB	HCS	HHT	PFT			
Northam *W. Davies*			PFT				
Obiit *W. Parratt*	AHB	HCS	HHT	HS	PP		
St Audrey *B. Harwood*					✓		
St Thomas (Holywood) *Traditional Melody*	✓	2	✓	✓	✓	✓	
878777							
Aethelwold *S. H. Nicholson*					✓		
All Saints *Darmstadt Gesangbuch*	✓	2	✓	✓	✓	✓	WOV, AHB; AHB (8787D)
St Leonard *J. C. Bach*	✓		✓	✓		✓	WOV, SW

VARIED TREATMENTS	BEST PLAIN VERSION	THEMATIC INDEX
NCH (improved h line 2): EP line 7		$s_1 l_1 s_1 d \mid \widehat{d t_1} \, \widehat{d} r m r$
Very impressive when sung slowly	AMR	$d r m d \mid \widehat{m r} \, \widehat{m} f s m$
SP (difficult d)	EH = AMR	$d' - m's' \mid d' t l s \mid l t d' \widehat{t l} \mid s f m$
BP (u + h)		$s m r d \mid l s \widehat{l} t d'$
BHB (d) = SP; AHB = AMR (d)	EH	$d r m d \mid m f s s$
AMR = SP = AHB (d)		$d d d d \mid r m f m$
HS (h)		$l_1 t_1 d r m - m r \mid m - m -$
HCS (d): AHB (d): Camb. (d)	AMR	$s s s s \mid d' t l - \mid s -$
AHB (d, Choir, u)	EH	$s m d' s \mid m' r' d' s$
		$d d d d \mid m d r_1 s_1$
		$d' d' d' m \mid l s m r$
8787D in MHB; SP (d)	EH	$d r m f \mid s f m r$
AHB (d). Use Grafton for v. "To this temple where we call Thee"	EP	$m - s \mid m - d \mid f - r \mid t_1 - s_1$
	EH	$\widehat{m m} \mid l t \mid \widehat{d' d'} d' t$
Extended version in AHB, HCS		$d d r m \mid m m f l$
		$s s d' t \mid d' s \widehat{l} s f$
		$d d \mid r d \mid f m \mid l s$
O (u)		$d r m \mid r - d \mid d r m \mid r - r$
	EH = AMR	$d r m d \mid r m f m$
		$s_1 s_1 d d \mid \widehat{r d} \, \widehat{r m} f f$
SP (fa − b): AHB (melodic differences)	EH	$d' s l l \mid s f m d$
		$m \widehat{r d} r s \mid d \widehat{r d} t_1 s_1$

METRE—TITLE—COMPOSER	BHB	CH3	CP	MHB	AMR	EH	SUPPLEMENTS
8787D							
Abbot's Leigh *C. V. Taylor*	√	√	√		√		CH3, EP, HHT, HS, PP
Austria *J. Haydn*	√	√	√	√	√	√	
Blaenwern *W. P. Rowlands*	√	√					MHT
Ebenezer (Ton-y-botel) *T. J. Williams*	√	2	√	√		√	
Ermuntre dich (c) *J. Schop*	√	√	√				
Hyfrydol *R. H. Pritchard*	√	√	√	√	√	√	PP, SW
Ivinghoe *G. Cooke*	√						BP, HS
Megerran (Iambic) *W. K. Stanton*			BBC				
Marathon *R. Vaughan Williams*			AHB SP				
Mead House *C. V. Taylor*	√						BHB
Rex Gloriae *H. Smart*	√	2	√	√	√	√	MHT
Rustington *C. H. H. Parry*	√	√	√		√		HS
See also **Everton** *H. Smart*	√	2		√	√	√	
Exile (c) *English Melody*			SP WOV				
Hermon (c) *C. V. Pilcher*			PFT				
Twigworth (c) *H. Howells*			BP HCS HS				
Würzburg (c) *German*	√		√	√		√	WOV
8787887							
Allein Gott (Elberfeld, Stettin, Atolle Paulum) (c) *German 16th c.*		√		√	S	√	CH3, HHT
Aus tiefer noth (Coburg) (c) *German 16th c.*	√		√				
Es ist das heil (Wittenberg, Saving Health) (c) *J. S. Bach*		√		√	√	√	
Luther (Nun freut euch Luther) (c) *M. Luther*	√	√	√	√	√	√	
Nun freut euch (Erk) (c) *J. S. Bach*					√	√	

VARIED TREATMENTS	BEST PLAIN VERSION	THEMATIC INDEX
		s - m | d - d | d'tl | ls -
SP (d): BHB (d)	AMR	drmr | fmr̂t₁d
		s₁ - s₁ | l₁ - l₁ | s₁dm | m - r
Bairstow OUP (u)		lſtd'tl | ttd'r'd̂'t l
AHB, CH2 (Bach)		d | drm̂fes | sfes
	EH	d - r | drm | f - m | rdr
		s₁mrs | dr̂d t₁s₁
		d | mrdt₁ | l₁ĺ₁d r
		mmrm | dl₁s₁l₁
		s₁s₁ds₁ | drmd
		ds₁dr | mfmr
		· ddfm | rdt₁s₁
Bright tempo needed		mf sd' | ltd's
		f f mf | sdt₁d
		dmsd' | sf̂mfs
		sld'd' | tsls
		s₁dt₁d | r̂mr̂d t₁s₁
SS (16th century − m + h)	EH	d̂r | mfsf | mrm
		m - | l₁mfm̂r | drm -
SS (16th century − m + h)	EH	s | sssta | lsf
SS (16th century − m + h)		d | d̂rmrd | rrm
SS (16th century − m + h)	EH	d | ds₁df | mrd

METRE—TITLE—COMPOSER	BHB	CH3	CP	MHB	AMR	EH	SUPPLEMENTS
See also **Dolberrow** (Trochaic) *W. K. Stanton*					√		
Irvine Waterside *K. G. Finlay*	√		√				
Lindeman *L. M. Lindeman*			√				EP, HHT, WOV
Mit freuden zart *Bohemian Brethren*	√	√		√	√	√	WOV
Newnham *H. Howells*			HCS				
Palace Green *M. Fleming*			MHT				
87878887 **O Christe Rex piisime** (c) *Piae Cantiones*		√	√				(EP)
878788 **Eisenach** (Mach's mit mir Gott: Schein) *J. S. Bach*						√	
See also **Llanherne** (87887) *G. Thalben-Ball*	√						
Lanteglos (884) *J. D. Bower*			HHT				
Sales (886) *G. F. Champneys*					S		
886D **Allgütiger mein Lebelang** (Erfurt) (c) *G. P. Weimar*	√	2		√	√		
Chapel Royal *W. Boyce*					√		
Cornwall *S. S. Wesley*	√		√		√		BP, NCP, HHT
Manna *J. G. Schicht*					√		BP, HS
8877D **Genevan Psalm 86** (Mon Dieu, prête moi l'oreille) (c) *L Bourgeois*			√		√	√	
887887D **Psalm 36** (Genevan Psalm 68 Old 113) (c) *M. Greiter*		√	√	√	√	√	
887D **Alles ist an Gottes segen** (Evangelists) *J. S. Bach*					√		HHT
Ascendit Deus *J. G. Schicht*	√	√	√				WOV, CH3, (MHT)

VARIED TREATMENTS	BEST PLAIN VERSION	THEMATIC INDEX
AMR (h): Others (u)		ds₁mr │ d̂t₁d l₁s₁ s │ mrdm̂f │ sls l₁l₁m │ d - l₁ │ d - r │ m d - mf │ s - d' - │ tls - s │ lld't │ lsl d - dr │ fmls │ d' - -
	CP	d̂r │ m - mm - r │ dt₁l₁s -
SS (17th century m + h) BHB (Bach), CH3, CP, AMR, MHB all L.M.		d̂r │ mfss │ fmr ds₁l₁s₁ │ d̂t₁d̂rmd dd̂rm̂f s │ mdr - s₁ │ drfm │ rdt₁
BBC (m)		s │ mrdd │ rm̂ f̂sm d │ ddrm │ frm m │ sm̂rdd' │ tls d │ mdl₁l₁ │ rrt₁
SS: AMR (h)		l - l - │ sltd' │ t - l -
HCS = EH = CH2 = SP: BHB poor: SS	EH	d - dr │ mdmf │ s -
BHB = CH3 = CP (good)	BBC	ddss │ fsmd s₁ │ l₁t₁dt₁ │ drm

METRE—TITLE—COMPOSER	BHB	CH3	CP	MHB	AMR	EH	SUPPLEMENTS
Dresden (Lucerne) *Würtemburg Gesangbuch*	√		√	√			
Stabat Mater *French Church Melody*		√		√	√	√	
887D 4848 **Wie schon leuchtet** (c—especially BBC) *P. Nicolai*		√					EP, HS
888 **O mensch sieh** (Bohemia) *Bohemian Brethren*		√				√	
8884 **Gelobt sei Gott** (Vulpius) *M. Vulpius*	√	√	√		√		EP, HHT, HS
Meyer (Es ist kein tag) *Meyer's Seelenfreud*	√	√	√	√	√	√	HHT
O filii et filae *French Church Melody*	√	√	√		√	√	PP
Victory *Palestrina (adapted)*	√	2	√	√	√	√	
See also **Ripponden** (c) *N. Cocker*	√	√					MHT, BP
St Gabriel *F. A. G. Ouseley*	√	2	√	√	√		
8886 **Childhood** *Student's Hymnal*	√	√	√	√		√	
Saffron Walden *A. H. Brown*	√	√	√	√	√	√	
See also **Isleworth** *S. Howard*		√		√		√	
Misericordia *H. Smart*	√	2	√	√	√		
See also **Blairgowrie** (888646) *R. G. Thomson*	√		√	√			MHT
8887 **Charing** *S. L. Russell*						√	
Quem Pastores *German 14th c.*	√	√	√	√	√	√	HHT
88886 **Ashbourne Road** *G. A. Morgan*	√						
88887 **Praises** *B. L. Selby*					√		

VARIED TREATMENTS	BEST PLAIN VERSION	THEMATIC INDEX
888D effective for "I'll praise my Maker" (CP)		s | msd't | d'r'm'
	EH = CH3	drmr | msfm
Mendelssohn and Bach versions in SP	BBC (Wagner)	d | smds | lls
		mmm | r - - drf | m - -
HS (d)	Not AMR, CP	d'tl | s - s | l - t | d' - -
		s | d'tl̂sl̂s | f̂m r d
SS: 2 versions in CH3 and EH		llt | lsl | d'tl | m - -
MHB, EH omit introductory Alleluias		sss | l - s | sfm | s - -
		dms | sfmr | f
Use Victory in E flat for final verse with rhythmic modification of last line		m | sfmf | mrd
	CH2	d̂m | slŝf̂mr | ddd
		mrd | s - d' | d'tl | s - -
		m | lmfr | dt₁l₁
		mrd | f - m | l - l | s - -
See also Exultate Deo BBC		m | sfmf | mrd
		drmr | msls
BBC 8877: Orig. rhythm in CH3 also		d - m | s - m | fsl | s - r
Repton may be adapted easily to fit "O Love that wilt not let me go"		d | rrdd | f̂mrm
		s | lmsl̂t | d'd'r'

METRE—TITLE—COMPOSER	BHB	CH3	CP	MHB	AMR	EH	SUPPLEMENTS
8888888							
Abingdon *E. Routley*	√		√				MHT, NCP
David's Harp *R. King*	√	2	√	√		√	
Leicester *J. Bishop*		2	√	√		√	
Melita *J. B. Dykes*	√	√	√	√	√	√	HHT
St Petersburg (Wells, Russia, Wellspring) *D. S. Bartnianski*	√	2	√	√	S		HHT, (MHT)
Surrey *H. Carey*	√	√	√	√	√	√	HHT
Toc H (c) *M. Shaw*					√		
Vater Unser (Old 112th, Psalm 112) (c) *Geistliche Lieder*	√	√	√	√	√	√	
Veni Creator (c) *T. Attwood*	√	√		√		√	
Veni Emmanual *French Missal*	√	√	√	√	√	√	
See also **Colchester** *S. S. Wesley*	√	2	√	√	√		(BP)
Jabbok *C. V. Taylor*			BBC				
Ryburn *N. Cocker*	√						BP, HS, MHT
St Jerome *F. Champneys*			√		S		
Sidmouth *B. J. Dale*	√			√			MHT, HS = BP
Warwick Gardens *T. C. Gregory*				√			
Wrestling Jacob *S. S. Wesley*	√			√	√		
888D							
Judicium (c) *P. C. Buck*			HCS Camb.				
See also **Stamford** *S. Reay*				√			
898D 66488							
Wachet Auf *P. Nicolai*		√	√	√	√	√	
8989D							
Crossings (c) *C. A. Gibbs*			HCS HS SP				

VARIED TREATMENTS	BEST PLAIN VERSION	THEMATIC INDEX
		mfs │ l - s │ d' - r' │ s - -
		m ȓd t₁d │ r m l̑ m
	AMR	m │ mlsel │ ȓ d' t̑lse
Camb. (d)		d │ mmss │ lls
Numerous metrical variants		s │ smf │ s - d' │ r'd't │ d' -
	EH	s │ fml │ dt₁d │ fmr │ m -
		d' │ tlmrdr │ m
SP (fa − b): BHB = EH = CH3 (Bach): SS		m │ mdrm │ dt₁l₁
		s │ sd'l̑ │ s - m │ d - r │ m -
	EH	l₁dmmmrfmrd
Camb. (d)		m │ sdfr │ dt₁d
		s │ msd'd │ f m̑r m
		dmfs - s │ l - sd
		s │ ls l̑ m l̑ s │ r r d
		m │ l₁t₁rd │ fmm
		d' │ tlsel │ ttl
		d │ msr m̑r │ drm
		mmmr │ mmll
Impressive if sung with dignity		ds₁d │ mrd │ s - f │ m - -
BBC (2 vers.); CH3 (Mendelssohn); EH = CP = SP (Bach) SS (pre-Bach)		dm │ ssss │ l - s -
See Clarendon for extended version		dmr │ t₁ - s₁ │ l₁ - l₁ │ s₁ - -

METRE—TITLE—COMPOSER	BHB	CH3	CP	MHB	AMR	EH	SUPPLEMENTS
See also **Hambleden** (c) *W. K. Stanton*		√					HHT = NCP
9898 **St Clement** *C. C. Scholefield*	√	√	√	√	√	√	
Sunset (c) *G. G. Stocks*		√					NCP, AHB, CH3
See also **(Les) Commandment(s)** *Genevan Psalter 1543*			√	√	√	√	√	HS = WOV = EP = CH3 = HHT
Padstow *C. S. Lang*			HCS				
989888 **Bremen** (Neumark, Wer nur den lieben) *E. Neumark*	√	√	√	√	S	√	CH3
9898D **Rendez à Dieu** (Genevan Psalm 98) (c) *French Psalter*	√	√	√	√	√	√	EP, MHT = NCP
9899 **Sheng en** (God's grace) *Su yin-lan*		√					
10 4 6666 10 4 **Luckington** *B. Harwood*	√	√	√	√	√		(EP)
10 4 10 4 10 10 **Alberta** (c) *W. H. Harris*	√		√		√		(HS), SW, AHB
10 10 **Song 46** *O. Gibbons*	√	2	√	√	√	√	WOV
See also **Garden** *English Traditional Melody*	√						
10 10 and chorus **Crucifer** *S. H. Nicholson*		√			√		(HS)
10 10 7 *See also* **Martins** (St Sebastian) *P. C. Buck*	√	√	√		√		EP (HS)
10 10 10 **Löwenstern** (Heut' ist O mensch) *M. Von Löwenstern*				√			

VARIED TREATMENTS	BEST PLAIN VERSION	THEMATIC INDEX
		m - rd | s - m - | l t d' -
Hereford L.M. would provide an alternative		s₁ | mfm | smr | drl₁ | dt₁ d | r͡m f m r͡d r s₁
HS (u) SS		d - dr | m - mffm - r - lms | l d' t | l s m͡r | mm -
SS, CH3 (Mendelssohn harmonies) 4/4; CP in 3/4; EH 3/4 more elaborate		m | l t d' t | l t͡l s e
SS (h)		d' - ls | ddrf | m - r -
		d | drm - drm | d l₁ l₁
		d | m - s - | d' - - d | r l s f | m
BBC (u + h)		d - dr | mrfmrd | l -
		d - md | s - - d | fffm | r - m | mfsm | l - - s | fmr -
		s - d' l | f - - s | mfsl | r - -
PSHB (d)		s | l s͡f s d' | t l s m | d
		m - sl | t d' t l | r' - d' - | t -

METRE—TITLE—COMPOSER	BHB	CH3	CP	MHB	AMR	EH	SUPPLEMENTS
10 10 10 4							
Engelberg (c) *C. V. Stanford*	√	√	√		√		HHT, HS, NCP, CH3, AHB
Sine Nomine *R. Vaughan Williams*	√	√	√	√		√	
See also **Laleham** *J. Wilson*			**HS HCS**				
Woodchurch *S. H. Nicholson*					√		
10 10 10 6							
Mundays *M. Shaw*			**PTL SP WOV**				
10 10 10 10							
All Souls *J. Yoakley*	√	2		√		√	
Congleton (c) *M. Wise*		2				√	
Eventide *W. H. Monk*	√	√	√	√	√	√	
Farley Castle *H. Lawes*	√	√	√		√	√	HHT, WOV
Magda *R. Vaughan Williams*	√	√			√	√	HHT
Morestead *S. Watson*			**BP HCS HHT PFT**				
O Quanta Qualia (Regnator Orbis) (Dactylic) *La Feillée Method*	√	√	√		√	√	SW
Quedlinburg *J. C. Kittel*			√			√	HHT = PFT
Sheldonian (c) *C. V. Taylor*	√						
Song 22 *O. Gibbons*		√	√		√	√	PP (fits badly)
Song 24 *O. Gibbons*	√	√	√	√	√	√	HHT, CH3
Trisagion *H. Smart*		2			√		
Woodlands *W. Greatorex*	√	√	√	√			EP = HHT = PP = SW = WOV; WOV
See also **Birmingham** *F. Cunningham*	√			√		√	
Cliff Town *E. Routley*			√				MHT
Julius *M. Shaw*					√		BP, SW

VARIED TREATMENTS	BEST PLAIN VERSION	THEMATIC INDEX
AMR = BHB = CP = HCS (Extended versions) CH3 (u + h versions only): BBC (h)		$s_l d m r s_l \mid l_l t_l d l_l \mid s_l - -$ $s m r \mid d - - s_l \mid l_l d r s_l \mid m - -$
HS (u + h)		$m - \mid l s d d \mid r f m r \mid m -$ $s d r \mid m r d d r m \mid f -$
		$m^l \mid t r^l d^l l \mid s l s f \mid m - -$
AHB (d) Camb. (d)		$m - r d \mid f - m - \mid l l s r \mid m - -$ $l \mid d^l - t d^l l \mid s e l s f \mid m - -$ $m - m r \mid d - s - \mid l s s f \mid m$ $d - m f \mid s m f s \mid l t d^l -$ $s d^l l \mid s - m \mid d r m \mid f - s \mid m - -$ $d - m s \mid d^l - l - \mid s m d r \mid m$
SP (d): AMR (h): EH (u) PFT poor version	EH = SP EH	$d - d r \mid m - d d \mid f - m r \mid r - d$ $d m f \mid s s d \mid l s f \mid m -$ $m - m s m r \mid d r m s l$
HCS (u): SS: O (h) AMR repeats lines 3 and 4: O	EH	$s - s m \mid l - s - \mid s f m s \mid r -$ $d d r \mid m m r d \mid t_l t_l l - -$ $s s l \mid s m r \mid d r r \mid m - -$ $s s s \mid d^l - - s \mid l \widehat{m} f s r \mid m - -$ $d - m d \mid s - - m \mid l s l t \mid d^l - -$ $m \mid r d r s \mid l s d r \mid m - -$ $m - r d \mid r s d t_l l_l t_l \mid s_l - -$

METRE—TITLE—COMPOSER	BHB	CH3	CP	MHB	AMR	EH	SUPPLEMENTS
Present Tense *Frankfurt Chorale Book*			PP				
Song 4 (c) *O. Gibbons*						√	
Winton *G. Dyson*			HCS	NCP			
10 10 10 10 10 **Old 124** *Genevan Psalter*		√	√	√	√	√	EP, (PFT)
10 10 10 10 10 10 **Northumbria** *W. K. Stanton*	√						
Song 1 *O. Gibbons*	√	√	√	√	√	√	(HHT), WOV
Unde et memores *W. H. Monk*	√	2		√	√		
10 10 10 14 **Tidings** *W. Llewellyn*			AHB				
10 10 11 11 (55556565) **Hanover** *W. Croft*	√	√	√	√	√	√	
Old 104 (Ravenscroft) *Ravenscroft Psalter*	√	2	√	√	√	√	BP, MHT
Paderborn (Maria zu leben) *Paderborn Gesangbuch*	√				√		(EP)
See also **East Head** (10 11 11 6) *B. Rose*			BP				
10 11 11 11 and chorus **Maccabeus** *G. F. Handel*	√	√		√			(EP), (HHT)
10 11 11 12 **Miniver** *C. V. Taylor*		√					(HHT), PFT
Slane *Irish Melody*	√	√	√	√			SW, WOV, HHT, (EP), CH3, AHB
See also **Snowshill** *W. K. Stanton*			BBC				
11 10 10 11 **Noel nouvelet** *French Carol*		√					MHT, PP
11 10 11 10 **Donne Secours** (Genevan Psalm 12; Comfort Ye) *L. Bourgeois*		√	√		√	√	PP (fits badly)

VARIED TREATMENTS	BEST PLAIN VERSION	THEMATIC INDEX
		d'tl | m'r'd' | td'l | se
		m | lselt | d'sls | m -
		s₁ | drs - - s | fmdr | d - -
BBC (u): EH (fa − b): Holst arr. in HCS: 22		d - rm | f - m - | rddt₁ | d -
BHB (h): BBC (u). *See also* Rejoice O People (CP) (c)		s | d'drm | fslsf̂ | s - - s₁ - s₁s₁ | drmm | rrd - m | mddr | mmmf | s - -
		s₁dr | mf | s - mr̂d r | d -
AMR = AHB (d): CP (d): CH2 = SP = ChP (fa − b): Camb. (d): HCS (d) *See* HCS for footnote. AMR, BHB, CP (melodically equal: Ditto EH + MHB): AMR (d) PTL (melodic variants)	EH	s₁ | ddr | m - s | drt₁ | d - l₁ | dt₁l₁ | m - d | rfm | r - s₁ | ddr | m - m̂r̂ | smr | d - l₁dm | l - l - | slmr - m
		s - mf | s - d - | r̂m̂fsfm | r -
		mmd̂r̂msl | smrd - dd r̂d | l₁s₁ŝ₁l₁ | ddr | m - dmdsss | lfld' - -
		rlts | l - f - sŝlfm | r - ₗ
AMR, CH3, CP, HCS (h): SS (h): BBC, CH2 (u); BHB extd. version		d - dr | m - s - | mdrd | t₁ - l₁

METRE—TITLE—COMPOSER	BHB	CH3	CP	MHB	AMR	EH	SUPPLEMENTS
Highwood *R. R. Terry*	✓			✓			MHT, SW, WOV
Intercessor *C. H. H. Parry*	✓	✓	✓	✓	✓		NCP, BP, HS, MHT
L'Omnipotent (Genevan Psalm 110) *Genevan Psalter*		2			✓	✓	✓
Liebster Immanuel (Emmanuel) (c) *J. S. Bach*	✓	2	✓		✓	✓	
Northbrook *R. S. Thatcher*		✓					SW = PFT
Russia (n) **(Anthem)** *A. F. Lvov*			✓	✓	✓	✓	SW
Spean *J. F. Bridge*				✓			
Stonor *S. Watson*					✓		
Welwyn *A. S. Gatty*	✓	2		✓		✓	WOV

See also
  Crudwell
  W. K. Stanton
	✓	✓					BP = BHB

Eastwood *E. Shave*			✓				
Jesmian *G. Thalben-Ball*	✓						
Lexham *S. Watson*			HCS				
Ready Token (Dactylic) *W. K. Stanton*	✓						
Zu meinen Herrn *J. G. Schicht*		2	✓	✓		✓	PP
11 10 11 10 10 **Langham** *G. Shaw*			SP WOV				
11 11 11 5 **Christe fons jugis** *Rouen Church Melody*					✓	✓	
Christe sanctorum (C – HHT) *La Féillée*	✓	✓	✓		✓	✓	HHT: HS = MHT = PP = WOV = NC
Coelites plaudant (Rouen) *Rouen Church Melody*	✓				✓	✓	MHT
Diva Servatrix (Bayeux) (c–HHT) *Bayeux Church Melody*	✓	✓	✓		✓	✓	EP, MHT, CH3
Herr deinen Zorn (Lobet den Herrn) *J. Crüger*					✓	✓	MHT
Herzliebster Jesu (c) *J. Crüger*	✓	✓	✓	✓		✓	

VARIED TREATMENTS	BEST PLAIN VERSION	THEMATIC INDEX
BBC (u)		s - lm' | r' - - t | d'lsm | d - r -
		lsf | mmfld'd' | t - l
SS (h)		l - sl | t - d' - | r'm'r'd' | t - l
AMR 9898		d'd'd' | tls | lf m | r - d
		s | lsfsd | rmsfmr | d - t₁
also 11 10 11 9		s - ll | smd - | d' - tl | s - l -
		m - dl₁ | s₁ - dm | s - f r | d - t₁
		smf | s - - d | fslt | d' - s -
		m - rd | t₁ - - d | rfmr | d - t₁
		sdrmrd | fsls - m
		m₁ - s₁d | m - - r | dt₁l₁d | sfm
		m - rd | s - mr | slmd | r - m
		dmf | s - s | l - t | d'tl | ss -
		mrd | smd | rmf | m - r
		s₁ - l₁t₁ | dt₁ddrr | md
		m - rd | t₁ - l₁ - | drmd | s - m
BBC (u + h): AMR (h)		m - mr | m - d - | mfsm | f - m -
H. Celeb.: AMR (h)		s - mf | mrd - | mfss | l - s -
	EH	d' - sl | sfm - | ltsd' | d'td'
SS (m + h)	EH	m - mf | m - d - | rdrm | r - d -
AMR (h) poor	EH	s - d't | l - s - | mfss | f - m -
EH = AHB = SP (2 versions): HCS; SS (m + h); O (m + h)		l | llsem | ltd'd' | r'd't

METRE—TITLE—COMPOSER	BHB	CH3	CP	MHB	AMR	EH	SUPPLEMENTS
Iste Confessor (Rouen) *Rouen Church Melody*	✓	✓	✓		✓	✓	WOV
See also **Die Nacht ist kommen** (c) *P. Nigidius*			SP				
11 11 11 11 **Arncliffe** *H. D. Statham*					✓		
St Denio (Joanna) *Welsh Hymn Melody*	✓	✓	✓	✓	✓	✓	
Town joys (Polzeath) *English Carol Melody*		✓					NCP
See also **Datchet** *G. J. Elvey*				✓			
Maldwyn *D. Evans*			SP				
Stowey *English Melody*	✓		✓				PP
11 11 11 11 and chorus **To God be the glory** *W. H. Doane*	✓			✓			
See also **Mason** (Old German) (11 12 11 10) *J. Mason's Companion*				✓			
11 12 12 10 **Nicaea** *J. B. Dykes*	✓	✓	✓	✓	✓	✓	
12 10 12 10 **Was lebet, was schwebet** (Üttingen) *Reinhardt Mss*	✓	✓	✓		✓	✓	HHT, WOV
12 12 12 12 **Seventh Mode Melody** (c) *T. Tallis*						✓	
13 13 13 13 13 13 **Thaxted** *G. Holst*	✓			✓	✓	✓	
13 13 14 14 **Gosterwood** *English Traditional Melody*		2	✓			✓	
14 14 478 **Lobe den Herren** (Praxis Pietatis) (c) (Hast du denn Jesu) *Stralsund Gesangbuch*	✓	✓	✓	✓	✓	✓	

VARIED TREATMENTS	BEST PLAIN VERSION	THEMATIC INDEX
SP (d): BBC (u + h): HCS (d)		l_i - md | r - m - | $l_i t_i$ dr | $dt_i l_i$
SS (m + h)		d - rm | f - m - | r - rder | m - r
HCS (d)		drmsd't | lslrs - d' | lfr' | tsd' | m'm'r' | d' - s | ss$\widehat{ls}$ | mmd | fmr | d - s_i | ddr | $t_i s_i t_i$ | ddr | m - m | llt | d'd't | ld'$\widehat{tl}$ | lse $\widehat{dr}$ | mrd | $l_i s_i f_i$ | rrr | r -
AHB only tolerable version		s | s - $\widehat{lt}$ | d'sd' | r'sr' | m| -
	SP	$\widehat{mm}$ | ltse | l - t | d'r't | l -
AHB (d). cf. respective fortunes of Bromley Common (SP) and Tersanctus (HF) as rivals to Nicaea, with their merits		ddmm | s - s - | l - ll | s - m
		s | ddr | mms | fmr | mmm
		d | srmf | s
		$\widehat{ms}$ | ld'$\widehat{ts}$ | d'$\widehat{r'}$d't' | $\widehat{ltls}$ | m -
		d | d$l_i t_i$d | rmds | fm$\widehat{rd}$r | d - -
BBC (Bach) HCS (d) SS (Old version – m)		dds | mrd | $t_i l_i s_i$ | $l_i t_i$d | r - - | d - -

METRE—TITLE—COMPOSER	BHB	CH3	CP	MHB	AMR	EH	SUPPLEMENTS
14 14 14 15 **Sheen** *G. Holst*				✓	✓	✓	
Irregular **Battle Hymn of the Republic** *W. Steffe*		✓	✓	✓			SW
Benson *M. D. Kingham*	✓		✓		✓	✓	
Laredo *American Cowboy Melody*		✓					
Lord of the Dance *Shaker Tune*	CH EP HHT HS NCH PFT PP PTL SW WOV Camb.						
Salve feste Dies *R. Vaughan Williams*		✓					
Sebaste (c) *J. Stainer*	✓	✓	✓	✓	✓		
Standish *J. Dykes Bower*					✓		
Vision *H. Walford Davies*			✓	✓	✓		PFT
See also **Culrathain and Ramelton** *Irish Melodies*		✓					
Cumulus *S. H. Nicholson*					✓		
Jacob's Ladder *Traditional Melody*			EP MHT				
Rangoon *C. Wood*				✓	✓		
Water-End *G. Shaw*			SP				

VARIED TREATMENTS	BEST PLAIN VERSION	THEMATIC INDEX
See also St Keverne CH3		s₁ | l₁dr | mdt̂₁l₁ | s₁df | mrd | d -
		s | ŝŝŝm̂sd̂r' | m̂'m' m̂'r'd -
		ssld̂'d'| tlss | lr'd't | d' - - -
		s | sfm | fsf | mrd | ds₁ -
(Original version "Tis the gift to be simple")		s₁ | dd̂rm̂rm̂l̂ | ssm
MHT the only practicable version		dsf̂mr | d - -
See also Lessington AHB BBC HCS		m -fsm | l -sdmrr
		l̂t | d'tl̂s | ls
		dr | mrms | lsmd | rmfm | m -
		d̂r | mmm | m - m₁ | l₁t₁d | t₁m
		d̂r | m̂mrdl₁ | d -
		d'tld' | tllse
		s₁ | dd̂d̂d̂mr̂d | rr̂rr̂fm̂r
		dm̂m ss | d' - -
		sm̂d rm | s₁ - -

Contemporary tunes

A list of roughly one hundred tunes together with their sources follows. They use idioms which differ from the "contemporary" tunes of a generation ago, such as those which found their way into the *BBC Hymn Book*, the *Baptist Hymn Book, Hymns Ancient and Modern Revised,* and *Congregational Praise*. In their differing ways, almost all offer a degree of challenge but it is one worthy of acceptance. A personal evaluation of difficulty is offered, but it must be borne in mind that the age and outlook of a congregation can markedly affect the speed of learning or willingness to accept a new idiom.

Some of the tunes featured in modern collections, whilst being contemporary in time are hardly so in outlook; others date from a previous generation. These are included in the main index.

By way of postscript it may be pointed out that one of the commonplaces of hymnological criticism is to say how quickly the idioms of *Songs of Praise* became dated. Whilst this may indeed be true of some tunes, it is by no means true of all. A good deal of the ethos of *Songs of Praise* as well as some of the actual contents found their way into the *Cambridge Hymnal* a generation later *as if they were new or newly discovered*, a matter on which reviewers were strangely silent.

In general, only one tune has been recommended for each contemporary hymn, because it is believed that a united effort to propagate the association of a hymn with one tune only offers the best hope of ultimate popularity. The source is underlined where the tune is set to the quoted words. As a general guide, some of the most radical material is contained in the *Church Hymnary: Third Edition* and *New Church Praise,* the more traditional in the *Anglican Hymn Book* and *Hymns for Church and School,* and the simplest in *Partners in Praise* and *Songs of Worship.* The numbers selected from the various books and supplements is *PFT* (28), *NCP* (24) and *CH3* (20). The two latter contain forty-three different recommended tunes, and all three a total of sixty-one. *PP* (20) *MHT* (14) *HS* (13) *WOV* (11) *NCH* (10) *HCS* (9) *SW* (9) *BP* (8) *PTL* (8) *EP* (6) *HHT* (6) *CH* (5) *AHB* (5) *EHSB* (2) *H. Celeb.* (2) *CW* (1) *WH* (1).

The writer has sought to bring to bear an equivalent critical judgment in the examination of tunes of all periods. To show a greater degree of tolerance toward contemporaneity would render no service to the composer. Similarly, he has tried to show equal partiality for different idioms, but has tended to exclude items (often of a highly syncopated nature) that would be effective only when performed by a "group" with attendant guitars, amplification, etc. Many of these ditties, when stripped of their syncopation are embarrassingly trivial and are often set to equally poverty-stricken words. There are some fine words which still await a worthy musical setting, e.g. "Beyond the mist of doubts" by Donald Hughes in *Hymns and Songs* and *New Church Praise.*

As will be seen from reference to the main index, a number of older tunes are set to modern verse in the Supplements, etc. The sources are left unbracketed where this occurs. In some instances, a hymn was written with an older tune in the author's mind; in others, it is frequently remarkable how much strength such music can impart to newer words.

An inevitable question is, "Have these tunes permanent worth?" In view of the high hopes entertained by many "contemporary" tunes of the past, one hesitates to assume the mantle of the prophet and answer in the affirmative. Just as many tunes written earlier in this century suffered from a contrived avoidance of the obvious — which means in fact the singable — so one fears that some tunes of the present day will not make the grade. This apparent fear of the conventional by the composer in respect of harmony is likely to be the biggest obstacle to a tune's popularity. The evasion of an implied perfect cadence and the use of a plentiful quantity of secondary triads is just the thing to give harmonic piquancy to a last verse, but it is an entirely different matter to present such harmony in verse one and repeat it as the *only* harmony in subsequent verses. Geoffrey Shaw's "Dymchurch" (93, *SP*) which has been taken up by no other hymn book, is a tune that makes a number of appealing gestures and yet fails to convince as a whole because of the harmonic and melodic oddities to which I've referred. These stem basically from trying to reconcile modality in harmony and diatonicism in melody or vice versa. Similarly, dare one suggest that a C sharp for the penultimate note of line five in "Hampton Lucy" (270, *BBC*) would help the tune's popularity without diminishing its quality? Might one also suggest some gestures of harmonic simplification in the form of more primary triads and clearer cadences on the part of organists, at any rate until a tune is well-known?

Of course, one does not wish to prescribe a predictable mediocrity for all tunes, but it is nevertheless remarkable how an unexpected or unusual interval can prove a stumbling block. Even today, after nearly forty years of frequent performance, many congregations have still not come to terms with the final line of "Abbot's Leigh". If the falling major 6th had occurred at some point earlier in the tune, would it have proved fatal to its popularity?

Those contemporary tunes whose idioms tend to be more orthodox are listed in the main index. All their sources are indicated in bold type.

METRE—TITLE—COMPOSER	WORDS
S.M.	
Hillsborough (e) *J. Gardner*	O day of God, draw nigh
C.M.	
Divine Image (m) *P. Aston*	To Mercy, Pity, Peace and Love
In armour bright (m) *E. N. Hay*	The eternal gates are lifted up
McKee (e) *Negro Melody*	In Christ there is no East and West
Metropolitan (m) *M. Cook*	Come Holy Ghost, our hearts inspire
Niamryl (m) *G. Laycock*	Forgive our sins as we forgive
San Rocco (m–d) *D. Williams*	Lord of the boundless curves of space
L.M.	
Cross Deep (e–m) *B. Rose*	Come, dearest Lord, descend and dwell
Dunedin (m) *V. Griffiths*	Give to our God immortal praise
Felinfoel (c) (d) *M. Dawney*	See, Christ was wounded for our sake
Fudgie (m) *A. Hutchings*	Creator of the earth and skies
St Mary's (e–m) *D. Potter*	Christ is alive! Let Christians sing
Wesley's Chapel (e–m) *F. Westbrook*	Savagely beat the desert sun
Woodbridge Road (e–m) *J. Wilson*	My God, and is Thy table spread
37688933	
Laudate Pueri (d) *H. W. Zimmerman*	Praise the Lord! Praise, you servants
45538883	
Lord Jesus Christ (Living Lord) (e) *P. Appleford*	Lord Jesus Christ, you have come to us
4776	
Concord (e) *R. J. B. Fleming*	Let there be light
5457	
Swaffham (e) *C. G. Hambly*	A is for Advent
5554	
Ridgeway (e) *B. R. Hoare*	After darkness light
5554D	
Addington (e) *C. V. Taylor*	This day God gives me

SOURCES

CH3, HCS, HS (Additional Unison version in HCS)

BP, NCH

CH3

BP, CH, EP, HCS, PP, PTL, WOV, HS (*See also* Pityoulish in CH3)

H. Celeb.

NCH, PFT

BP, MHT, NCP

BP

MHT, NCH

NCH, WOV

CH3, EHSB, NCP, PFT (*See also* Penitence in HS)

NCP

PP, HS

HS

NCP

CH, HHT, HS, PFT, PP, SW, WOV

PFT

PP

PP

MHT

METRE—TITLE—COMPOSER	WORDS
565D **Swithen** (m–d) *P. Cutts*	Where is God today
56 12 **Glencaple** (e) *C. Micklem*	Lord you give to us
5856 **Bitter was the night** (e) *S. Carter*	Bitter was the night
64446 **Emley Moor** (m) *P. Cutts*	Joy wings to God our song
6464D **Euroclydon** (c) (m) *C. S. Lang*	Fierce was the wild billow
6464664 **Blackford** (d) *K. Leighton*	Teach me to serve Thee, Lord
6564 **Into thy keeping** (e) *G. Foote*	Into Thy loving care
666565 **Mayfield** (d) *K. Leighton*	Christ who knows all his sheep
6666 **Ackergill** (m–d) *L. Blake*	Into a world of dark
Growing (Iambic) (e) *R. Sheldon*	Now let us learn of Christ
6666336 **Sharpethorne** (m) *E. Routley*	What does the Lord require
66668 **Rawthorpe** (m–d) *P. Cutts*	Lord bring the day to pass
6684 **Transfiguration** (e) *C. Dearnley*	Once on a mountain-top
6775 **Lord of Lords** (e–m) *Traditional Melody*	Jesus Christ, Son of God
7777 **Harrowby** (m) *J. Gillespie*	Sinful, sighing to be blest
Lauds (e–m) *J. Wilson*	There's a spirit in the air
767666446 **Oasis** (m) *J. McCarthy*	As water to the thirsty

SOURCES

NCP

NCP, PP

EP

NCP (*See also* Caerlaverock in NCP)

HCS

CH3

CH3

CH3

HCS, NCP

SW

BP, HHT, PFT, WOV

NCP, PFT

EP, NCP

SW

AHB

BP, HS, MHT, NCH, NCP, PFT, PP

PP

METRE—TITLE—COMPOSER	WORDS
7676D	
Soldiers Marching (e)	Easter Glory fills the sky
D. Kingsley	
777777	
Christ whose glory (m)	Christ whose glory fills the skies
M. Williamson	
Elsmere (e–m)	God of concrete, God of steel
G. L. Barnes	
Jordan (m)	Come, thou Holy Paraclete
D. Swann	
84844444	
Hadlow (c) (m)	God's saints are shining lights
J. Wilson	
84848884	
East Acklam (m)	For the fruits of his creation
F. A. Jackson	
868686	
Sancta Civitas (m) (c)	O Holy City, seen of John
H. Howells	
8787	
Birabus (m)	All who love and serve your city
P. Cutts	
Great Wilkins (m)	Rise and hear! The Lord is speaking
I. A. Copley	
Sheet (e)	Where is this stupendous stranger
C. V. Taylor	
87876	
Bridegroom (m)	As the bridegroom to his chosen
P. Cutts	
878787	
Cotton Weaver (e)	Jesus is the Lord of living
Lancashire Folk Song	
Finnian (e)	Sing to Him in whom creation
C. Dearnley	
Kensington (m)	God who spoke in the beginning
H. Howells	
Litherop (e–m)	Life is great! So sing about it
P. Cutts	
New Malden (e)	God who spoke in the beginning
D. McCarthy	
Tredegar (e)	Lord, enthroned in heavenly splendour
G. Foote	
Wolvesey (e)	God whose city's sure foundation
E. T. Sweeting	
8787D	
Geneva (m)	Sing we of a modern city
G. H. Day	
Salisbury (c) (d)	Holy Spirit ever dwelling
H. Howells	

PP

CH3, CW

PFT (*See* New Horizons in HS and SW and Minterne in HHT) But Arfon
captures the rugged strength of these words better than any contemporary tune

CH3

HCS

BP, HS, MHT, PFT, PP, PTL

CH3, HCS (descant version), HHT

HS, NCP, PTL, WOV (*See also* Charlestown in NCP and Citizens in HS)

MHT

MHT

HHT, NCP, PFT, PP, BP (u + h)

SW

EP

HS

MHT, NCP, PFT, PP

BP, MHT, PP (Set to When our confidence is shaken—
Fred Pratt Green)

CH3, EHSB

HCS

PFT

HCS

METRE—TITLE—COMPOSER	WORDS
8787887	
Conquering love (d)	Let all the multitudes of light
D. Willcocks	
Palace Green (m)	You, living Christ, our eyes behold
M. Fleming	
88586	
Hampton Poyle (m)	Lord Christ, the Father's mighty Son
P. Cutts	
8866	
Harpenden (e–m)	When Jesus walked by Galilee
F. B. Westbrook	
887D	
Grove Hill (m)	Praise the Lord, let earth adore Him
L. Blake	
Sarum New (m)	Behold the temple of the Lord
R. Lloyd	
8884	
Norfolk (c) (d)	With wonder, Lord, we see your works
H. Howells	
8888	
Maer Down (e–m)	Inspirer and Hearer of prayer
R. Sheldon	
88884	
Mayfield (m–d)	For the bread that we have eaten
P. Cutts	
888888	
Reading (e–m)	Almighty God, lift up our eyes
F. B. Westbrook	
Woodmansterne (m)	O God, by whose almighty plan
C. Micklem	
8897 10 7	
Cresswell (e–m)	Love is his word, Love is his way
A. Milner	
8987	
Colinton (d)	O Christ, who sinless art alone
K. Leighton	
89894	
Courtney (m)	When from the darkness comes no light
C. Mawby	
9766 11	
Abergevenny (m)	We are of that honoured company
C. G. Hambly	
Westholme (m)	Fire is lighting torch and lamp at night
E. Reid	
998 12	
Trotting (d)	Trotting, trotting through Jerusalem
E. Reid	
99997	
Ashton (m–d)	Go ye, said Jesus
R. Barrett-Ayres	

SOURCES

AHB

MHT (*See also* Vinolanda in H. Celeb.)

EP, HHT, NCP, PP

PFT

HCS

AHB

NCH, PFT

AHB

NCP, PFT

HS, WOV

NCP

CH, PFT, PTL, SW, WOV (Catholic Supplement)

CH3

NCH, PFT

PP

HS, NCP

HS, NCP, PFT, PP, WOV

CH3

METRE—TITLE—COMPOSER	WORDS

10 7 10 74666
Jucunda Laudatio (m)   Reap me the earth as a harvest to God
A. G. Murray

10 8 10 9 and ref.
Sing Hosanna (e)   Give me joy in my heart
Traditional Melody

10 10 and ref.
Let us break (Let us praise) (e)   Let us break bread together with the Lord
Negro Spiritual

10 10 10 7
Philippian (m)   We praise you, Lord, for all that's true and pure
C. Micklem

10 10 10 9
George (m)   Father eternal, Lord of the ages
A. Hutchings

10 10 10 10
Blackbird Leys (m–d)   { Come, risen Lord (HHT)
P. Cutts   { The voice of God (NCP)

Blessing and honour (e)   Blessing and honour and glory and power
Scottish Melody

Dunoon (d)   Most glorious Lord of Life
K. Leighton

In Manus tuas (c) (d)   This world, my God, is held within your hand
H. Howells

Munda Cor Meum (e–m)   Filled with the Spirit's power
W. Trotman

Stonelaw (d)   I greet thee, who my sure redeemer art
T. Wilson

Unity (m)   Glory to you, dear Christ
E. Knight

11 6 11 6
Headington (d)   Lover of souls and Lord of all the living
K. Leighton

11 10 11 10
Broadwalk (m)   What thou hast given us
R. Ashfield

Rerum Creator (m–d)   O Lord of every shining constellation
J. Wilson

Victoria (m)   We turn to you, O God of every nation
G. Ridout

11 11 11 5
Baxter Gate (m)   Lord as we rise to leave this shell
G. Towers

12 12 12 12 and chorus
Ubi caritas (e–m)   God is love
A. G. Murray

14 14 478
Caus a Divina (d)   God who has caused to be written
F. R. C. Clarke

SOURCES

PFT, PTL (*See also* Worlebury MHT, NCP, PTL)

CH, MHT, NCP, PP, SW, WOV (Two sets of words in SW)

CH, HS, MHT, PFT, PP, SW, WOV. The first line is best as quoted and Cleall's arrangement in HS, PFT and WOV the best

NCP

EP

CH3

CH3

NCH, PFT

PFT, PTL

CH3, WOV

NCH, PFT

CH3

AHB, CW

HCS, PFT, PTL , HS (*See also* NCH, Lord of the Universe)

PFT

PFT

BP, CH, MHT, NCH, NCP, PFT, WH

MHT, PFT

H

METRE—TITLE—COMPOSER	WORDS
Irregular	
Caribbean Lord's Prayer (e) *West Indian Calypso*	Our Father who art in heaven
Egton Bridge (c) (d) *J. Joubert*	Today I arise
Monikie (d) *D. Dorward*	Spirit of Light – Holy
Pax (e–m) *A. Percival*	We pray for peace
Pettronsen (c) (d) *M. Dalby*	God be in my head
The Beatitudes (c) (d) *W. Llewellyn*	Show us your ways, O Lord

SOURCES

CH, HS, PP, PTL (PP best and clearest version)

CH3

CH3

PP

CH3

NCP, SW

Hymns as anthems

The list of 124 hymn anthems is made up of items from the early sixteenth century down to the present day. All the good contemporary sources of a tune are listed, and though there may be textual variants these are seldom significant except where stated. The sources underlined indicate where the listed words are set. A simple graded system of easy (e), moderate (m), and difficult (d) has been employed, but the relevance of this will depend on resources available, and whether a performance in unison or harmony is intended. It is far better to sing in unison than attempt harmony with a missing part. Again, available resources will determine a suitable mode of treatment on the lines suggested earlier. There is, of course, no need to adopt a uniform tempo throughout, and changes may be necessary to accommodate different styles of treatment from verse to verse.

Some seventy-five or so tunes from the main index and marked (C) are also suitable for Choral treatment. These are generally easier than the ones in the following list. Some of the contemporary tunes are also suitable, and in many instances should be performed *by the choir* before being attempted by the congregation.

Interesting arrangements and harmonizations in the *Oxford Hymn Book* (O) and *Songs of Syon* (SS) are marked where appropriate.

METRE—TITLE—COMPOSER	WORDS
S.M.	
Aylesbury (Wirksworth) (e) *Chetham Psalms 1715*	Breathe on me, Breath of God
Drumcondra (e) *D. F. R. Wilson*	O Holy Spirit, God
Garelochside (e) *K. G. Finlay*	The first day of the week
Redemptor (m) *J. Wilson*	The Saviour's precious blood
C.M.	
Hunnys (m) *7 Sobs of a sorrowful soul*	Lord when we bend before Thy throne
Lindens (d) *E. Rubbra*	That Virgin's Child
Searching for lambs (e) *English Traditional Carol*	The Lord's my Shepherd
Shepherd Boy's Song (e) *J. H. Alden*	He that is down needs fear no fall
D.C.M.	
Bicclescombe (d) *J. Gardner*	The God of love my shepherd is
Bishops (d) *J. Joubert*	To Mercy, Pity, Peace and Love
First Mode Melody (m) *T. Tallis*	Lord, teach us how to pray aright
Old 22 (m) *Day's Psalter*	O Unity of Threefold Light
Old 44 (m) *Anglo-Genevan Psalter*	The Lord is in his holy place
Old 81 (Old 77th) (m) *Day's Psalter 1562*	The Son of God goes forth to war
Old 137 (m) *Day's Psalter 1563*	How shall I sing that majesty
Second Mode Melody (m) *T. Tallis*	Behold the Bridegroom draweth nigh
L.M.	
Ave vera virginitas (m) *Josquin des Prés*	O Son of God eternal Love
Babylon's Stream (e) *T. Campion*	A voice upon the midnight air
Bodley (e) *84 Church Tunes*	We sing the praise of Him who died
Calvisius (Ach bleib be uns) *J. S. Bach*	Now cheer our hearts this eventide
Hilariter (Die ganzewelt) (e) *Cölner Gesangbuch*	The whole bright world rejoices now
Komm, Gott Schöpfer (m) *J. S. Bach*	Come Holy Ghost, our souls inspire

SOURCES

AMR (best version) Needs a slow tempo AHB also good

MHB = SP

AHB = HS = PFT = Ch P

BP (u + h), HS (u)

EH = SP

BP = NCH = Camb. Tenor Solo v. 3 (ATB accomp.)

CH3 Use in alternation with Crimond

BP = HCS = NCH Use Marlow Bottom (BP) in E Flat as unaccompanied middle
verse: *See also* Plumstead Camb. H

Camb.

Camb.

AMR: CH2 = EH = SP: O gives original version

CH2: CP: CW: EH, SP (SP differs in rhythm and harmony: EH in harmony)

AMS: CH3, MHB (poor), CP (good): EH = SP (best) WH

AMR (more interesting rhythm), CH2, EH, SS, SP (Faux-bourdon) "O" gives fine
unison version by Basil Harwood
(AMS) CH2: CP: EH = SP: SS (2 16th-century settings): O (2 16th-century settings)

EH Faux-bourdon given too

EP, NCH = WOV (Catholic Supplement)

AMR: BBC: CH2: CP = EH = SP (MHB) WH: WOV: O

AHB = Ch P

EH = CH3 = WH = SP = BBC

EH = CH3 = SP (PTL) : SS

Camb. Use nos 120, 121, 123, 124 in one performance of vv. 1–4

METRE—TITLE—COMPOSER	WORDS
Nuremburg (e) *J. S. Bach*	Nature with open volume stands
Schutz (m) *H. Schutz*	Where e'er the appointed sacrifice
Seraphinen (m) *J. A. Freylinghausen*	The Lord reigns clothed in strength and power
Veni Creator (m) *T. Tallis*	Come Holy Ghost, our souls inspire
D.L.M. **Jesus Christ the Apple Tree** (m) *E. Poston*	The tree of life my soul hath seen
St Olaf's (d) *J. Gardner*	The water stood like walls of brass
44776 **O Traurigkeit** (e) *German Melody (arr. F. Layritz)*	O Sorrow deep!
44 11D **Wir Christenleut** (e) *J. S. Bach*	Shall God not share
4 10 **Spring** (e) *M. Shaw*	Spring bursts today
557D **Schönster Herr Jesu** (e) *Münster Gesangbuch*	O most merciful
558855 **Westron Wynde** (m) *W. Llewellyn*	Lord Thy word hath taught
6466 **Binham** (d) *L. Berkeley*	The sun is sinking fast
6565D **Requiem** (e) *J. E. Hunt*	Think, O Lord, in mercy
665D7876 **Jesu meine Freude** (m) *J. S. Bach*	Jesu, priceless treasure
666565 **Cambridge** (e) *C. Wood*	Christ who knows all His sheep
6665D **Lemon's Farm** (m) *M. Shaw*	Sing men and angels, sing
6666 and chorus **Angel roll'd the stone** (e) *Negro Spiritual*	The angel rolled the stone
666688 **Auctor Vitae** (e) *H. Walford Davies*	Author of life divine

SOURCES

BP = CP = EP = HCS = HS = MHT

EP

EP

SP

Camb.

Camb. (d) = CH3 without (d)

AMR: BBC: SS

SP

SP

EH = ICH = SP

AHB = BP = MHT

CH3

BBC

AHB = BBC = BHB = Ch P = HCS = MHB = NCH = SP = WOV:
SS (pre-Bach): CP (simplified Bach)

BBC, CP, HCS, HHT, HS, MHB, SP

SP

EP

AMS = CH2

METRE—TITLE—COMPOSER	WORDS
6676 and chorus **Go tell it** (e) *Negro Spiritual*	Go, tell it on the mountain
68888 and Alleluia **Trier** (Christus ist erstanden, Victor King) *Trier Gesangbuch (arr. C. Wood)*	Jesus Christ is risen
7474D and Alleluia **Salve Cordes Gaudium** (m) *J. R. Ahle*	King of glory
7676D **Little Baddow** (m) *C. A. Gibbs*	O God of earth and altar
76767876 **Llangeitho** (e) *Welsh Melody*	Open, Lord, my inward ear
76768877 **Werde Munter** (m) *J. Schop*	
767688787 **Song of the Holy Spirit** (m) *Dutch Melody*	Upon that Whitsun morning
7773 **Brookend** (m) *G. Holst*	In this world, the Isle of Dreams
777444 **Heiliger Geist** (e) *German (arr H. G. Ley)*	Holy Spirit, make us strong
7775 **Guildford Cathedral** (m) *G. Ives*	Gracious Spirit, Holy Ghost
7777 **Come my way** (d) *A. D. Smith*	Come, my way, my truth, my life
The Call (d) *R. Vaughan Williams*	Come, my way, my truth, my life
Long Mynd (d) *R. S. Thatcher*	Christ, of all my hopes the ground
Nun lasst uns Gott (Selnecker) (e) *Selnecker's Psalmer*	Christ was the Word who spake it
Peacefield (e) *Irish Lullaby*	Holy Spirit, truth divine
View me Lord (m) *T. Campion*	View me, Lord, a work of Thine
777777 **Pressburg** (Nicht so traurig) (m) *J. A. Freylinghausen*	Dark the day on Calvary's Cross
7777774455 **Meistersinger Chórale** (m) *R. Wagner*	Holy God, we show forth here

SOURCES

CH, NCH (h), PP (u), SW (u)

EP (arr. C. Wood) SP: PTL: CP (arr. G. Shaw)

AMR

HCS (Is set to Stand up, stand up for Jesus in SP)

CP

Numerous metrical variants PTL = WH: NCH = ICH (Jesu joy): EH = SP, PP

EP

SP = BP

SP

BP

BP = HCS = HS = NCP

Camb. = PTL = WOV

SP

BBC: EH = HCS = SP (BBC gives Bach version)

AHB = BHB = EH = MHB, PTL (Dawney harmonization) SP

Camb. (u) O (h – original version)

CH2, EH = SP: MHB

EH = SP

METRE—TITLE—COMPOSER	WORDS
7777777 **In Natali Domini** (m) *Andernach Gesangbuch*	Cometh sunshine after rain
7777 14 10 **Cologne** (d) *Cologne Gesangbuch*	Sing, all ye Christian people
7777779 **O Lamm Gottes** (e) *J. S. Bach*	O Lamb of God
777788 11 676 **Angelus ad virginem** *Medieval Irish Melody*	Gabriel to Mary came
787877 **Jesus ist mein Aufenthalt** (Meinhold) (m) *J. S. Bach*	Love of live, and Light of light
78787888 **Grasmere** (d) *J. A. Freylinghausen*	Saviour, who didst healing give
78878787 **Sebastian** (Jesu meines glaubens zier) (d) *J. S. Bach*	It is finished! Christ hath known
847D **Chastleton** (e) *W. K. Stanton*	Love, unto thine own who camest
Geneva Psalm 38 (m) *Genevan Psalter 1542*	Darkening night the land doth cover
8484884 **Lower Marlwood** (m) *B. Harwood*	Lift up your heads
8484 10 10 **Fountains Abbey** (e) *G. Slater*	More lovely than the noonday rest
8486D **Fifth Mode Melody** (e) *T. Tallis*	Enter Thy courts, Thou Word of life
848484 **Exon** (e) *T. Armstrong*	Close by the heedless worker's side
8787 **Parsifal** (m) *R. Wagner*	O King most high
87877 **Il Buon Pastor** (e) *Canzuns Spirituelas*	Lord of health, thou life within us
878787 **Lingwood** (e) *C. A. Gibbs*	Judge eternal, throned in splendour
87877787 **Jesus ist das schönste Licht** (e) *J. S. Bach*	Jesus is this dark world's light

SOURCES

SP

SP

BBC: SS

AMR

BBC

AMR

SP, EH

BBC

BBC = O: SS

AHB = BBC = CH3, HCS, ICH (Ending added in HCS)

SP

CH3: SP (CH2 faux-bourdon)

SP

EH

SP

AHB, HCS (Same extended setting for other words)

BBC: NCH

METRE TITLE COMPOSER	WORDS

87877874
Christ lag in Todesbanden (m)
M. Luther

Christ Jesus lay in death's strong bands

878788
Dies ist der Tag (e)
P. Schren

Thou hallowed chosen morn of praise

8787887
Laus Deo (e)
J. S. Bach

Thee, living Christ, our eyes behold

888 and Alleluia
Salus Mortalium (e)
Gesangbuch Erfurt

Our Lord the path of suffering trod

886D
Psalm 6 (e)
French Psalter 1542

O Lord, how happy should we be

8875
Wonder (d)
A. Bax

Lord, Thou hast told us that there be

8884
Pen Selwood (d)
A. Bliss

Sweet day, so cool

88887777
Oakley (d)
R. Vaughan Williams

The night is come like to the day

8888
Gynach (d)
W. Wordsworth

Ah! my dear Lord! what could'st Thou spy

88888
Ich fah dahin (m)
arr. J. Brahms

There's heaven above, and night by night

888888
Font Hill (e)
E. Routley

Wide as His vast dominion lies

Gesius (Heut' triumphiret) (m)
arr. J. S. Bach

I praised the earth, in beauty seen

88108
Cransley (e)
G. Cooke

Here beauty dwells

8989D
Psalm 138 (Genevan Psalm 138) (e)
Genevan Psalter

Thee will I love, my God and King

9898 (Irregular)
Pimlico Road (m)
M. Shaw

O world invisible, we view thee

9898
Weisse (Gott lob es geht) (e)
J. S. Bach

Before the day draws near its ending

9898D
Henham (m)
M. Shaw

O Thou that movest all

SOURCES

HF = NCH (Bach version) BHB = CH3 = CP = MHB; WOV

EH = SP

AMR

AMR

CP = CH2

SP

Camb.

SP

Camb. H.

SP

CP

EH = SP: SS

BBC

BBC = BHB = CP = SP, SS

SP

BHB = CH3 = NCH = SP. Because T + B cross, the latter must be
supported at 16 foot pitch

SP

METRE—TITLE—COMPOSER	WORDS
10 46666 10 4 **Augustine** (m) *E. Routley*	Let all the world in every corner sing
10 10 10 10 84 **So giebst du** (Dresden) (m) *J. S. Bach*	Wilt Thou forgive that sin
10 10 10 10 4 **Tambaram** (e) *C. V. Taylor*	Gather us in
10 10 14 10 **Were you there** (e) *American Folk Hymn*	Were you there when they crucified my Lord
10 14 (5568) **Song of Joy** (m) *T. Campion*	Sing a song of joy
11 10 10 11 **Grain of wheat** (e) *E. Routley*	Now the green blade riseth
11 10 11 6 **Stanstead** (m) *S. L. Russell*	When on my day of life
11 10 11 10 **Erwin** (d) *H. Howells*	Lord by whose breath all souls and seeds are living
11 11 11 5 **Wansbeck** (m) *E. Routley*	Lord as we rise to leave this shell of worship
12 3 **Rasumovsky** (Russian Melody) (e) *Russian Melody*	Praise to God in the highest bless us o Father
12 12 **Garden of Jesus** (e) *Dutch Carol*	King Jesus hath a garden full of divers flowers
12 12 and chorus **Dieu nous avons vu ta gloire** (m) *J. Langlais*	God your glory we have seen
13 10 **When I needed** (e) *S. Carter*	When I needed a neighbour
13 10 13 10 **Crasselius** (m) *J. S. Bach*	O Worship the Lord in the beauty of holiness
13 13 15 13 **Weather beaten sail** (e) *T. Campion*	Never weather-beaten sail more willing bent to shore
Irregular **Boar's Hill** (d) *L. Berkeley*	Hear'st thou my soul
Constantia (m) *R. O. Morris*	God be in my head

CH3, HCS

EH = SP. *See also* Donne (Camb.)

BBC

CH, EP (u), HS (h), MHT, NCH (u), PP (u), PTL (u), SW (u),
| WOV (h), Camb. (best versions underlined)

BP: SP: Camb. (u + d)

PTL. *See also* note on Noel nouvelet and "L'Empereur"

EH = SP

Camb.: *See also* Wiveton (Camb.)

NCP, SW

NCP: PP (simpler version) *See also* OBC

EP

CH3, NCH, NCP, WOV

CH, HHT, HS, PFT, PP, PTL, WOV (All different arrangements)

SP (*See also* Dir dir Jehovah — different metre in SS)

SP (h), Camb. (Good 2 part with accomp.)

Camb. H

SP. *See also* God be in my head (Walford Davies)

METRE—TITLE—COMPOSER	WORDS
Death and Darkness (d) *G. Jacob*	Death and darkness get you packing
Delganey (m) *P. C. Buck*	Into this world of sorrow
Es ist vollbracht (m) *J. S. Bach*	It is finished! ah, grant, O Lord
Freshwater (e) *C. H. H. Parry*	Sunset and evening Star
Gott lebet noch (e) *J. S. Bach*	God liveth still
Jesus unser Trost und Leben (e) *J. S. Bach*	Christ our helper
Kieff Melody (e) *Russian Melody*	Give rest, O Christ
Legend (e) *P. Tchaikovsky*	When Jesus Christ was yet a child
Melfort (d) *L. Berkeley*	Hail gladdening light
Monk's march (m) *Welsh Melody*	What are these that glow from afar
Pleasure it is (d) *A. Ridout*	Pleasure it is to hear i-wis
Prayer (d) *E. Rubbra*	Jesus Lord that madest me
Santa Barbara (d) *A. Bliss*	He is the way

SOURCES

Camb. H

BBC

BBC

AMS = BBC (Try Gillam SP)

BBC

BBC: SS

BBC, EH

BBC

CH3. *See also* Gladdening Light, AHB (m)

EH = SP

Camb. H.

Camb. H.

Camb. H.

Roman Catholic hymnody

In his article "Roman Catholic Church Music in Britain" in the *Oxford Companion to Music,* Dr Percy Scholes shows how the disabilities against Roman Catholics precluded the development of a school of church music composition, and how, when freedom at last came in the mid-nineteenth century, English Music generally was at a low ebb. Thanks to the efforts of Sir Richard Terry and other twentieth-century Catholic musicians progress was made, and this was reflected in the various editions of the *Westminster Hymnal.* That of 1940 as a whole represented a creditable standard for its time, even though one regretted a general reluctance to admit that many of the tunes came from Protestant sources. Apart from composing some dignified modern tunes, many standard tunes were re-harmonized by Dom A. Gregory Murray in a modern though not incongruous idiom. But little real progress was possible whilst vernacular hymns were excluded from the Mass.

A tremendous leap forward followed the second Vatican Council. The Constitution on the Sacred Liturgy 1963 provided for a wider use of the vernacular in worship (section 36) and encouraged the use of hymns other than the traditional Office hymns (section 93). Arising from this, there was an upsurge of new, biblically based hymnody by Catholic writers at the very time when some Protestant hymn writers were venturing outside Christian orthodoxy. Some of this new material was antiphonal in character, in which a solo or choir verse was answered by a congregational antiphon or chorus, and may be regarded as a distinctively Catholic contribution to contemporary hymnody. Alongside this was an enthusiastic adoption of Protestant words and music, particularly since 1964, when vernacular hymns were used at Low Mass.

In addition to the publication in booklet form of material of a transient nature, contemporary Catholic writers such as James Quinn have produced work of more lasting value, which has found its way into such Protestant collections as *Praise for Today* and the *Church Hymnary.* More substantial (in bulk) has been *Praise the Lord,* whose first edition of 1966 was quickly overtaken by virtually a new book of the same title in 1972, which contains material of some interest to the church musician but unfortunately much that is rendered null and void by untasteful arrangements. *The Parish Hymn Book* (1968) appears to be the equivalent of a Catholic *Hymns Ancient and Modern,* balanced and eminently sensible. It acquainted congregations with what their Protestant brethren sang, but it made few gestures towards developing "contemporary" trends. Nevertheless, it represents a considerable step forward from the *Westminster Hymnal,* and perhaps suits the average Parish church better than the more challenging *New Catholic Hymnal* of 1971. This offers scope for a "Radio 3" type of service and looks confidently towards the twenty-first century. Reference has been made elsewhere to the wholesale modernizing of older hymns, which many will regard as artistically indefensible, and which may limit the *New Catholic Hymnal's* use. But there are over fifty new musical settings, some of outstanding quality, as for instance Michael Dawnay's of Brian Foley's "See Christ was wounded for our sake" based on Isaiah 53. But, in common with many other hymn books, it is overloaded with editorial contributions. *Celebration Hymnal,* with Supplement, 1978 is clearly aimed at the pop market and contains many choruses and musical idioms associated with radical nonconformity, together with syncopated contemporary material of the more "with it" kind. Only a small proportion of the whole requires the musician's serious critical attention. Some of the musical material of the above is listed in the other indexes, but the following list includes tunes that have not yet found their way into Protestant collections. Since the prejudice against using non-Catholic material has broken down, many of the standard items of English hymnody have found their way into Roman Catholic worship, and some reciprocity is to be welcomed.

Few of the words, except those marked (x) would be unacceptable to most Protestant congregations. Only one source is listed for each tune. The material in the *Westminster Hymnal* and the *Parish Hymn Book* is of the traditional congregational type and therefore no grading was deemed necessary.

The other tunes are graded (e), (m), (d) respectively, easy moderate or difficult, though categories will vary from place to place.

The tunes have also been graded into types:

1. Congregational (cong) denoting music in a broadly traditional idiom.

2. Contemporary (contemp) denoting music whose melodic character, rhythm, tonality or harmony represents a challenge to traditional values.

3. Choir (ch) denoting music whose intimacy of words and/or music, or whose complexity would make the hymn more suitable for choral performance.

ROMAN CATHOLIC HYMN TUNES
WESTMINSTER HYMNAL

METRE	TITLE	COMPOSER
D.C.M.	**New Prince**	*A. G. Murray*
888888	*×* **Mysterium Fidei**	*A. G. Murray*
10 10 10 6	*×* **St Joseph**	*A. G. Murray*
11 11 11 5	*×* **Nocte surgentes**	*Cassinese Melody*
10 4 10 4 10 10	**Lux in tenebris**	*A. G. Murray*
776D	*×* **Ne vueilles pas**	*L. Bourgeois*
7777	**Surge**	*A. G. Murray*

PARISH HYMN BOOK

METRE	TITLE	COMPOSER
7676D	**O King of might**	*A. G. Murray*
10 10 10 10	**Wilcox**	*J. Rush*
11 11 11 5	**Theophilia**	*J. Rush*
878787	*×* **Cheam**	*J. Rush*
767777	**Te Deum**	*J. Rush*
L.M.	*×* **New Malden**	*J. Rush*
8888553	*×* **Cheyne Row**	*W. S. Lloyd Webber*

NEW CATHOLIC HYMNAL

METRE	TITLE	COMPOSER	CATEGORY	
6767	**Divine Paradox**	*J. Dowland*	ch	(e)
C.M.	**Maker's Praise**	*L. Berkeley*	contemp	(d)
10 10 10	**Praise God**	*E. Poston*	contemp	(m)
8787	**Lumen Christi**	*N. Caplin*	contemp	(d)
8884	**Commemoration**	*J. Battishill* (adapted)	ch-cong	(e)
8787	**Kas dziejada**	*Latvian*	cong	(e)
10 9 10 9	**New River**	*K. D. Smith*	contemp	(m)
Irregular	**Komm süsser Tod**	*J. S. Bach*	ch	(m)
	(New words needed for general use)			
10 10 10 10	**St Anthony**	*G. Laycock*	contemp-ch	(m)
12 12 12 12 and refrain	**Toronto**	*S. Somerville*	contemp	(m)
7777	**Resurrexit**	*R. S. Johnson*	contemp	(m)
878787	**Verbum Dei**	*G. Laycock*	contemp	(m)
C.M.	**Newtondale**	*B. Sargent*	contemp	(m)
Irregular	**How mighty are the Sabbaths**	*G. Holst*	ch	(m)
	(First introduced into the Clarendon Hymn Book)			
Irregular	**Liebster Herr Jesu**	*J. S. Bach*	ch	(m)
88788	**Jesu Rex Admirabilis**	*Palestrina*	ch	(e)
10 8999	**In dirist Freude**	*Gastoldi*	ch	(e)
D.C.M.	**Tye**	*C. Tye*	cong-ch	(e)
	(Compare the truncated version Southwark in CH3)			
7777	**Semper Laudate**	*G. Laycock*	cong	(e)
88586	**M.J.G.**	*W. Tamblyn*	ch	(d)
5454 and refrain	**St Peter's Song**	*E. Poston*	contemp-ch	(e)
10 10 10 10	**Now bless the Lord**	*G. Laycock*	contemp	(m)
L.M.	**De Profundis**	*G. Laycock*	contemp	(d)
8888	**Felinfoel**	*M. Dawney*	ch	(d)
7775 and refrain	**Seek the Lord** (Venantius)	*R. Connolly*	cong	(m)
11 10 569	**Trumpet Carol**	*Burgundian Carol*	cong	(e)

L.M.	**Potentia Domini**	*M. Tolles*	contemp	(d)
9888	**My dancing day**	*Sandys' Christmas Carol*	cong-ch	(e)
10 10 10 10	**Unitas vera**	*I. Gundry*	cong	(m)
C.M. and refrain	**Semper nobiscum**	*R. B. Rowsell*	contemp	(m)
10 10 11 11	**The tree springs to life**	*W. Tamblyn*	contemp	(d)
8886	**O Domine**	*Palestrina*	ch	(e)
7777 and refrain	**Mater Dolorosa**	*R. S. Johnson*	ch	(d)
7676D	**Nous voici dans la ville** (Compare Chartres 8787D in CH2)	*Provençal Carol*	cong	(e)

PRAISE THE LORD

METRE	TITLE	COMPOSER	CATEGORY	
	Responsorial Psalm 2	*S. Wolff*		
10 10 10 10	**Ellenborough**	*J. Ainslie*	cong	(m)
Irregular	**Lord I am not worthy**	*L. Bévenot*	contemp (group)	(m)
Irregular	**Sons of God hear his holy word**	*J. Thiem*	cong	(e)
8887	**Edge Hill**	*R. Shaw*	cong	(m)
L.M. and Alleluia	**Pangamas melos gloriae**	*Analecta Hymnica*	cong-ch	(m)
888777	**Marantha**	*S. Somerville*	contemp	(d)
8787	**En clara vox**	*R. L. Pearsall*	cong	(e)
8484	**Providence**	*R. R. Terry*	cong	(e)
7777 and Alleluias	**François**	*D. Kingsley*	contemp	(e)
4555D	**Celebration Song**	*C. A. Gibson*	contemp	(e)
L.M.	**Mein Seel, O Gott**	*M. Praetorius*	cong	(e)
767776	**Llanelli**	*M. Dawney*	cong	(m)
8787D	**In principio**	*R. Shaw*	contemp	(m)
12 4 12 6 and refrain	**Confido**	*A. G. Murray*	ch	(m–d)
9494 and refrain	**Beguine**	*A. G. Murray*	contemp	(d)
L.M.	**Surrexit Christus**	*14th c. Melody*	cong	(e)

CELEBRATION HYMNAL

METRE	TITLE	COMPOSER	CATEGORY	
12 12 and refrain	**The King of Glory**	*Israeli Melody*	contemp	(e)
L.M.	**Suantrai**	*Irish Melody*	contemp	(e)

WITH ONE VOICE (CATHOLIC SUPPLEMENT)

METRE	TITLE	COMPOSER	CATEGORY	
11 10 and refrain	ˣ**Sandy Bay**	*R. Connolly*	contemp	(m)
888 and refrain	ˣ**Helen**	*R. Connolly*	contemp	(m)
10 10 10 10 and refrain	ˣ**Jeremy**	*R. Connolly*	contemp	(m)
7874 and refrain	ˣ**Travalli**	*R. Connolly*	contemp	(m)
7777 and refrain	ˣ**Sancta Sophia**	*R. Connolly*	contemp	(m)

Distribution of tunes

In compiling the various indexes, no attempt was made to select equally from the standard hymn books, or to show partiality to the contents of one over another. In reaching these totals, no tune was excluded because it was presented in a poor arrangement. Taken together, the books contain approximately 570 recommended tunes. They are distributed as follows:

Approx. 350

Songs of Praise
Congregational Praise
Baptist Church Hymn Book
Anglican Hymn Book.

Approx. 335

BBC Hymn Book
English Hymnal
Hymns Ancient and Modern Revised. (There are additionally nearly 20 tunes in the Standard Edition not included in *Hymns Ancient and Modern Revised.*)

Approx. 325

Methodist Hymn Book
Church Hymnary: Third Edition. (There are additionally over 80 tunes in the *Church Hymnary: Second Edition* not included in the *Church Hymnary: Third Edition,* most of which are well-represented in other hymn books in current use.)

245

Approx. 270   *Christian Praise*
                               Christian Worship
                               Hymns of Faith.

Taking into account the diversity of the books' contents, their sizes, and the "congregations" they are intended to serve, the closeness of the totals is very remarkable. Most people would, I imagine, produce a rather different "pecking order" if called upon to list, on reputation alone, the chief hymn books in order of the excellence of their musical content.

Range of Idiom

Again, whilst the list was compiled with merit as its criterion, and not with a view to striking some kind of artificial idiomatic balance, it is nevertheless gratifying that the various styles have secured a fair, if fortuitous, representation. Tunes have been assigned to the following categories on the basis of style rather than on strict historical fact:

Psalter tunes, Gibbons, Tallis, etc.	8.8%
English seventeenth and eighteenth centuries	17.2%
French and German seventeenth and eighteenth centuries	9.8%
Chorale type tunes	8.8%
Victorian tunes	16.2%
Twentieth-century tunes	23.8%
Welsh tunes (traditional and composed)	3.1%
Folk/Modal tunes	7.3%

The Top Twenty (One)

I am indebted to the Rev. David Perry's *Hymns and Tunes Indexed* for information concerning tunes featured in 25 or more contemporary hymn books:

In 28 books   Franconia, Lasst uns Erfreuen.

In 27 books   St Bernard (C.M.).

In 26 books   Herzlich thut mich verlangen, Hyfrydol, Rockingham.

In 25 books   Carlisle, Duke Street, Melcombe, Monkland, Nicaea, Nun danket alle Gott, Orientis Partibus, Praise my soul, Ravenshaw, St Anne, St George's Windsor, Stuttgart, Tallis' Canon, Westminster, Winchester New.

I believe that the average hymn buff — even with a hymn book at his side to jolt his memory — would do well to list more than half the above titles, when "Melita", "Wir pflügen", "Repton", "St Gertrude", "St Clement" and many others seem to be more obvious candidates in the popularity stakes. What is really so special about "Franconia" and "St Bernard" one may ask?

But just as the candidates for inclusion in other top twenties are subject to change, so we may expect similar changes in the representation of the standard tunes in future hymn books. It may well be that an edition of *Hymns and Tunes Indexed* in the next century will include "East Acklam", "Abbot's Leigh" and "Michael" among those with the widest representation. If this takes place, we may rest assured that our successors' choice of hymn tunes has been made using sounder criteria than that witnessed in so many quarters today.

LIST OF HYMN BOOKS EXAMINED

A Student's Hymnal, 1923
Anglican Hymn Book, 1965   AHB
Hymns Ancient and Modern Revised, 1950   AMR
Hymns Ancient and Modern, standard edition, 1916   AMS
Hymns Ancient and Modern, 1904
BBC Hymn Book, 1951   BBC
Baptist Hymn Book, 1962   BHB
Baptist Hymnal, 1933
Broadcast Praise, 1981   BP
Cambridge Hymnal, 1967   Camb.H.
Celebration Hymnal, 1978   CH
The Church Hymnary: Second Edition, 1927   CH2
The Church Hymnary: Third Edition, 1973   CH3
Christian Hymns (Welsh), 1977
Christian Praise, 1957   Ch.P.
Clarendon Hymn Book, 1936   Clar.
Congregational Praise, 1951   CP
Christian Worship, 1976   CW
English Hymnal, 1933   EH
English Hymnal Service Book, 1962   EHSB
English Praise, 1975   EP
Fellowship Hymn Book, 1933
Hymns for Celebration, 1979   H.Celeb.
Hymns for Choirs, 1976
Hymns for Church and School, 1964   HCS
Hymns of Faith, 1964   HF
Hymns for Worship (Unitarian), 1962
One Hundred Hymns for Today, 1969   HHT
Hymns and Songs, 1969   HS
(Irish) Church Hymnal, 1960   ICH
Methodist Hymnal, 1964 (USA)
Methodist Hymn Book, 1904, 1933   MHB
More Hymns for Today, 1980   MHT
New Catholic Hymnal, 1971   NCH
New Church Praise, 1975   NCP
Oxford Hymn Book, 1909   O
Oxford Book of Carols, 1928   OBC
Praise for Today, 1974   PFT
Parish Hymn Book, 1968   PHB

Partners in Praise, 1979   PP
Public School Hymn Book: Third Edition, 1949   PSHB
Praise the Lord, 1972   PTL
Redemption Hymnal, 1955   RH
Salvation Army Tune Book, with supplements 1 and 2, n.d.   SA
Songs of Praise, enlarged edition, 1931   SP
Songs of Syon, 1919   SS
Songs of Worship, 1980   SW
The Hymn Book (Canada), 1938
The Hymnal (USA), 1940
Westminster Hymnal, 1939   WH
With One Voice, 1979   WOV

BIBLIOGRAPHY

Andrews, J. S., *A Survey of Current English Hymnals*, (Evangelical Quarterly, July 1980).

The Archbishop's Committee's Reports on Church Music 1922, 1951.

Barkley, J. M., (ed.), *Handbook to the Church Hymnary: Third Edition*, (OUP, 1979).

Bell, M. F., *Church Music*, (Mowbray, 1904).

The Bulletins of the Hymn Society (see *HSB* in text).

Cleall, C., *Sixty Songs from Sankey*, (Marshall, Morgan and Scott, 1960).
The Selection and Training of Mixed Choirs in Churches, (Independent Press, 1961).

Coleman, H., *The Amateur Choir Trainer*, (OUP, 1932).
The Amateur Organist, (OUP, 1955).

Curwen, J., *Studies in Worship Music*, (Curwen, 1880).

Dakers, L., *Church Music at the Crossroads*, (Marshall, Morgan and Scott, 1970).
Handbook of Parish Music, (A. R. Mowbray, 1976).
Making Church Music Work, (A. R. Mowbray, 1978).

Davies, H. Walford and Harvey Grace, *Music in Worship*, (Eyre and Spottiswoode, 1935).

Davies, H. Walford, *Church Anthem Book*, (OUP, 1934).

Davison, A. T., *Church Music Illusion and Reality*, (Harvard, 1952).

Dearmer, P., *Songs of Praise Discussed*, (OUP, 1933).

Douglas, W., *Church Music in History and Practice*, (Scribner, 1937).

Dunstan, A., *These are the hymns*, (SPCK, 1978).

English Church Music (an annual publication of the Royal School of Church Music; see *ECM* in text).

Fleming, J. R., *A Highway of Praise*, (OUP, 1937).

Fox, A., *English Hymns and Hymn Writers*, (Collins, 1947).

Frost, M., *An Historical Companion to Hymns Ancient and Modern*, (Clowes, 1962).
English and Scottish Hymn and Psalm Tunes c1543–1677, (OUP, 1953).

Goldhawk, N. P., *On Hymns and Hymnbooks*, (Epworth Press, 1979).

Grace, H., *The Complete Organist*, (Richards, 1947).

Gregory, A. S., *Praises with Understanding*, (Epworth Press, 1936).

Hutchings, A., *Church Music in the Nineteenth Century*, (Jenkins, 1967).

Jefferson, H. A. L., *Hymns in Christian Worship*, (Rockliff, 1950).

Julian, J., *Dictionary of Hymnology*, (Murray, 1925).

Leaver, R. A., *The Liturgy and Music*, (Grove Liturgical Studies, 1975).
A Hymn Book Survey 1962–1980, (Grove Worship Series, No. 71, 1980).

Lightwood, J. T., *Music of the Methodist Hymn Book*, (Epworth Press, 1935).

Long, K. R., *Music of the English Church*, (Hodder and Stoughton, 1972).

Lowther Clarke, W. K., *A Hundred Years of Hymns Ancient and Modern*, (Clowes, 1960).

Nicholson, S. H., *Church Music*, (Faith Press, 1920).

Quires and and Places where they sing, (re-issue SPCK, 1942).

Northcott, C., *Hymns in Christian Worship*, (Lutterworth Press, 1964).

Parry, K. L. and Routley, E., *Companion to Congregational Praise*, (Independent Press, 1953).

Patrick, M., *Story of the Church's Song*, (OUP, 1927).

Perry, D. W., *Hymns and Tunes Indexed*, (RSCM, 1980).

Phillips, C. H., *The Singing Church*, (Faber, new and revised edition, 1968).

Phillips, C. S., *Hymnody Past and Present*, (SPCK, 1937).

Principles and Recommendations of the Royal School of Church Music, (RSCM, 1950).

Quinn, J., *New Hymns for all Seasons*, (Chapman, 1969).

Rhys, S. and Palmer, K., *ABC of Church Music*, (Hodder and Stoughton, 1967).

Routley, E., *The Church and Music*, (Duckworth, 1950).

Church Music and the Christian Faith, (Collins, 1980).

Church Music and Theology, (SCM Press, 1959).

Music of Christian Hymnody, (Independent Press, 1957).

Organist's Guide to Congregational Praise, (Independent Press, 1957).

Twentieth Century Church Music, (Jenkins, 1964).

Hymns today and tomorrow, (Darton, Longman and Todd, 1966).

Hymn Tunes, a short history, (RSCM, 1981).

Scholes, P. A., *Oxford Companion to Music*, (OUP, 1938).

Shaw, M., *Principles of Church Music Composition*, (Musical Opinion, 1921).

Staples, H. J., *The Choirmaster and Organist*, (Epworth Press, 1939).

Taylor, C. V., *Way to Heaven's Door*, (Epworth Press, 1955).

Temperley, N., *Music of the English Parish Church*, (CUP, 1980).

Thiman, E. H., *Varied Harmonisations of Hymn Tunes*, (OUP, 1934).

The Beginning Organist, (Ascherberg, 1954).

Whitley, W. T., *Congregational Singing in England*, (Dent, 1933).

Wilson, A. W., *The Chorales, their origin and influence*, (Faith Press, 1920).